Learning

Organisations

CW00815991

DISCLAIMER

No person should rely on the contents of this publication without first obtaining advice from a qualified professional person. This publication is sold on the terms and understanding that (1) the authors, consultants and editors are not responsible for the results of any actions taken on the basis of information in this publication, nor for any error in or omission from this publication; and (2) the publisher is not engaged in rendering legal, accounting, professional or other advice or services. The publisher, and the authors, consultants and editors, expressly disclaim all and any liability and responsibility to any person, whether a purchaser or reader of this publication or not, in respect of anything, and of the consequences of anything, done or omitted to be done by any such person in reliance, whether wholly or partially, upon the whole or any part of the contents of this publication. Without limiting the generality of the above, no author, consultant or editor shall have any responsibility for any act or omission of any other author, consultant or editor.

Learning
from High
Reliability
Organisations

CCH

a Wolters Kluwer business

Edited by
Andrew Hopkins

CCH AUSTRALIA LIMITED

GPO Box 4072, Sydney, NSW 2001

Head Office North Ryde
Phone: (02) 9857 1300 Fax: (02) 9857 1600

Customer Support
Phone: 1 300 300 224 Fax: 1 300 306 224

www.cch.com.au

Book Code: 39027A

ABOUT CCH AUSTRALIA LIMITED

CCH Australia is a leading provider of accurate, authoritative and timely information services for professionals. Our position as the 'professional's first choice' is built on the delivery of expert information that is relevant, comprehensive and easy to use.

We are a member of the Wolters Kluwer group, a leading global information services provider with a presence in more than 25 countries in Europe, North America and Asia Pacific.

CCH — *The Professional's First Choice.*

Enquiries are welcome on **1300 300 224**

National Library of Australia Cataloguing-in-Publication Entry

Hopkins, Andrew, 1945-

Learning from high reliability organisations/Andrew Hopkins

ISBN: 978 1 921485 97 8 (pbk)

Includes index

Subjects: Reliability — Case studies
        Success in business — Case studies

Dewey number: 650.1

© 2009 CCH Australia Limited

All rights reserved. No part of this work covered by copyright may be reproduced or copied in any form or by any means (graphic, electronic or mechanical, including photocopying, recording, recording taping, or information retrieval systems) without the written permission of the publisher.

Printed in Australia by McPherson's Printing Group

FOREWORD

Kim Beazley, Chancellor, Australian National University

This book epitomises what the Australian National University is about.

Professor Andrew Hopkins has developed a distinctive area of research on the cultural and organisational causes of major accidents. Arising out of this work, he created and taught a course on "the sociology of disasters". Students who took the course were excited by it, and some moved on to do honours and even PhD theses with him. This book is a product of that process, and includes contributions from both honours and PhD students. It is, if you like, a celebration of an intellectual partnership between a teacher and his students.

My first portfolio was Minister for Aviation. My nightmare was the possibility of a major aircraft accident. Though none occurred on my watch, there were plenty of smaller ones, each with its own sorrowful story. I embedded myself in the safety aspects of the portfolio and came to deeply appreciate the training and performance of our air traffic controllers in particular. I am glad this book sees them in the context of a successful operation whose outcomes are worthy of a broader audience.

Professor Hopkins is a major national asset. His work on the causes of disastrous accidents has made him internationally known — an element of our national capacity to intellectually "punch above our weight". He is not selfish with his reputation or his chosen area of research. He takes pride in the capacity displayed by those he has supervised and is pleased to share the platform with them.

Not only is this book the product of a collaboration between teacher and students, it is also a product of a collaboration between the ANU and two industry partners. One partnership, with Airservices Australia, attracted an Australian Research Council linkage grant to fund a PhD scholar. A second partner, the Defence Science and Technology Organisation, directly funded a PhD scholar. Both scholars are represented in this collection.

Given the way that this work has grown out of a particular academic environment, its authors decided to return publication royalties to that environment in a way that reflects their interests and commitments. The money will be used to provide awards to ANU staff who have given of their time voluntarily as part of the network of OHS representatives on campus.

CCH ACKNOWLEDGMENTS

CCH Australia Ltd wishes to thank the following team members who contributed to this publication:

Publishing Director
Matthew Sullivan

Editor-in-Chief
John Stafford

Editor
Deborah Powell

Indexing
Beverley Kirkby

Portfolio Projects Manager
Kate Aylett-Graham

Production
Lata Prabakaran

Typesetting
Jenny Hedges, Midland Typesetters

Marketing
Antonina Cocilovo

CONTENTS

Foreword..v

Contributors viii

Preface.. xi

PART 1: The air traffic control study

Introduction to Part 1 3

Chapter 1   The problem of defining high reliability organisations..................5

Chapter 2   Why study Australia's air traffic control agency?........................ 17

Chapter 3   Identifying and responding to warnings....................................33

Chapter 4   Risk management: from hazard logs to bow ties 59

PART 2:   Other studies

Introduction to Part 2 89

Chapter 5   From risk to resilience: assessing flight safety incidents
                 in airlines...95

Chapter 6   Incident reporting: a nuclear industry case study 117

Chapter 7   Operational discipline 135

Chapter 8   Operational decision-making..149

Chapter 9   The "no-blame" approach: investigating blame in systemic
                 accident analyses..179

Chapter 10   Guidelines for AcciMap analysis..193

Chapter 11   The importance of "counterfactual" thinking: the case of
                 the 2003 Canberra bushfires..213

Bibliography...225

Index..237

CONTRIBUTORS

Richard J Angiullo is currently a part-time management consultant at DuPont Safety Resources, and Adjunct Professor in the Graduate School of Business Administration at Wilmington University, Delaware, in the United States. He previously held various vice-presidential positions with DuPont companies during a career that spanned 35 years. Richard served on numerous boards during the later part of his career. He has an MChE from the University of Delaware (1975), and a BChE from the City College of New York (1969). He is a member of the American Institute of Chemical Engineers, and Tau Beta Pi and Omega Chi Epsilon (National Engineering Honor Societies).

Max Bice has worked at Airservices Australia for over 30 years and currently holds the position of Manager Safety Services. He leads a diverse and distributed team that provides frontline support in the application of Airservices' safety management system within project and operational service delivery.

He has a broad knowledge of operational systems in Airservices, ranging from communication and navigation systems to air traffic management systems. For the last 10 years, Max has been intimately involved in establishing, maintaining and enhancing Airservices' safety management system to meet the regulatory requirements and social expectations placed on the organisation.

Max has provided safety, quality and risk management consultancy services to international air navigation service providers in the Asia-Pacific region. In addition, he has undertaken work in the rail industry, most notably in executive and senior management safety training, and probabilistic risk assessment of passenger egress for emergency situations. In a "sabbatical" to the US, Max worked with Outcome Engineering under the leadership of David Marx, undertaking probabilistic risk assessment of patient harm in the delivery of healthcare. This was an invaluable learning experience and provided tangible evidence of the value of "just culture" as a cornerstone to enhancing safety outcomes.

Kate Branford is a human factors specialist with Dédale Asia Pacific in Melbourne. Her PhD research, completed in 2007, involved developing guidelines for the AcciMap approach (a systems-based technique for analysing organisational accidents) and investigating the validity and reliability of the approach. This research was funded by the Defence Science and Technology Organisation, and supervised by Dr Neelam Naikar from the DSTO and Professor Andrew Hopkins from the Australian National University. Kate obtained a BA with first class honours from ANU in 2003, and received the University Medal for her honours thesis investigating the attribution of blame in accident analyses. Prior to this, she worked as an intern for the Civil Aviation Safety Authority's Fatigue Management Committee as part of the Australian National Internships Program. Kate's current areas of work include accident and incident analysis, safety culture enhancement, and teamwork and training in safety-critical industries.

Jan Hayes has 25 years' experience in safety and risk management. Her project experience covers a range of industries, including offshore oil and gas, onshore petrochemicals, gas pipelines, mining, manufacturing and transportation (including air traffic control). She has worked as a consultant for operational sites, major projects and regulators. She began her career in 1983 in oil and gas process plant operations, and then moved to detailed design. She was involved in the initial Australian oil industry response to the Piper Alpha incident in 1988, and has been working almost exclusively in industrial safety since then. Jan was a director and part-owner of Qest Consulting Pty Ltd (one of Australia's best-known industrial risk and safety consultancies) between 1991 and 2004. Holding a number of operational roles, she managed up to 50 staff and was personally responsible for projects ranging from technical safety studies (such as safety cases, HAZOP studies, quantitative risk assessments and reliability studies) to organisational psychology reviews and human factors studies. She is currently completing a PhD on operational decision-making with Professor Andrew Hopkins at the Australian National University. She also works part time with a small group of clients on safety performance improvement projects. She holds a BEng from the University of Adelaide and an MBusLOD from Swinburne University.

Andrew Hopkins is Professor of Sociology at the Australian National University in Canberra. His recent books have focused on the organisational and cultural causes of major accidents. He was an expert witness at the Royal Commission into the causes of the fire at Esso's gas plant at Longford in Victoria in 1998, and subsequently wrote *Lessons from Longford: the Esso Gas Plant Explosion*. In 2001, he was the expert member of the Board of Inquiry into the exposure of Air Force maintenance workers to toxic chemicals. He has been involved in various government OHS reviews and has done consultancy work for major companies in the resources sector. Andrew was a consultant to the US Chemical Safety and Hazard Investigation Board during its investigation into the Texas City accident, and subsequently wrote *Failure to Learn: the BP Texas City Refinery Disaster*. He received the 2008 European Process Safety Centre Award for extraordinary contribution to process safety. He speaks regularly to audiences around the world about the causes of major accidents. Andrew has a BSc and an MA from ANU, a PhD from the University of Connecticut, and is a Fellow of the Safety Institute of Australia.

Carl Macrae is special advisor to the National Patient Safety Agency within the United Kingdom National Health Service. His research focuses on the analysis and management of risk, knowledge and resilience, particularly in safety-critical and high-consequence industries. Carl has previously held posts at the Economic and Social Research Council Centre for Analysis of Risk and Regulation, London School of Economics and Political Science, and in the regulatory risk group of an investment bank. He completed his PhD at the University of East Anglia in 2005, funded by the ESRC in collaboration with a large airline, and had the pleasure of being an ESRC Visiting Scholar at the Australian National University in 2004. He is a chartered psychologist and has taught on risk management and regulation courses at LSE and UEA. Carl's book, *Risk and Resilience: Near-Miss Management in the Airline Industry*, is forthcoming from Palgrave Macmillan.

Neelam Naikar is the lead scientist at the Centre for Cognitive Work and Safety Analysis. She joined the Defence Science and Technology Organisation as a research scientist in 1996, and was promoted to senior research scientist in 1999. Some of Neelam's major projects at the DSTO have involved the extension of cognitive work analysis to support the acquisition of complex military systems (such as Airborne Early Warning and Control and F/A-18), and the application of AcciMap analysis and the critical decision method to enhance safety in complex military systems (such as the F-111). Her current research interests include the development of theories and methods for analysing cognitive work and safety in complex systems. Neelam obtained a BSc (Hons) in psychology from the University of New South Wales in 1993, and a PhD in psychology from the University of Auckland in 1996. Neelam is a member of the Board of Editors for the *International Journal of Aviation Psychology*.

Madeleine E Rowland is an undergraduate student at the Australian National University. In 2008, she received first class honours in sociology after completing a thesis under the supervision of Professor Andrew Hopkins. Her thesis is entitled "Blame and Cause" and examines the coronial inquest into the 2003 Canberra firestorm. She has given several talks to Canberra community groups on the findings in her thesis. Madeleine is currently completing her LLB, and hopes to pursue a career in disaster analysis, mitigation and prevention when she graduates. This is Madeleine's first academic publication.

PREFACE

Andrew Hopkins

Train crashes, space shuttle accidents and oil refinery fires all have very different physical causes. But at the organisational and cultural levels, the root causes are surprisingly, and distressingly, similar. Mindless cost cutting, incentive schemes that divert attention from safe operation, failure to consider the safety implications of organisational changes — all these are regularly found to have contributed to major accidents. Because this is so well established, it may be that research into the causes of accidents is at a point of diminishing returns.

There is, however, another way that we can hope to prevent accidents, and that is by studying organisations that don't have them — so-called high reliability organisations. What are these organisations doing that enables them to operate safely? What can other organisations learn from them about accident prevention? Answering these questions is a primary purpose of this book.

But it is not the only purpose. Another is to showcase the work of some of the people I have been associated with (both colleagues and students), in particular, some of my honours and PhD students at the Australian National University. Academics in the hard sciences take it for granted that their students will work on topics closely related to their own interests — indeed, will often contribute to their own research agendas. This is not nearly such a common pattern in the social sciences, and I count myself fortunate to have had students at both honours and PhD level work on topics that are close to my own research interests.

The book is organised as follows. Part 1 is a study of Australia's navigation service provider, Airservices Australia, which was judged to be an organisation from which other organisations could learn. The study was funded by an Australian Research Council linkage grant, with Airservices as the linkage partner. The lynchpin of this partnership was Dr Claire Marrison, then safety manager at Airservices. It was she who made the whole project possible. The grant was, in part, to provide a PhD scholarship, which was awarded to Jan Hayes. Hayes is therefore a prominent contributor to this book.

Part 2 of the book moves away from the Airservices study and looks at other high-hazard organisations from which we can learn. It also contains three chapters on the logic of accident analysis — a topic that has fascinated various research students I have worked with. Part 2 is introduced with some editorial commentary that highlights important points and identifies common strands.

Canberra, September 2009
andrew.hopkins@anu.edu.au

PART 1

The air traffic control study

INTRODUCTION TO PART 1

Part 1 of this book is a study of Australia's air traffic control organisation, Airservices Australia. It takes as its starting point the literature on high reliability organisations (HROs). Chapter 1 is a critical discussion of the concept of an HRO and argues that HRO theorists have not defined the term clearly enough for others to be able to determine whether any particular organisation is or is not an HRO. For instance, while HROs are said to have remarkably low accident or incident rates, there is no way that this can be used as a decision criterion since the theory does not tell us how low an accident/incident rate needs to be to warrant classification as an HRO. I argue that, ultimately, the concept of an HRO is an ideal to which organisations may aspire, and that we can never expect to identify organisations that live up to this ideal in every respect. This means that we cannot expect to advance our understanding of safety by first identifying HROs and then studying how these HROs do business.

How can a study of a particular organisation like Airservices be justified in this context? Chapter 2 provides that justification. I argue that Airservices is the kind of organisation where aspects of HRO functioning are likely to be found. It is an organisation where a single error, if not contained, could cause not one fatality, but hundreds. Its staff are acutely aware of this potential, and act accordingly. Furthermore, because the stakes are so high, Airservices is closely scrutinised by an array of watchers — a circumstance that is known to be conducive to HRO behaviour. In short, this is not just one more organisation which is being studied to see how well it measures up to the HRO ideal; it is an organisation which can be expected to show some of the characteristics of an HRO. It is therefore an organisation from which other organisations can expect to learn. It is clear, then, that I have taken a liberty with the title of this book: strictly speaking, the book is not about learning from HROs but, rather, in the case of the Airservices study, learning from an organisation that can be expected to exhibit aspects of HRO behaviour. Two aspects are of particular interest: Airservices' incident reporting system, and its evolving hazard management system. These are discussed in Chapters 3 and 4.

Chapter 3 deals with incident reporting. Airservices has specified what it wants reported and has gone to great lengths to create a culture of reporting. The chapter shows how these reports are responded to, how they are prioritised, and how Airservices tries to learn from them. There are certainly lessons here for other organisations. The research on which the chapter is based was carried out in the first half of 2007. It is thus a snapshot of the situation that existed at that time. Airservices has already used the chapter for self-educational purposes.

Chapter 4 is a discussion of a hazard management system that is being developed, based on "bow tie" thinking. Airservices was dissatisfied with the way it identified, analysed and responded to hazards. The chapter describes the introduction of a system that more readily and transparently identifies the controls required for each hazard. This chapter is co-written by Max Bice, the Airservices manager responsible for the introduction of the system, and Jan Hayes, who worked as a consultant on the project.

CHAPTER 1

THE PROBLEM OF DEFINING HIGH RELIABILITY ORGANISATIONS

Andrew Hopkins

Introduction

So-called "high reliability organisations" (HROs) are frequently seen as models for others to follow. For instance, the presidential inquiry into the 2003 space shuttle *Columbia* disaster chose to evaluate the National Aeronautical and Space Administration (NASA) against the way that an HRO would have performed. It found that NASA fell a long way short of this standard. The report was a clear invitation to NASA, and more generally to all organisations using complex and risky technologies, to examine how HROs operate and to learn from them.

But if we are to learn from HROs, we must first be able to identify them. How do we know one when we see one? This is an important question from a practical point of view. Where should NASA turn if it wants to learn from a real HRO? I am frequently asked to name a specific HRO in Australia that other organisations can use to benchmark their own performance. How should I respond to such requests? Are there any criteria that would enable me to decide whether a particular organisation is an HRO and therefore worthy of attention by other organisations? This is the question that motivates the present chapter.

The original HRO research

The term "high reliability organisation" originated in the 1980s with a group of researchers at the Berkeley campus of the University of California. They observed that there had been much research on organisations that had experienced disaster, but very little on organisations that, despite operating highly hazardous technologies, appeared to function without mishap. Here are their words:

> "[In 1984] three interdisciplinary faculty members at the University of California, Berkeley, joined forces because they were in a position to capitalise on an amazing and quite unique opportunity to examine, in depth, three organisations in which errors could have catastrophic consequences, but which seemed to manage their tasks well despite great technical complexity and pressure to perform. The three

organisations ... were not so much selected as offered to us, by a conjunction of personal contacts and previous research. Although the selection process was far from 'objective' ... the opportunity was not resistible." (Mannarelli, Roberts & Bea 1996, p 84)

The three organisations concerned were, first, the United States Federal Aviation Administration's air traffic control (ATC) system, second, an electricity company operating both a nuclear power station (Diablo Canyon) and an electricity distribution system, and third, the US Navy's nuclear aircraft carrier operations.

It was only after the work began that the researchers turned their attention to defining an HRO more carefully. Perhaps the most considered attempt was the following:

"Within the set of hazardous organisations, there is a subset which has enjoyed a record of high safety over long periods of time. One can identify this subset by answering the question, 'how many times could this organisation have failed, resulting in catastrophic consequences, that it did not?' If the answer is in the order of tens of thousands of times, the organisation is 'highly reliable'." (Roberts 1990, p 160)

Critics have pounced on an obvious problem with this definition. Many organisations could fail catastrophically at each and every second of the day. There are 86,400 seconds in a day. An organisation could therefore undergo a major accident every day and still count as highly reliable by the above definition. Indeed, say the critics, by this criterion "it is difficult to think of any low reliability organisations" (Marais, Dulac & Leveson 2004, p 3).

Perhaps in order to avoid this kind of objection, HRO researchers have also defined HROs in a less precise way, by saying that they are hazardous systems that produce "nearly accident-free performance" (La Porte 1996), or function in a "nearly error-free fashion" (La Porte & Consolini 1998, p 848). Various statistics are then produced to support the claim that the three organisations studied are indeed HROs in this sense.

Consider, first, nuclear aircraft carriers. The original HRO researchers note that, in one typical year, the US Navy had 1.93 accidents involving fatalities, or property damage of half a million dollars or more, for every 100,000 flight hours. However, such evidence does not mean much until it is put into comparative perspective. The researchers claim, without data, that compared with "ordinary organisational performance", this is "very safe" (Roberts 1989, p 114). On the other hand, critics claim, also without data, that "the accident rate in aircraft carrier landings (a commonly cited example of an HRO) is relatively high compared to many other high-risk activities" (Marais, Dulac & Leveson 2004, p 3). These differing interpretations indicate just how difficult it is to use statistics to support any claim of "near accident-free performance".[1]

Second, in relation to the electricity company, HRO researchers cite various figures demonstrating the reliability of the electricity supply to consumers. In one period, for instance, the supply was "99.965% reliable in terms of outages" (Roberts 1989, p 114). The researchers also refer to the reliability of the company's nuclear reactors, noting that, in 1991, one of these power stations set a reliability record by running for 481 consecutive days without interruption (Klein, Bigley & Roberts 1995, p 777).

The problem with these data, however, is that reliability, especially reliability of supply, is not always equivalent to safety. Indeed, the two may pull in opposite directions. Reliability of supply over a particular period may be achieved by running plant in a dangerous way and, conversely, safety may sometimes depend on shutting off supply.[2] The fact that the nuclear power station achieved a record run without interruption is not necessarily an indicator of how safely it was being run.

Third, in relation to ATC, HRO researchers make statements of the following type:

> "While there were 44,450 highway fatalities in 1990 [in the US], there were 827 aviation accidents. In that same year, air route traffic control centers handled 37 [million] aircraft and airport towers handled 63 [million] aircraft." (Roberts 1993, p 169)

It is difficult to draw any conclusions about air safety from this statement, as a moment's reflection will make clear. More importantly, it tells us nothing about the safety of the ATC system, since many of the 827 aviation accidents referred to above would have been outside controlled airspace and would have had nothing to do with ATC.

Far more relevant is the observation that "in the past ten years there has been no instance of a midair collision when both planes were under positive control"

---

1 The HRO researchers note that, during a trip aboard the USS *Enterprise* in 1987, it took its 250,000th arrested landing without the kind of error in arrestor wire settings that could have led to the loss of an aircraft overboard (Rochlin, La Porte & Roberts 1987, p 85). Such evidence of absolute error-free operation makes the claim to high reliability more plausible. On the other hand, the researchers also note that none of the six US nuclear aircraft carriers has ever been destroyed (Roberts & Gargano 1990, p 147). The interpretation of this information depends crucially on the standard of comparison. It is rare for large ships to be destroyed in peace time and, from this point of view, the fact that none of the nuclear aircraft carriers has been destroyed seems hardly remarkable.

2 Railways are another context in which reliability and safety can be in direct conflict. Insisting that trains run on time can sometimes be at the expense of safety (Hopkins 2005, pt B).

(Roberts 1989, p 114). This is obviously a carefully worded statement, and one is left wondering about the possibility of collisions where only one plane was "under positive control". Nevertheless, this record supports the status of the US ATC system as an HRO, in that ATC has been accident-free, not just *near* accident-free, for at least 10 years. Of course, this conclusion leaves open the question of how many midair collisions it would take to undermine ATC's status as an HRO. Swiss ATC was responsible for a disastrous midair collision in 2002, with large-scale loss of life (BFU 2004). If such an event occurred in the US, would US ATC still be regarded as an HRO?

It is clear from this discussion that most of the figures provided by the HRO theorists cannot readily be used to justify their decisions to study these particular organisations. They lend plausibility to those decisions once made, but they do not provide the kind of criteria that would enable us to identify other HROs.

Although HRO theorists deploy statistics in the manner discussed above, they do acknowledge that these statistics are not definitive. In an article devoted specifically to this question of definition, Rochlin admits that "no truly objective measure is possible". He continues:

> "What distinguishes reliability enhancing organisations is not their absolute error or accident rate, but their effective management of innately risky technologies … There is, therefore, no a priori way to evaluate … the mathematical or statistical performance of the organisation … relative to any theoretical optimal condition." (Rochlin 1993, p 17)

Here, then, is a very explicit statement that, strictly speaking, statistical data are of no use in identifying additional HROs beyond those that have already been studied.[3]

Other approaches to identifying HROs

Let us consider some alternative approaches to identifying HROs. Based on their empirical investigations, HRO theorists have made various lists of organisational characteristics that describe the three organisations studied. In principle, these lists of characteristics can be used to evaluate the extent to which other organisations qualify as HROs.

---

3 Another HRO researcher candidly admits that the three organisations studied cannot be assumed to be a random sample and, indeed, "no one now knows what the population of HROs might be" (La Porte 1996, p 69).

One set of characteristics that has been identified relates to the nature of the technology in use: complex, demanding, tightly coupled (in the sense that sequences of events are rapid and difficult to interrupt), and highly hazardous. Interestingly, HRO theorists have sometimes used this set of technological characteristics to rule out whole industries as potential locations in which HROs might be found. So, for example, Rochlin (1993, p 22) argues that no organisation in the railroad industry can be an HRO, mainly on the grounds that the technology is "reasonably simple and straightforward" and the hazards are considered by the public to be "self-limiting". Similarly, Roberts and Rousseau argue that petroleum refineries cannot be HROs because:

> "… these and many other continuous processing facilities do not specifically involve compressed time frames or simultaneously critical outcomes. The technology itself has a high degree of predictability, unlike that found in high-reliability organisations." (Roberts & Rousseau 1989, p 133)

This is bad news for organisations in industries that have been influenced by some of the HRO literature and are aspiring to join the HRO ranks. Projects have been undertaken in the oil and gas industry to encourage the growth of HRO modes of operation, but HRO theorists appear to be arguing that such projects are misconceived from the outset. This is clearly an unsatisfactory conclusion and one would have to say, therefore, that it is not useful to define HROs in terms of the technology in use.

Fortunately, there is another way of describing the organisational characteristics of the three HROs studied that is potentially more useful than focusing on the nature of their technologies. The alternative is to examine how these organisations go about their business. This approach does not limit the possibility of achieving HRO status to certain industries and it broadens the range of organisations that might aspire to HRO status. It has been developed most extensively by Karl Weick, not one of the original HRO researchers. Perhaps because of this, he has been able to free himself more effectively from the original context and to extract from it the ideas of broadest relevance. In so doing, he has reconceptualised HROs as "mindful" organisations. This is a useful change of terminology since it gets away from questions of just how safe an organisation has to be before it can be considered an HRO, and it highlights instead what an organisation needs to do in order to reach the required end state. As Weick and Sutcliffe say:

> "Other people who had examined these organisations were struck by their unique structural features. We saw something else: these organisations also think and act differently." (Weick & Sutcliffe 2001, p xiii)

The following passage both identifies the five characteristics that Weick and Sutcliffe have distilled from the HRO literature and demonstrates the conceptual shift from HRO to mindful organisation:

> "HROs manage the unexpected through five processes: (1) pre-occupation with failures rather than successes, (2) reluctance to simplify interpretations, (3) sensitivity to operations, (4) commitment to resilience and (5) deference to expertise, as exhibited by encouragement of a fluid decision-making system. Together, these five processes produce a collective state of *mindfulness*." [emphasis in original] (Weick & Sutcliffe 2001, p v)

Let us consider these five characteristics in more detail.

Preoccupation with failures rather than successes

High reliability organisations understand that long periods of success breed complacency and they are therefore wary of success. They are preoccupied with the possibility of failure. They hunt for lapses and errors, recognising that these may be the precursors to larger failures. They therefore have well-developed systems for reporting near misses, process upsets, and all kinds of small and localised failures.

Putting this another way, errors and other small failures amount to warnings of danger, indicators of how things might be about to go disastrously wrong. High reliability organisations are alert to the warnings of danger and operate on the basis that, if warnings are identified and acted on, disaster can be averted.

Critics, however, have argued that the warning signs are only obvious in retrospect and that it is often not possible to discern their significance beforehand. The point is often put in terms of the signal/noise metaphor. For instance, Perrow argues that, although there were warnings prior to the near disaster at the Three Mile Island nuclear power station in 1979, it would have been impossible to distinguish signal from noise beforehand. "Signals are simply viewed as background noise until their meaning is disclosed by an accident" (Perrow 1982, p 175).

Weick and Sutcliffe allude to this criticism: "… some experts argue that it is impossible to anticipate the unexpected both because there are almost an infinite number of weak signals in the environment and because the ability to pick up these weak signals is far beyond the existing technological capabilities of most organisations" (Weick & Sutcliffe 2001, p 53). In their view, however, the evidence does not support these critics.

To take a particular example, the warnings prior to the near meltdown of the Three Mile Island nuclear power station in 1979 were not weak signals, lost in the background noise; they were explicit letters and memos from engineers foreshadowing exactly what happened (Hopkins 2001). They were ignored, not because they were indistinguishable from noise, but because the organisations concerned had no capacity to listen. (It was the experience of Three Mile Island which transformed nuclear power stations, at least in the US, into HROs (Rees 1994).)

The signal/noise metaphor is central in the analysis of HROs. "The key difference between HROs and other organisations in managing the unexpected often occurs at the earliest stages, when the unexpected may give off only weak signals of trouble. The overwhelming tendency is to respond to weak signals with a weak response. Mindfulness preserves the capability to see the significant meaning of weak signals and to give strong responses to weak signals" (Weick & Sutcliffe 2001, pp 3-4).

Warning signs are usually ambiguous and may well have innocent or unproblematic explanations. The important point is not to default to the assumption of normalcy but to investigate the signals which are appearing until they are either demonstrated to have an innocent explanation or, alternatively, are confirmed as unambiguous indicators of danger. This is exactly what mindful organisations do. "Mindfulness involves interpretative work directed at weak signals" (Weick, Sutcliffe & Obstfeld 1999, p 90). It is the interpretive work which reveals their true significance.

Before moving on, it should be noted that there is another line of research that converges on this same conclusion, namely, research on organisational safety cultures. Reason (1997) identifies various aspects of a developed safety culture but, above all else, he says a safety culture is a reporting culture in which people are prepared to report errors, near misses, unsafe conditions, inappropriate procedures, and any other concerns that they may have about safety. These are the warning signs of ways in which things might go disastrously wrong. Of course, these reports will be to no avail unless the organisation has some way of analysing and responding to them or, to use Weick's term, doing the interpretative work. Both the HRO and the safety culture research therefore converge on the need to identify warning signs, analyse their significance, and act on the analysis.

Neither the HRO researchers (Weick and his associates) nor those working on safety culture (Reason and his followers) have devoted much attention to the issue of how to distinguish signal from noise, that is, how to decide whether reported events are insignificant glitches or symptoms of deeper and potentially disastrous problems. Given the prevalence of the signal/noise metaphor and the general scepticism about the possibility of distinguishing between the two beforehand, there is surprisingly little social science literature on this issue. One of the aims of Part 1 of this book is to shed light on just how an HRO goes about analysing and prioritising the warning signs that it receives.

Reluctance to simplify interpretations

All organisations must simplify the data which confront them in order to make decisions and move forward. Simplification means discarding some information as unimportant or irrelevant. But this is inherently dangerous, for the discarded information may be the very information necessary to avert disaster. "Simplifications increase the likelihood of eventual surprise" (Weick & Sutcliffe 2001, p 94). High reliability organisations are therefore reluctant to discard information. "High reliability organisations take deliberate steps to create more complete and nuanced pictures. They simplify less and see more … they position themselves to see as much as possible" (Weick & Sutcliffe 2001, p 11). They socialise their workforces to notice more, and they employ more people whose job it is to explore complexity and to double-check on claims of competency and success. Cost cutting organisations regard such people as redundant and work on the assumption that redundancy is the enemy of efficiency. High reliability organisations treat redundancy as vital for the collection and interpretation of information that is necessary to avert disaster.

Lawson puts this another way:

> "Organisational slack, in terms of time and human resources that are not constantly subject to measures of short-term efficiency, is important for organisations coping with the challenges of the 21st century." (Lawson 2001, p 125)

For Lawson, "slack" can be defined as "the pool of resources in an organisation that is in excess of the minimum necessary to produce a given level of organisational output" (Lawson 2001, p 126). She goes on, "learning organisations require slack in the form of time to develop, and time for learning must be part of the organisation's design" (Lawson 2001, p 131).

The essential point here is that this is a matter of organisational design. In practice, this means that there must be staff whose exclusive job is the collection and analysis of relevant information. Indeed, HROs employ whole departments of people to carry out this function. These are the people who do the analysis of weak signals and determine the significance of warning signs that are picked up. In short, HROs embrace the principle of organisational slack as a vital ingredient of organisational mindfulness.

Sensitivity to operations

A third feature of HROs is that their frontline operators strive to maintain situational awareness, or sensitivity to operations, that is, they strive to remain as aware as possible of the current state of operations. Moreover, they strive to understand the implications of the present situation for future functioning. All of this presupposes frontline operators who are highly informed about operations as a whole, about how operations can fail, and about strategies for recovery.

The significance of this feature can be seen by contrasting it with the situation in many organisations where "silo" thinking prevails, that is, where employees operate within their own small sphere of influence without thought of the more remote impact of their activities. A culture of silos has been implicated in many organisational accidents (Hopkins 2005, pt B).

It is not only frontline operators who must be sensitive to operations. Managers must be sensitive to the experience of their frontline operators, in particular, by encouraging them to report on their experiences. Weick and Sutcliffe note that "people who refuse to speak up out of fear enact a system that knows less than it needs to know to remain effective. People in HROs know that you can't develop a big picture of operations if the symptoms of those operations are withheld" (Weick & Sutcliffe 2001, p 13). Here we see again the crucial importance of reporting systems backed up by an organisational capacity to learn from what is reported. Interestingly, "the big picture in HROs is less strategic and more situational than is true for most other organisations". More so than other organisations, HROs "are attentive to the front line, where the real work gets done" (Weick & Sutcliffe 2001, p 13).

Commitment to resilience

According to Weick and Sutcliffe, mindful organisations show a commitment to resilience, by which they mean that mindful organisations are not disabled by errors or crises but mobilise themselves in special ways when these events occur so as to be able to deal with them. "The signature of an HRO is not that it is error-free, but that errors don't disable it" (Weick & Sutcliffe 2001, p 14). High reliability organisations work on the assumption that errors will occur and they put back-up systems in place to catch and correct errors. A commitment to resilience is actually a commitment to learn from error:

> "To learn from error (as opposed to avoiding error altogether) and
> to implement that learning through fast negative feedback, which
> dampens oscillations, are at the forefront of operating resiliently."
> (Weick & Sutcliffe 2001, p 69)

The commitment to resilience, then, is clearly an aspect of the preoccupation with failure discussed above.

Deference to expertise

The final characteristic is deference to expertise. When operations are being carried out at a very high tempo, decisions "migrate" to the people with the greatest expertise or knowledge about the events in question. These people may be relatively low in the hierarchy but, at such times, more senior managers will defer to their expertise. Researchers have identified this as a consistent pattern in flight operations on aircraft carriers, for example. They note that even the lowest level seaman can abort a landing, without reference to higher authority. When the tempo returns to normal, the locus of decision-making moves back up the hierarchy.

Although HRO researchers have emphasised this final characteristic, critics have questioned its significance. They point out that decisions must inevitably be made by people at the front line in time-critical situations. In such situations, there is no possibility of referring matters up the chain of command. However, these frontline decision-makers are highly trained and they make their decisions in accordance with their training. Typically, too, these decisions are in one direction only — in the case mentioned above, to abort landings — and the decision-making process is relatively simple (Marais, Dulac & Leveson 2004, p 8). Air traffic controllers routinely abort landings and order aircraft to go around for another attempt, but it is hard to see how this contributes to ATC's HRO status in the US.

The principle of deference to expertise has rather more substance in situations that are not so time-critical. The decision to launch the *Challenger* space shuttle was made against the advice of the expert engineers. This was a case where decision-making did not migrate to the experts; had it done so, seven lives would not have been lost. Or to take another example, the Piper Alpha platform fire was fed by fuel from a neighbouring platform. Managers on this platform were aware of what was happening but did not shut down production because they had not been authorised to do so. As these examples make clear, the principle of transferring decision-making power to those who are most knowledgeable has much to be said for it, particularly where that decision is about whether to shut down or abort in the interests of safety.

But it is not clear how generalisable this principle is. There is now much evidence that accidents may be the result of decisions made in many parts of an organisation by people who are unaware of the full implications of their decisions. As the critics note: "… the type of bottom-up decentralized decision-making advocated for HROs can lead to major accidents in complex socio-technical systems" (Marais, Dulac & Leveson 2004, p 9).

Whatever judgment we end up making about this fifth characteristic of HROs, it is in some respects the odd man out. The other four characteristics hang together in an obvious way; they are all, in one way or another, about organisational learning. The fifth characteristic is about the locus of decision-making. Leaving aside this final characteristic, one thing is clear from Weick's account: above all else, HROs are learning organisations.

Implications

The preceding elaboration of what it means to be an HRO or a mindful organisation can be treated as a definition: an HRO is an organisation that exhibits the five characteristics described above. Moreover, if we think in these terms, it is clear that being an HRO is not an all or nothing matter. Organisations may exhibit the characteristics of an HRO to varying degrees. Indeed, the concept of an HRO is best regarded as an ideal type, to use Max Weber's famous concept (Bendix 1966): real organisations may hope to approximate this ideal, but never to achieve it in its entirety, not even the organisations studied by the original HRO researchers. The advantage of this definition is that it gets away from disputes about whether an organisation is or is not an HRO.

The definition of an HRO in terms of organisational characteristics suggests an obvious research strategy. The investigator can compare an organisation of interest to the ideal type and assess how well it measures up. As noted earlier, this was the strategy adopted by the Columbia Space Shuttle Accident Investigation Board. The research design involved comparing the NASA culture revealed in the inquiry process with other theoretical models. In the board's words:

> "To develop a thorough understanding of accident causes and risk, and to better interpret the chain of events that led to the *Columbia* accident, the Board turned to the contemporary social science literature on accidents and risk and sought insights from experts in High Reliability, Normal Accident, and Organizational Theory … insight from each figured prominently in the Board's deliberation … The Board selected certain well-known traits from these models to use as a yardstick to assess the Space Shuttle Program, and found them particularly useful in shaping its views on whether NASA's current organization … is appropriate." (CAIB 2003, p 180)

In fact, the insights on which the board ultimately relied came almost exclusively from HRO theory, and its conclusion was that NASA fell a long way short of the ideal.[4]

Treating the HRO as an ideal in this way resolves one of the difficulties that HRO researchers have found themselves in. In 1989, three years after the *Challenger* space shuttle disaster, they described NASA as an HRO (Roberts & Rousseau 1989, pp 133, 137), but in 2001, they concluded that it did not exhibit the characteristics of an HRO (Roberts & Bea 2001a, p 179). While it is conceivable that NASA had

---

4 Showing how organisations fall short of the HRO ideal is not only a research strategy — it is also a way of developing what it means to be an HRO. Weick and Sutcliffe's influential book is structured in just this way. They elaborate on the ideal by showing how the Union Pacific railway company in the US and the Moura coal mine in Queensland fell short (Weick & Sutcliffe 2001).

reverted from HRO to non-HRO status in this two-year period, it is far more likely that NASA at no stage measured up completely to what was in fact an unattainable ideal, and that the researchers had different aspects of this real world organisation in mind at the times they were writing about it.[5]

More generally, Weick and Sutcliffe have developed checklists of questions that can be used to assess where organisations stand in relation to the various HRO characteristics (Weick & Sutcliffe 2001, pp 90, 95, 96, 100, 102, 104, 106, 108, 110). These are of value to any organisation which is seeking to operate more mindfully. The checklists are a practical application of HRO theory (a good example of theory in use). They offer a way forward for organisations that feel they have stagnated in their efforts to enhance safety.

Since the initial investigations by the Berkeley group in the 1980s, there has been a growing body of work that situates itself in the HRO literature. For instance, there have been studies of hospital intensive care units and of US wildfire fighting organisations that cite this literature. However, the researchers do not claim to be studying organisations that have been previously identified as HROs. Indeed, some of the organisations studied are found *not* to be performing as HROs (Weick & Sutcliffe 2007, pp 3-18, 126-137).[6] In much of this work, the HRO concept has been subtly transformed into a model, a yardstick, an ideal, against which real organisations can be measured.

This chapter began by asking how we might go about identifying real live HROs in order to learn from them. It turns out that these are very elusive creatures that inhabit the realm of theory more than the real world. That being the case, we must find a different way of advancing our understanding of them — a task to which I now turn.

---

5   That said, it is possible that NASA approximated the HRO ideal more at one time than another. According to the Columbia Space Shuttle Accident Investigation Board: "NASA's *Apollo*-era research and development culture and its prized deference to the technical expertise of its working engineers was overridden in the space shuttle era by 'bureaucratic accountability'" (CAIB 2003, p 198, quoted in Buljan & Shapiro 2005, p 149). It is possible to read this as a statement that NASA had operated closer to the HRO ideal during the *Apollo* era than it did during the space shuttle era.

6   Large numbers of deaths occur each year in hospitals as a result of medical errors (Rosenthal & Sutcliffe 2002, p x). Some of these fatal errors occur in intensive care units (Dekker 2007).

CHAPTER 2

WHY STUDY AUSTRALIA'S AIR TRAFFIC CONTROL AGENCY?

Andrew Hopkins

Introduction

Chapter 1 showed how the high reliability organisation (HRO) has been subtly transformed from a real object of study into an ideal against which real organisations can be assessed. Real organisations can improve their safety performance by evaluating themselves against the ideal and identifying ways in which they are falling short. All this makes good sense.

But giving up on HROs as real world organisations means that they are no longer available for study and we are no longer able to refine our understanding of how best practice organisations behave. If our aim is to know more about HROs, we must find new real world organisations that approach the ideal in some respects, and examine how they operate. In particular, Chapter 1 highlighted the fact that HROs are, above all, learning organisations. If we want to examine in more detail *how* they learn, we need to go back to the empirical study of organisations that do this well. Where, then, should we look for new objects of study? Where are we most likely to find organisations with highly developed learning strategies?

At least one organisation in Australia claims (at least implicitly[1]) that it functions as an HRO. That organisation is Airservices Australia, a government-owned entity that provides a variety of air navigation services including, most importantly, air traffic control (ATC).[2] Given that the HRO is being treated in this study as an unattainable ideal, Airservices' claim cannot be accepted at face value. Nevertheless, the fact that Airservices is prepared to make such a claim suggests that it may be an organisation worthy of attention. This chapter will not seek to establish that Airservices is an HRO, or even to measure how close it has come to that ideal. The aim is simply to demonstrate that it is likely to be an organisation from which others can learn.

---

1   Airservices Australia, *Safety plan 2004–2005*, Airservices Australia, Canberra, 2005, p 18; Airservices Australia, *Annual report July 2005–June 2006*, Airservices Australia, Canberra, 2006, p 25.
2   Airservices Australia also provides firefighting and rescue services, as well as a variety of information services.

It is worth making this point another way. High reliability organisation researchers write about the organisations that they have studied with great fondness and enormous enthusiasm. At times, they seem breathless with excitement. This is not a state of mind conducive to objectivity and one wonders about the organisational flaws that may have escaped the researchers' notice. The literature on regulation talks about the "capture" of the regulator by the organisations that they are supposed to be regulating. There is a similar risk of researchers being captured by the organisations that they study.[3] Perrow describes the problem well:

> "It is easy to be awed by these behemoths and the intense level of activity in some of them, such as flight exercises at night on the rolling deck of an aircraft carrier. I cannot even walk through a nuclear power plant without being awed by the immensity of controlled power and danger. The reflection that the plant that I am in has been safe for 15 years and might be for ten more, erodes the critical scrutiny I should maintain. I remember being very impressed by one such visit and chastened to later read that it was closed down for gross violations after a series of near misses." (Perrow 1994, p 215)

This study seeks to avoid such capture. It will do so by avoiding any suggestion that Airservices is indeed an HRO. Rather, it will be argued that both the context in which Airservices operates and the nature of work done by air traffic controllers are conducive to the development of HRO behaviour. This is what makes Airservices worthy of study.

The context

The HRO literature provides a number of leads about where HROs are likely to be found. First, they operate in situations where the stakes are extremely high, that is, where the consequences of failure are so great that organisations cannot afford to fail. Roberts and Gargano put it this way:

> "[HROs] do not have the luxury to learn by trial and error. The consequences are often so great that when a major error occurs, the organisation effectively ceases to function or there is sufficient public outrage that it is significantly altered or put out of operation." (Roberts & Gargano 1990, p 147)

The nuclear power industry exemplifies this situation. The near meltdown of the Three Mile Island nuclear power station in the United States in 1979, and the enormous public reaction to what was, in effect, a near miss, put the industry

---

3   I am indebted to Jan Hayes for this point.

on notice. It became clear that, if a US nuclear power station ever suffered a catastrophic failure such as that which actually occurred at Chernobyl in the former Soviet Union in 1986, the entire industry would be threatened with closure (Rees 1994). Such an event would be a catastrophe, not only in terms of the number of people killed or poisoned, but also in terms of its impact on the industry itself.

A second factor conducive to the emergence of HROs is the presence of "aggressive, knowledgeable watchers" (La Porte 1996, p 65). These include effective regulatory agencies, active public interest groups, and strong groups of interested professionals. Again, this situation is well exemplified by the nuclear power industry in the US where there is an extensive array of watchers — indeed, watchdogs.

The airline industry is another industry in which these conditions prevail. In order to develop this point, we need to make a distinction between the aviation industry in general and the airline industry in particular. The aviation industry is quite heterogeneous, consisting, at one end, of high-capacity regular public transport which is operated by nationally recognised airline companies and, at the other end, an amorphous general aviation category which includes recreational and light commercial aircraft. General aviation aircraft crash not infrequently and, while tragic, such crashes do not cause the kind of public reaction of which HRO theorists speak. However, when a small aircraft carrying paying passengers crashes, there is a major inquiry, perhaps even a parliamentary inquiry.[4] The crash of a large passenger-carrying aircraft triggers an even greater public response.

Moreover, the airline industry is replete with watchers. In Australia, there is detailed legislation governing air safety and there are various government bodies charged with implementing this legislation, including the Civil Aviation Safety Authority, the Department of Transport and Regional Services and, within this department, the Australian Transport Safety Bureau. There are also vocal industry associations and even high-profile individuals who make it their business to watch and criticise.[5]

The result has been impressive worldwide, but particularly in Australia. No Australian jet airliner has ever suffered a fatal crash (Braithwaite 2001, p 17). Data back to 1960 show that no Qantas aircraft (jet or propeller driven) has been involved in a fatal crash. The data also show that no other significant Australian airline has suffered a fatal crash at least as far back as 1977 (Braithwaite 2001, p 11).[6]

---

4 For example, Staunton, J (QC), *Commission of inquiry into the relations between the CAA and Seaview Air*, 1996.

5 See, for example, www.dicksmithflyer.com.au.

6 Australia's worst civil aviation accident in recent decades was the crash of a small passenger-carrying aircraft in Far North Queensland in 2005. Fifteen people, including the two pilots, died (Australian Transport Safety Bureau, Occurrence number 200501977).

By any standards, the performance of the Australian airline system has been remarkable. This is perhaps just as well. In the case of airline safety, the public and politicians are not impressed by a "very low" accident rate (Matthews 2005). One major accident is one too many. In effect, the public expects a zero accident rate and that is what the airline industry in Australia has delivered. In terms of their accident record, the major airlines in this country can certainly lay claim to HRO status.

Airservices is a special player in this industry. To understand its special nature, consider for a moment a claim made by certain critics of HRO theory (Marais, Dulac & Leveson 2004, p 6). They argue that HRO theory is not generalisable to most industrial contexts because the organisations studied by HRO researchers in the US had a special characteristic: they were organisations for which there were no performance or output goals other than safety. United States aircraft carriers were studied during peace time when there were no war-fighting goals. In these circumstances, operations were for training purposes, and the primary goal was to get aircraft launched and landed safely. If the weather was unfavourable, flight operations could be delayed without major consequence. Similarly, the primary goal of ATC, say the critics, is to maintain aircraft separation, that is, to avoid collisions, either in midair or on the runway.[7] In so far as this is indeed the primary purpose of ATC agencies, it increases the likelihood that they will function as HROs.

It has to be said, however, that while safety may be the primary goal of ATC, it is not the only goal. The point is very clear in the legislation by which Airservices is constituted. The *Air Services Act 1995* specifies that Airservices "must regard the safety of air navigation as the most important consideration",[8] but it also states that one of the functions of Airservices is "promoting and fostering civil aviation".[9] To give an example of what this means, airline operators prefer a system of flexible routing on long hauls that enables them to take advantage of tailwinds and so reduce fuel ("wind surfing", as it is sometimes called). Airservices is therefore increasingly offering airlines this opportunity, and international carriers have reported flight reduction times of over 20 minutes and fuel savings of up to four tonnes per flight.[10] At the time of writing, Airservices had not offered this opportunity on the trans-Tasman route because it was realised that air traffic controllers would not be able to manage these arrangement safely. In this case, safety took precedence over other considerations.

---

7   The critics have obviously overstated their case since their claim is clearly inapplicable to nuclear power stations.
8   *Air Services Act 1995*, section 9(1).
9   *Air Services Act 1995*, section 8(1)(b).
10 Airservices Australia, *Annual report July 2005–June 2006*, Airservices Australia, Canberra, 2006, p 6.

The significance of this industry-promoting function was demonstrated by an award that Airservices won in 2005. In that year, the airline industry's peak body, the International Air Transport Association, judged Airservices to be the world's best ATC provider. Airservices notes that "the award recognises our commitment to our customers for price certainty and cost reduction through flexible tracking, new routing arrangements and airspace harmonisation".[11] These considerations are largely to do with the economic interests of the airlines.

What this means is that, in principle, Airservices could find itself in a position where it is required to weigh safety against the economic interests of some or all of the players in the industry. Its circumstances are not therefore quite as pristine as suggested above. Nevertheless, although Airservices does have multiple and potentially conflicting goals, it is set apart from other organisations by the fact that its primary purpose is to assure safety.

There is one other feature of the way Airservices is constituted that is conducive to safety, namely, the fact that it is essentially a monopoly service and is therefore not under immediate pressure from competitors to cut costs or reduce its fees to users. If it can argue convincingly that the delivery of its services requires a certain level of fees, then it will be authorised to charge these fees.[12] To this extent, it is shielded from the market forces that tend to undermine safety in other contexts. Moreover, while its owner, the Australian Government, does expect a dividend, Airservices is not expected to maximise revenue: the legislation specifically states that all that is required is a "reasonable dividend" and "a reasonable rate of return".[13]

Notwithstanding this legislative situation, Airservices has a variety of incentives to cut costs. For one thing, the users of navigation services want lower costs and are vocal in their demands. Furthermore, Airservices is seeking to offer its air navigation services in other parts of the world, which requires it to compete with other air navigation service providers in terms of the cost of the service. In the final analysis, then, there remains a potential for cost cutting to be at the expense of safety.[14]

An Airservices restructure in 2006 was designed to address this potential conflict.[15] Prior to that time, Airservices had been organised as a series of decentralised profit centres that were expected to deliver commercial growth. Top management became

---

11   Airservices Australia, *Annual report July 2004–June 2005*, Airservices Australia, Canberra, 2005, p 2. Fees are set by the Australian Competition and Consumer Commission.
12   *Air Services Act 1995*, sections 53, 54 and 55.
13   *Air Services Act 1995*, section 13.
14   Airservices staff themselves identify cases where this has happened. See Airservices Australia, *Systematic review of breakdown of separation occurrences — January 2000 to April 2003*, Airservices Australia, Canberra, 2003, pp 50, 51.
15   Details taken from Airservices Australia, *Operational restructure, all phases, safety assessment report*, Airservices Australia, Canberra, 2006, pp 10-12.

concerned that this was leading to dysfunctional behaviour, that is, behaviour that might be in the interests of the particular centre but not in the interests of Airservices as a whole. It decided to reorganise Airservices into so-called "functional" groups that would be responsible for carrying out specific activities across the whole organisation, for example, ATC, engineering/asset management, firefighting and rescue, etc. One specialised group within Airservices would be dedicated to commercial development. This new design would enable most of the organisation to focus on core, specialised activities, leaving business development to others. Since the constituent groups were more dependent on each other than previously, this structure required more centralised control. Accordingly, a management group was created, numbering among its members the head of the ATC function, as well as certain individuals with responsibility for Airservices' commercial goals. This structure means that, in principle, the head of ATC is not personally responsible for maximising profit and can argue at the highest level for a budget to facilitate the safest way to do things. Of course, this person is not oblivious to cost pressures; indeed, at interview he spoke of a social responsibility to minimise costs. But the system does ensure that safety considerations get a hearing at the highest level.

It is interesting to note that many large organisations structure themselves as a series of independent profit centres, operating with as little control as possible from the corporate centre, apart from an overriding imperative to operate profitably. This decentralised, hands-off approach by the corporate centre has been implicated in numerous major accidents (Hopkins 2000a, pp 34-37; 2008, ch 10). It is perhaps a mark of HROs that they are *not* structured in this way.

In summary, Airservices operates in the same arena as the major airlines, sharing with them a dread of catastrophic failure, and scrutinised by an array of watchers. But the fact that its primary function is to assure safety sets it apart from other organisations in the airline industry and makes aspects of HRO operation especially likely in its case.

The job of the air traffic controllers

As shown in Chapter 1, HRO theorists insist that HROs will only be found where the technology in use is complex and tightly coupled. These terms are drawn from Charles Perrow (1999) who popularised them in his widely quoted book, *Normal Accidents*.[16] A system is complex if there is a possibility of multiple, unforeseen interactions. A system is said to be tightly coupled if errors or perturbations propagate rapidly throughout the system, allowing very little time for human

---

16   I have argued elsewhere that normal accident theory is incoherent, but that is beside the point here (Hopkins 2001).

intervention. I argued in Chapter 1 that this was not helpful as a way of defining HROs because it meant that other organisations that did not have these technological characteristics were precluded from aspiring to HRO status. Nevertheless, HRO theorists claim that these things are conducive to HRO operation. In making the case for studying Airservices in the present context, therefore, it would be useful to demonstrate that ATC is a complex, tightly coupled system.

As soon as we set out to do this, however, a problem emerges. It turns out to be difficult to determine what complexity and tight coupling mean in practice. The HRO theorists assert that ATC systems display these characteristics, while Perrow asserts that they do not, and there is no way to resolve this disagreement (Hopkins 1999). Rather than waste time on this dispute, the approach adopted here will be to describe just what it is that air traffic controllers do. In so doing, I hope to show that the ATC system is one in which small problems can rapidly escalate into major incidents and that air traffic controllers must be constantly alert to prevent this from happening. Readers can then decide for themselves whether this is the type of socio-technical environment that promotes HRO functioning. The following descriptions are based on observations made at the Melbourne ATC centre.

Air traffic controllers can be divided into two broad groups — tower controllers and in-flight controllers.[17] Their jobs are very different and to some extent they operate as distinct subcultures.

At Melbourne's Tullamarine airport, tower controllers manage traffic on the taxi ways, they authorise aircraft to line up on the runway, and they clear them for take-off after visually scanning the runway. They also clear aircraft to land. One of the most critical parts of this job is to insert a take-off aircraft into the stream of landing aircraft. Controllers must decide whether there is sufficient separation between two consecutive landing aircraft to be able to do this safely. At a busy airport, there is pressure to get aircraft away as quickly as possible, but if the controller misjudges the situation, the second landing aircraft may need to abort the landing, go around and rejoin the queue of landing aircraft. This of course is an undesired outcome, but such is the tightness of the timing that it happens perhaps once a week at Tullamarine.

Once an aircraft has taken off, responsibility for it is handed over to other controllers. In the Melbourne control room, there may be dozens of controllers working at any one time, each with a screen and each with responsibility for controlling all of the aircraft in one particular sector or segment of airspace. Some of these sectors centre on major airports extending outwards for many miles, and controllers in these sectors will spend much of their time ensuring that aircraft seeking to land at these airports are appropriately separated, both horizontally and

---

17 I am deliberately glossing over the distinction between "terminal manoeuvring area" and "en route" controllers at this point so as to simplify the discussion.

vertically. Other sectors are concerned largely with high-altitude, en route flight. Responsibility for an aircraft is passed from one controller to another during its journey, and the system ensures that passenger aircraft flying on trunk routes in Australia are under ATC at all times.

Each controller may have a dozen or more aircraft moving slowly across the screen at any one time. He or she is in some form of communication with each of them, monitoring their movements, and sometimes issuing a sequence of instructions about the direction and speed of flight and even how tightly to turn in order to ensure an orderly flow of traffic approaching a major airport. There is a certain level of stress associated with this process. I heard one controller, who was closely monitoring the rate at which an aircraft was turning, muttering to himself "come on, tighten up, tighten up". His body language exuded tension as he watched, and he eventually found it necessary to ask the pilot to tighten his turn.

A high level of concentration is required and the control room is quiet, with casual conversation discouraged. As an observer, I found myself having to wait several minutes before there was a lull in which the controller could explain to me what was going on. Then the tempo would pick up again and it would be minutes more before further interaction was possible. Even a supervisor coming over to talk to a controller may find it necessary to wait for an appropriate moment. Because of this high level of concentration, controllers in some circumstances take a half-hour break every two hours.

Controllers are not just monitoring a process, they are active players.[18] Their task is to juggle the icons on the screen to ensure that they remain appropriately separated. The contrast with control rooms in petrochemical facilities is instructive. Controllers in such facilities are monitoring a process to ensure that it remains within specified limits. Their intervention is required only when things are in some respects abnormal or some change in functioning is needed. In steady state functioning, they have relatively little to do and the control room atmosphere is relaxed. There is no such thing as a steady state for air traffic controllers. The situation is constantly changing and controllers may be engaged in almost continuous decision-making to ensure that aircraft remain appropriately spaced. Furthermore, if things go wrong in a petrochemical plant for some reason, operators can push an emergency shutdown button to buy time. There is no emergency shutdown button for air traffic controllers. When things are tight, they must manage their way out of the situation as best they can.[19] At such times, they say, the adrenalin is pumping.

---

18   Again, I am indebted to Jan Hayes for this observation.
19   Similar points are made by Kirwan (2007, p 160).

Here is an example of how things can get tight.[20] The airspace around Sydney airport is constrained in various ways. To the north, there is a sector of military airspace, controlled from the Air Force base near Newcastle. To the south, off the coast from Wollongong, a portion of airspace is used by the Navy for various exercises, including weapons firing. Access by civilian aircraft to these areas is restricted in various ways. When there are thunderstorms in the Sydney region, aircraft must diverge from their normal paths, without going into restricted areas, and in these circumstances controllers may feel that they are running out of airspace. They will tell you that a good day is one in which they have managed such a tight situation successfully.

Every controller has had a hair-raising experience at some point in their career. One will tell you how, years ago, he inadvertently turned one aircraft into the path of another. Another will tell you how she once ran out of airspace in which to locate aircraft, and so on. These things are always somewhere in the back of their minds.

Controllers take pride in their work. They see themselves as being on the front line when it comes to safety. As one told me: management lives in sideshow alley, we live in the real world; we talk to aircraft and we know very well that there are hundreds of people in metal cylinders up there whose lives depend on us.

This description leaves little doubt that this is an environment in which things can rapidly go wrong and in which controllers must be vigilant to ensure that they don't. According to HRO theorists, any organisation running a socio-technical system of this nature might be expected to display elements of HRO functioning.

An example of HRO functioning

A particular incident that occurred while I was doing observations at the Melbourne ATC centre provides a close-up view of Airservices functioning in HRO mode. A flight destined for Sydney had been cleared by the controller to descend to 35,000 feet. An aircraft travelling in the opposite direction was maintaining a steady 34,000 feet. A thousand feet is standard safe vertical separation in these circumstances. Nevertheless, slightly before the descending aircraft had reached its assigned altitude of 35,000 feet, an electronic collision alert was triggered in its cockpit. The pilot ceased his descent and climbed 300 feet. Any passenger who was alert to changes in engine speed would have wondered what was happening.

---

20   Weick argues that tight coupling need not be an invariant characteristic of a system and that tight coupling can develop in particular circumstances. He analyses the Tenerife aircraft crash in these terms (Weick 1990). Similarly, ATC exhibits tighter coupling at some times rather than others.

The pilot notified the controller who subsequently notified his manager. The controller was thereupon stood down.[21] Although this is standard practice, controllers inevitably feel condemned by this procedure and believe that they should not be stood down until there is some evidence that they made a mistake. Airservices believes, however, that controllers may be unnerved by what has happened and that it is safer to relieve them of any responsibility until the matter is resolved.

The next step in this case was immediately to assign an investigator to replay the audio and visual recordings to determine exactly what had happened. The investigation confirmed that the descending aircraft had not gone below its assigned level — in fact, had not even reached it — when the collision alert went off. In other words, there had been no breakdown of separation, and at no stage were passengers in any danger. The warning was in some respects a false alarm. The only explanation that the investigator could suggest was that the instrument on the incoming flight was unnecessarily sensitive.

However, there was a secondary issue that concerned the control room managers that night. The collision avoidance system would have told the pilot of the descending aircraft to climb. On the other hand, the controller twice told the descending pilot that he should maintain 35,000 feet. What should the pilot do, continue his descent to 35,000 feet, or climb? In fact, he chose to climb. It was the controller's instructions to the pilot to maintain 35,000 feet that had management worried. What had come immediately to mind was the world's worst midair collision, which occurred in the skies above Überlingen in Europe five years earlier in 2002. In that case, two aircraft had been on a collision course, and their collision avoidance instruments told them to take certain evasive action, but controllers gave contrary instructions. The pilot of one aircraft followed the controller's instructions, with catastrophic consequences. The worldwide response to this accident was a policy that, in these circumstances, aircraft should follow the advice of their collision avoidance systems, and that controllers should refrain from giving instructions and limit themselves to advising on the whereabouts of other aircraft. As can be seen, the Melbourne controller had not followed this policy and the Überlingen parallel clearly sent shivers down a number of spines. The controller was given additional training and re-instated, and a decision was made to give all controllers additional training on this matter.

This sequence of events demonstrates a number of things about the way Airservices operates. First, although the incident was not even a near miss, it triggered an immediate response. In the course of this response, Airservices identified a failure to follow procedure. The failure was in no way contributory to the incident, but it was the type of failure that in other circumstances could have, and indeed had

---

21   A similar process is followed in US ATC (Vaughan 2005, p 53).

had, catastrophic consequences. Airservices therefore took active steps to ensure future compliance with the procedure. Clearly, it had squeezed as much learning from this incident as it could. Notice that Airservices' response was not stimulated by its own experience but by lessons it had learnt from elsewhere. High reliability organisations cannot afford to wait to learn from their own experience. They must learn from the experience of others.

The accident record

It was argued in Chapter 1 that accident rates cannot be used to determine whether or not an organisation is an HRO. However, it would seem strange to propose Airservices as an object for study without saying something about its safety record. Two preliminary points must be noted. First, Airservices provides separation services to a range of aircraft, from major airliners to general aviation aircraft. In other words, the statistics to be discussed here refer to the aviation industry generally, not just the airline segment of the industry. Second, it must be understood that not all airspace is controlled by Airservices. Roughly speaking, Airservices controls all high-altitude airspace, as well as airspace down to the ground around major airports. The airspace around smaller airports is controlled to varying degrees. Most other airspace is uncontrolled. Collisions occurring in uncontrolled airspace are prima facie not the responsibility of ATC.

In order to obtain data on the accidents for which ATC was in some way responsible, an approach was made to the Australian Transport Safety Bureau (hereafter, the Safety Bureau). This is an official agency to which all safety-related incidents in the aviation industry must be reported. It is quite independent of Airservices and is therefore an unbiased source of information about Airservices' performance. The Safety Bureau makes judgments about who was responsible for an incident, in particular, whether it can be attributed to some failing on the part of ATC. Accordingly, there is a category of "ATC-attributable" events in the Safety Bureau database.[22] For the purposes of this research, the Safety Bureau provided a complete listing of ATC-attributable events from 1969 to 2006. During this entire period, only one midair collision was regarded as "ATC-attributable" by the Safety Bureau, and there were no ATC-attributable fatal aircraft incidents of any other kind.[23] The

22 The descriptor in the database is "ATS stream" but Safety Bureau personnel refer to this as "ATC-attributable".

23 Certain data errors and ambiguities needed to be clarified with the Safety Bureau in order to come to this conclusion. In particular, the list included: a collision between two light aircraft in 1969 at Parafield that was incorrectly attributed to ATC; an aircraft crash attributable to military ATC which is not the subject of this study (Australian Transport Safety Bureau, Occurrence number 199904842); and a midair collision between two light aircraft at Bankstown that was incorrectly attributed to ATC (Australian Transport Safety Bureau, Occurrence number 200201846). It did not include the Coolangatta accident discussed in the text, probably because of a coding error.

one midair collision involved two single-engine aircraft doing training circuits at the small regional airport of Coolangatta in 1988 (ATSB 1989). The aerodrome controller instructed one of these aircraft to perform a holding manoeuvre to allow an incoming passenger aircraft to land. In the process of performing the manoeuvre, it collided with the other light aircraft that was doing training circuits. Both occupants of each aircraft were killed.

This was not the only midair collision during the period for which data are available. In one year alone (2002), there were three such collisions, causing the Safety Bureau to carry out a review of all midair collisions from 1961 to 2003 (ATSB 2004a). It found that, during this period, there were 37 midair collisions, all involving small aircraft at general aviation airports. Since 1968, there had been approximately one per year. Most of these collisions involved aircraft that were taking off or landing. However, apart from the Coolangatta collision, none of these was in airspace controlled by ATC or in any other way ATC-attributable.

The meaning of "ATC-attributable"

At this point, we need to examine a little more carefully the concept of "ATC-attributable". Australian regulations specify that, in certain circumstances, the pilot in command is primarily responsible for separation from other aircraft (that is, for collision avoidance), while in other circumstances, primary responsibility lies with ATC. This language encourages industry participants to think of collisions, and incidents more generally, as primarily attributable to one party, usually pilots or ATC. The Safety Bureau classification reflects this thinking.

However, every thorough accident analysis reveals numerous causes, calling into question any idea of a single or even a primary cause. Accordingly, the Safety Bureau's detailed accident analyses do not limit themselves to apportioning responsibility but identify numerous causal factors. This often results in recommendations to various parties about how they might do things differently in order to reduce the likelihood of similar accidents in the future. Once this broader perspective is adopted, it becomes possible to argue that ATC policies may have contributed to certain midair collisions that have been formally classified as non-ATC-attributable.

A case in point is a midair collision at Bankstown general aviation airport in Sydney in 2002. The airport consists of three parallel runways, a left, a centre, and a right runway. When two aircraft are landing simultaneously, separation can be maximised by avoiding use of the centre runway. However, policy at the time was to allow two aircraft to land simultaneously on adjacent runways. On the occasion in question, two aircraft were landing simultaneously, one on the left and one on the centre runway, when one of the pilots strayed into the path of the other. Since aircraft separation was a pilot responsibility at this airport, the Safety Bureau did not attribute this accident to ATC. However, in its recommendations it urged Airservices to place limitations on the use of the central runway.

It should be noted that, on this occasion, Airservices did not take the view that, because aircraft separation at this airport was a pilot responsibility, Airservices was absolved from the need to learn lessons itself. On the contrary, it carried out a detailed analysis of what it might do at this and similar airports to reduce the risk of midair collisions and implemented its conclusions (ATSB 2004b, pp 70-71).[24]

The reality, then, is that accidents cannot be neatly categorised as ATC-attributable or non-ATC-attributable. This complicates any effort to specify ATC's accident record. Nevertheless, given that we want to be able to say something about ATC's performance, the Safety Bureau data provide the best available indicator. Moreover, it is the kind of data that led HRO researchers to regard ATC in the US as an HRO. In terms of this indicator, the ATC track record in Australia appears to be remarkably good. Indeed, if we restrict attention to aircraft involved in public transport, the record for collision avoidance is unblemished.

The organisation responsible for ATC

There is another complicating factor. I have described a safety record going back as far as 1969, but the organisations that are responsible for ATC have varied over the years. Prior to 1988, ATC was carried out by the Department of Civil Aviation. In that year, responsibility was transferred to the Civil Aviation Authority. In 1995, responsibility was handed to the newly established Airservices Australia. These various agencies had different legislative bases and performed different functions. They also differed in the extent to which they had commercial objectives that might interfere with the primary safety function. Moreover, Airservices itself has been through various organisational restructurings — some of which have emphasised commercial objectives more than others.[25] In short, the Airservices of today is not the Airservices of yesterday, and it does not equate with the organisations that ran

---

24 A further example of the ambiguity of accident attributions by the Safety Bureau is provided by the crash of a light aircraft as it was attempting to land at the small Benalla airport in 2004. The aircraft had been flying at altitude in controlled airspace. The lower-level airspace around Benalla airport is uncontrolled and the aircraft had to leave controlled airspace into order to land. Shortly after beginning its descent, an alarm sounded in the ATC room to indicate that the aircraft was off course. Because the aircraft was no longer in controlled airspace, the controller was not obliged to notify the pilot and did not do so, believing that the pilot, whom he knew to be very familiar with this airport, was aware of what he was doing. However, the pilot was apparently unaware that he was off course and crashed into a mountain side in cloud. The accident was not treated as ATC-attributable even though it could have been averted by an ATC intervention (ATSB 2004c).

25 See, for example, Airservices Australia, *Annual report 2003–2004*, Airservices Australia, Canberra, 2004, p 12.

ATC in earlier decades. In reality, therefore, the record back to 1969 is of limited value in judgments about how well Airservices is currently functioning.

Can ATC take the credit?

We have seen that the track record in relation to collision avoidance in Australia is virtually unblemished. Superficially, it might appear that, regardless of the nature of the ATC agency, the ATC function itself has been remarkably effective. This conclusion is not, however, inevitable. Hale and Heijer:

> "… ask whether one of the reasons why the aviation system has such good safety performance — particularly in the space between take-off and landing — is simply that airspace … is amazingly empty and so encounters, even without air traffic management (ATM) control, would be very rare."[26] (Hale & Heijer 2006, p 39)

One can make the point another way. Train safety depends, among other things, on maintaining the separation between trains. That is the job of the train traffic control system. If that system breaks down entirely, collisions are likely since trains may be running on the same tracks. Aircraft, on the other hand, even if following the same flight path, would be unlikely to be sufficiently aligned to collide.

The data provided earlier go some way to answering Hale and Heijer's question. The space around airports is sufficiently congested that, in the absence of ATC, Australia has been experiencing an average of one midair collision per year. The complete absence of midair collisions in the vicinity of the major airports controlled by ATC is therefore highly suggestive of an ATC effect.

However, there is a further complication. Larger passenger-carrying aircraft are generally better equipped than light aircraft to avoid collisions. In recent years, such aircraft have carried collision avoidance systems. Presumably, such equipment has contributed to the complete absence of midair collisions for regular public transport aircraft. Put another way, just as there are multiple causes of any accident,

---

26 They point out that, by comparison, there are an enormous number of encounters between road users each year where there is the potential for an accident (they calculate 6.5×10^{11} per year in the Netherlands). There are about 1,000 fatalities per year in the Netherlands which, after various adjustments, gives a fatality rate per encounter of 1.5×10^{-9}. By this reasoning, it is possible to arrive at the startling conclusion that the road safety record may be even more impressive than the air safety record.

Comparisons between transport modes often seem somewhat pointless. However, they become relevant when one is faced with a real choice about whether to make a particular journey by one mode or another. Thus, suppose one wishes to travel between two cities on the same continent. It makes sense to compare the fatality risk per kilometre for each of road, rail and air transport and to choose the one that involves the least risk. Such comparisons are likely to show that air travel is a much safer option than road travel.

there are multiple reasons for the absence of accidents. Air traffic control must therefore share the credit for the remarkable safety record in relation to aircraft under its control.[27]

The upshot of this discussion is that, although the record in relation to collision avoidance cannot be taken as evidence in support of Airservices' claim to HRO status, it does not provide a reason to reject it. We concluded in Chapter 1 that statistical evidence about failure or error rates could not be used to identify HROs, and the present discussion simply reinforces that finding.

Conclusion

If the HRO is an ideal, a search for real world HROs will be futile. Nevertheless, HRO theorists have identified certain features of organisational context, as well as certain technological features, that promote HRO functioning. Airservices displays these features and is therefore likely to have developed some of the characteristics of an HRO. In particular, it is likely to have highly developed mechanisms for learning from errors and failures. It is also likely to have advanced systems for identifying and controlling hazards. Other organisations aspiring to HRO status will thus benefit from an analysis of how Australia's air traffic controller goes about its business. It has been argued that "in a generation or two, the world will likely need thousands of high reliability organisations running … complex hazardous technologies" (Pool 1999, p 276). It is to be hoped that this study will assist the designers of these organisations.

Finally, it should be reiterated that this study does not attempt to make any overall evaluation of Airservices in terms of the HRO ideal. Inevitably, Airservices falls short of that ideal and there is room for improvement.[28] But that is not the point. The focus here is on what Airservices does well, and, as we shall see, there is much to focus on.

---

27   "It has been estimated that without ATC and in the absence of any ability to see-and-avoid, there would be thirty four times more midair collisions en route and eighty times more midairs in terminal areas" (ATSB 2004d, p 2). Unfortunately, these figures do not allow us to identify the contribution of ATC.

28   Airservices is not without its critics (see www.dicksmithflyer.com.au). For present purposes, there is no need to evaluate these criticisms.

CHAPTER 3

IDENTIFYING AND RESPONDING TO WARNINGS

Andrew Hopkins

Introduction

Chapter 1 demonstrated that one of the most distinctive things about high reliability organisations (HROs) is that they are alert to warnings of danger, that they have highly developed systems for picking up these warning signs and, of course, that they react effectively to these warnings. Chapter 2 provided a rationale for examining Airservices Australia, Australia's air navigation service provider. This chapter will explore how Airservices goes about identifying and responding to warnings. The focus of the chapter, therefore, is the reporting system or systems that Airservices operates.

Safety reporting systems differ across industries and organisations. In some environments, reporting systems focus on injuries that occur in the workplace. The number of injuries is used as an indicator of the safety performance of the industry or organisation: the lower the number of incidents, the better. However, individual injury rates tell us nothing about how well major hazards are being managed. It is quite possible for organisations to drive their annual injury rate to zero and remain at risk of a major accident — as is well demonstrated by accidents such the Longford gas plant explosion near Melbourne in 1998 (Hopkins 2000a).

Where an industry or organisation is trying to use its reporting system as an early warning system, it will encourage the reporting of occurrences that, while not themselves involving injury or damage, reveal that certain hazards are not adequately under control. In contrast to simple injury reporting systems, there is a sense in which the more hazard and occurrence reports there are, the better (Van der Schaaf, Lucas & Hale 1991).

Although the reporting of warning signs is vital for accident prevention, employees in organisations where such reporting systems exist are seldom given much guidance on the types of hazards and occurrences that represent the most significant precursors to injury in their environment. In short, seldom are they given guidance on what to report.

The aviation industry departs dramatically from this pattern. The industry has a relatively well developed idea of the precursor events that are worthy of reporting, and detailed guidance is provided on what to report. Indeed, Australian legislation spells out a number of things that must be reported to the Australian Transport Safety Bureau.[1] For instance, whenever an aircraft moves without authorisation onto a runway that is in use (a runway incursion), this must be reported. Or, when two aircraft under air traffic control (ATC) pass within less than a specified distance of each other in controlled airspace (a breakdown of separation), a report must be made to the Australian Transport Safety Bureau.

Partly in response to these legislatively prescribed reporting requirements, Airservices and all of the major airlines maintain their own reporting systems and provide guidance to their employees about what to report. The Airservices "safety incident" reporting system specifies a list of 18 "immediately reportable matters" that includes runway incursions, breakdown of separation incidents, difficulties experienced by pilots in controlling aircraft, failure by pilots to achieve expected performance during takeoff and landing, and so on. There is a second list of 16 "routinely reportable matters" that are judged to be less urgent but nevertheless have the potential to affect safety, and must also be entered into same the incident reporting system. This list includes matters such as failure by pilots to comply with instructions from air traffic controllers, and failure to pass on information. These lists cover the matters that by law must be reported to the Australian Transport Safety Bureau, but they are tailored to Airservices' particular circumstances so as to maximise the accident prevention potential of its reporting system. Airservices does not intend these lists to be exhaustive, and staff are encouraged to report other matters if they believe they may have impacted on safety.[2]

Apart from an incident reporting system oriented towards compliance with legislative requirements, Airservices maintains several other reporting systems which are all designed to pick up problems before they result in harmful outcomes. Two of these will be mentioned here. The first is a so-called "event reporting system". According to Airservices, this "is intended to encourage Airservices Australia staff to report an event which it is felt does not come within the meaning of an incident yet early reporting of the information may be useful in controlling risks by helping Airservices Australia anticipate failures and errors".[3] The second system is designed to allow staff to make confidential (not anonymous) reports about "safety concerns".[4] The subtle differences in focus of these various reporting

---

1   Transport Safety Investigation Regulations 2003 (Cth), regulations 2.3 and 2.4.

2   Airservices Australia, "Air safety occurrence and event reporting", in *Manual of air traffic services* (MATS), section 5, 7.5.4.3-7.5.4.7, Airservices Australia, Canberra.

3   MATS, 7.5.5.

4   MATS, 7.5.9. Airservices Australia also maintains a special system to report pilot navigation errors and aircraft deviations from authorised heights. It operates a system of General Aviation System Safety Enhancement Reports for minor matters occurring at general aviation airports. There is also a system for reporting Airservices' equipment defects (ASID). Finally, there is a reporting system that focuses on the health and safety of Airservices' employees.

systems go a long way to ensuring that deviations, errors, and various kinds of failures will be picked up and processed.

This chapter is organised as follows. First, it examines what gets reported through Airservices' main reporting systems. It also explores the reasons for Airservices' extraordinary reporting culture. The chapter moves on to consider how Airservices prioritises the incident reports that it receives. Finally, it examines the use that Airservices makes of these reports, for it is only if an organisation makes effective use of reports that it can reasonably claim to be a learning organisation.

Chapter

3

What is reported

Some sense of what is reported through Airservices' main incident reporting system can be gained by examining all reports for a randomly selected seven-day period (see Table 1).[5]

TABLE 1: Incident reports in sample week

Category		Number of reports
1	Violation of controlled airspace	29
2	Potential operational deviation	16
3	Failure to comply with ATC instructions/procedures	15
4	Emergency (such as emergency landings)	15
5	Birdstrike	10
6	Runway incursion	8
7	Information delivery/display error	7
8	Breakdown of coordination	7
9	Failure of Airservices' navigational equipment[6]	5
10	Aircraft accident	4
11	Go around	4
12	Breakdown of separation	3
13	TCAS resolution	2
14	Airprox	1
15	Loss of separation assurance	1
16	Other	8

5 Airservices Australia, *Occurrence review report, 13/11/2006 to 19/11/2006 inclusive*, Airservices Australia, Canberra.
6 These events may also be reported through ASID.

Some of these categories are self-evident or have already been explained. The meaning of the others is described below.

1. Violation of controlled airspace: broadly speaking, the sky is divided into controlled and uncontrolled airspace. In controlled airspace, pilots must only fly routes that are authorised by air traffic controllers, and the principal job of the air traffic controller is to ensure that aircraft remain well separated from each other. In uncontrolled airspace, pilots may fly where they wish, relying on their own resources to avoid collisions. Generally speaking, high-altitude airspace is controlled, and airspace nearer the ground is uncontrolled (except in the vicinity of large airports, where controlled space comes down to ground level). This means that airliners on major routes can fly in controlled airspace at all times. It also means that small aircraft, provided they stay away from large airports and fly at low altitude, can fly in uncontrolled airspace the whole time. Aircraft that fly in controlled airspace must pay for the privilege and must register their flight plans with ATC. Small aircraft operators generally prefer to fly in uncontrolled airspace to avoid these requirements. However, small aircraft sometimes stray into controlled airspace by accident. This is a violation of controlled airspace and most violations of controlled airspace are of this type.

2. Potential operational deviation: these are usually errors by ATC or pilot errors. After investigation, they are assigned into one or other of these categories (see categories 3 and 8 below). The incidents remaining in this classification are matters that have not been resolved.

3. Failure to comply with ATC instructions/procedures: almost invariably these are failures by pilots.

7. Information delivery/display error: these are cases where either air traffic controllers or pilots have not delivered or displayed the correct or appropriate information.

8. Breakdown of coordination: these are situations in which information supplied to pilots by ATC is deficient in some way (that is, delayed, incomplete, absent or incorrect).

10. Aircraft accident: the four accidents in the sample period included a light and an ultralight aircraft crash, one collapsed nosewheel landing, and one scraped engine landing. (These accidents, and indeed most aircraft accidents, have nothing to do with ATC.)

11. Go around: this is when an aircraft that is approaching a runway aborts the landing and goes around for another attempt. This may be as a result of an instruction from ATC or as a result of the pilot's own decision.

13. TCAS resolution: modern passenger aircraft are equipped with a traffic advisory and collision avoidance system (TCAS). When the system detects that the aircraft is on a potential collision course with another aircraft, it sounds a warning. Pilots may then need to change course to avoid a collision. Such an outcome is referred to as a TCAS resolution.

14. Airprox: this is when two aircraft that are *not under ATC* come too close for safety.

15. Loss of separation assurance: these are cases in which ATC was not effectively monitoring separation, as it should have been, but proper separation was neverthe-less maintained.

This last category is not specified by government regulations and is a very clear example of the lengths to which Airservices goes to pick up precursor events. Airservices' objective is to maintain, at all times, a specified minimum distance between aircraft under its control. Incidents in this last category involve no loss of separation, and therefore no danger. It is simply that, for some period of time, Airservices failed to monitor aircraft separation and hence was not in a position to provide *assurance* that aircraft were appropriately separated. There are various reasons why this might have happened, and investigating reports of this nature enables Airservices to improve the reliability of service. This attention to detail is characteristic of HROs.

When Airservices' staff make reports, they must provide a brief description of the incident and classify it into one of the categories described above. In addition, in the case of *incidents* (not events, which are discussed below), they make a preliminary judgment as to whether the incident can be attributed to an air traffic controller, a pilot or some other source. These attributions are checked by the line manager. In the sample week, 12% of reported incidents were attributed to Airservices' air traffic controllers, while 54% were attributed to pilots.[7]

Event reporting

I turn now to the second reporting system, which is designed to capture events that do not fit into the categories of the incident reporting system but are nevertheless judged to have safety implications that make them worth recording. There were 90 events reported in the sample week. This is a rather more difficult dataset to classify. Indeed, the largest single category is "miscellaneous", but it is worth mentioning three instances to give some indication of the breadth of what is reported:

1. as part of a weekly crash alarm exercise, ATC called the local police to pass on an "exercise scenario". The person receiving the call did not know what to do with

---

7   The problematic nature of these attributions was discussed in Chapter 2.

it. The call was transferred, not once, but twice, and ATC ended up conveying the message to three different people before the police were able to respond. The delay was such that air traffic controllers thought the matter worthy of reporting;

2. a Qantas pilot advised that, when he arrived at the parking bay he had been assigned at Sydney airport, it was already occupied. While it is hard to see that this event in itself had any safety implications, it is indicative of a communication failure that might, in some other circumstances, have safety consequences. Air traffic controllers decided to report the event into the Airservices event reporting system; and

3. a passenger reported to flight crew that they had seen a metal object on the runway as the aircraft was departing Brisbane airport. Flight crew reported this immediately to ATC, which put incoming aircraft in holding patterns while a runway inspection was organised. A 15 cm section of rubber door seal was found. This sequence of events was reported into the Airservices event reporting system.

This last event has interesting echoes in the HRO literature. The story is told of a seaman who thought he might have left a tool on the deck of an aircraft carrier. Such was the reporting culture on this vessel that the seaman reported the matter. Several aircraft were aloft at the time and, at considerable inconvenience, they were diverted to a shore base until the tool was found, after which they were brought back on board. The next day, the aircraft carrier commander summoned his crew for a ceremony on deck in which he praised the individual concerned for reporting his own error (Weick, Sutcliffe & Obstfeld 1999, p 93). This story is used to demonstrate the extraordinary reporting culture to be found in HROs. The Brisbane airport story demonstrates the extraordinary nature of reporting in the airline industry in general.[8]

These events give some indication of the diversity of matters that find their way into the Airservices event reporting system. Very few organisations capture such an array of safety-relevant information.

A culture of reporting

It is clear from the preceding discussion that Airservices has an active reporting culture. One piece of evidence indicates just how active this culture is. Airservices

---

8 The airline industry is acutely aware of the danger posed by foreign objects on runways. The Concorde crash in 2000 at Paris airport was caused by a foreign object on the runway — an object shed by the previously departing aeroplane. The acronym "FOD" is widely used to refer to such objects, although literally it stands for foreign object damage.

monitors the reporting behaviour of its staff in various ways (for instance, by routinely listening to samples of recorded conversations between air traffic controllers and pilots) in order to discover whether there are matters that should have been reported but weren't. This monitoring reveals less than a dozen such incidents each year.

Monitoring of this nature requires dedicated resources, and the willingness of Airservices to provide these resources to ensure that its reporting system is working optimally is one of the hallmarks of an HRO.

Many industries have difficulty in getting employees to report and it is worth enumerating some of the reasons why Airservices has been so successful in this respect. First, as discussed above, Airservices audits its reporting system in various ways which reveal whether or not its air traffic controllers are reporting. Second, Airservices has specified in considerable detail what it wants reported. Staff are not left to work out for themselves whether an incident may have safety implications and therefore be worth reporting; to a considerable extent, the organisation has done this for them. Third, there is the distinct possibility of disciplinary action if people fail to report. Fourth, in many cases, reports about the incident may be made by other parties into other reporting systems. For instance, pilots may report an incident into their own airline's reporting system. This information is shared with Airservices, and if an incident is of a type which should have been reported by an air traffic controller but wasn't, questions will be asked. Fifth, many of the reports by air traffic controllers attribute responsibility for an incident to a pilot. Since the pilots will not be known personally to the air traffic controllers, any impediments that they may feel about "dobbing in a mate" are removed.

The willingness to report survey

The energy which Airservices puts into maintaining this culture of reporting is extraordinary by the standards of most other industries, and is well illustrated by the following events. In one routinely monitored conversation, an air traffic controller was heard to say one thing when he obviously meant another. The pilot raised the matter and the air traffic controller corrected himself. However, the air traffic controller did not report his error into the incident reporting system. This is the kind of error that Airservices particularly wants reported. It is an error that has not been corrected automatically within the organisation and has only been picked up because it was identified by an external party — in this case, a pilot.

Two or three weeks later, routine monitoring identified a second failure to report. On this occasion, the air traffic controller had experienced problems that culminated in a collision avoidance alert sounding in one aircraft. The air traffic controller failed to report this occurrence at the end of the shift. The failure was obviously unintentional, as it was clear that the matter would have been reported through the reporting system of the airline concerned and thus come to the attention of Airservices in this way.

The safety management group within Airservices noted that this was the second failure to report within a matter of weeks. It generated the sense of disquiet that is so typical of HROs. In the terms of HRO theory, this was a weak signal requiring a strong response (Weick & Sutcliffe 2001, pp 3, 4). The matter was raised immediately at board level and various responses were set in motion. Most significantly, Airservices decided to carry out a study of air traffic controllers' willingness to report. Air traffic controllers are spread around Australia, some at quite small, remote airfields, and Airservices was particularly concerned about the possibility that subcultures resistant to reporting might develop at these locations. The study therefore examined reporting trends over time for different locations. It also surveyed 250 randomly selected air traffic controllers. The report found that no deviant subcultures existed and that willingness to report was high. In its words:

> "The results of the review have revealed a consistent culture which is increasing in its willingness to report breaches and failures of process or protocols. This willingness to report seemingly exists, even in the face of what may be perceived to be significant penalties, for example, the threat to ongoing employment, reduction in operating unit's reputation."[9]

The most significant negative finding of the survey was that many air traffic controllers believed that the organisation was not responding to incident reports adequately and that there was inadequate feedback to the groups in which the report originated. Airservices accepted that it was not communicating adequately about the lessons learnt. It is developing new techniques for providing feedback on incident reports and has employed additional staff to support this effort.

An aside on the meaning of "culture"

The preceding account provides a useful illustration of the meaning of "culture" in an organisational context. There are two rather different ways of thinking about organisational culture. The first sees culture as referring to the attitudes of people, while the second sees it as referring to their practices. Where the first meaning is emphasised, there is a tendency to talk about "mindset"; where the second is emphasised, there is a tendency to speak of culture as "the way we do things around here". These two ways of thinking about culture are of course complementary,

---

9　Airservices Australia, *Safety management group, willingness to report: review of reporting behaviours of air traffic controllers*, Airservices Australia, Canberra, 2006, p 7.

but they do suggest different strategies when it comes to changing organisational cultures. Where culture is seen as a matter of mindset, the aim will be to change the way people think, perhaps through various educational programs. Where culture is seen as a matter of practices, organisations will seek to change practices by providing a system of incentives and disincentives. In principle, this second approach is to be preferred. It is very difficult to change what is inside someone's head, and relatively easy to change behaviour with the right system of incentives (Hopkins 2005, ch 1). Moreover, from a practical point of view, it doesn't matter a great deal what people think, as long as they behave in the required way.

This analysis can be seen as supportive of behavioural safety programs. However, such programs are generally focused on relatively minor risks (Hopkins 2006a). What Airservices has done is to identify and promote a type of behaviour, namely, reporting, that facilitates the management of the most significant risks that it faces.

Airservices is concerned about maintaining a culture of reporting, that is, a culture in which reporting is the accepted practice: "the way we do things around here". Of course, it seeks to educate its air traffic controllers about the importance of reporting, but does not *rely* on education. Rather, it closely monitors reporting practices and ensures that there are consequences when people fail to report. It is this resource-intensive approach that has led to such high levels of reporting.

There is an interesting implication here. The willingness to report survey revealed some dissatisfaction by air traffic controllers with regard to the level of response that they were receiving from head office. Another employee survey carried out by external consultants revealed quite low levels of employee satisfaction in some areas. The consultants concluded that "safety culture does not seem to permeate top down". They justified this conclusion with the following words: "... there is no clear evidence of consistent and obvious information flow and communications emphasising safety."[10] As already noted, Airservices is responding to these criticisms and is now employing safety communicators. Moreover, it is conducting an annual staff satisfaction survey. But the consultants' conclusions about safety culture cannot go unchallenged. High reliability organisation theory suggests that a safety culture is first and foremost a reporting culture (Reason 1997, ch 9). From this point of view, the evidence is that Airservices has been successful in creating a culture of safety, despite some level of employee dissatisfaction.[11]

---

10 Dyson, L & Searles, B, "Ensuring a safety and high reliability culture", in *Feedback report to Airservices Australia*, 2005, p 3. The report (an internal Airservices' document) was based on 14 interviews.

11 For another example of successful culture creation, see Hopkins (2005, p 105).

Assessing the significance of incident reports

When an incident is reported into a system, it must be assessed for its significance. How serious is the incident and what does it suggest about the need for change? In some industries, there is considerable confusion about this process. It is worth describing some of this confusion before examining how Airservices deals with the problem.

The process by which incidents are assessed for their safety significance is sometimes described as risk assessment. Take the following example that was recounted to me by the manager of an outback production facility. A company vehicle, travelling on a road near the facility, had hit a pothole and swerved to the other side of the road before the driver recovered control. The incident was reported to the manager, who in turn had the job of determining a risk score. The facility was in a remote location and the chances of hitting an oncoming car were very slight. But if there had been a collision, it might have resulted in a fatality, he said. If he took this into account, the matter would receive a relatively high risk ranking and would need to be reported to corporate headquarters. How was he to assess the risk associated with the incident?

There is a fundamental problem with risk assessing incidents in this way. In order to identify this problem, we must first outline the standard risk assessment process, which uses a risk matrix with likelihood and severity as its two dimensions. A scenario is hypothesised, such as a being injured while operating a particular machine, or flying into a hillside while trying to land at a particular aerodrome in poor visibility. The risk assessment then involves making a judgment about the likelihood of the hypothesised event and its potential severity and, on this basis, assigning it a risk ranking. If the ranking is high, something must be done urgently to reduce the risk; if the risk is at the lower end of the scale, remedial action can be given a low priority.

The problem is that reported incidents are not hypothetical; they are actual. Furthermore, in the typical case, no harm has occurred. Strictly speaking, it makes little sense to carry out a risk assessment for an incident that has already occurred and which itself caused no harm.[12] Nevertheless, it is clear that certain incidents can sensibly be regarded as warning signs or indicators of danger, and the challenge remains as to how to evaluate their significance.[13]

---

12 In the case above, one could treat the incident as having identified a hazard — the pothole. One can then imagine a scenario, namely, a car hitting the pothole and swerving into the path of an oncoming car. This imaginary event can be sensibly risk assessed.

13 Dijkstra states that current practice in the airline industry is to assign a risk level to reported events using the International Air Transport Association risk matrix (Dijkstra 2006, p 189). As noted in the text, strictly speaking, this cannot be what is going on.

Airservices' strategy for assessing the significance of incidents

How, then, does Airservices deal with this problem? The primary function of ATC is to maintain separation between aircraft so as to prevent collisions. This very specific purpose has enabled Airservices to develop a distinctive way of evaluating the significance of incidents.[14] The evaluation involves two dimensions: the first concerns the degree of aircraft proximity involved in the reported event, and the second, whether or not the system defences functioned as intended. These two ideas will be explained below.

The proximity dimension has three categories:

1. the aircraft came dangerously close to each other (the guidelines spell out in more detail what "dangerous" means);

2. the separation requirements were not maintained but the aircraft did not come "dangerously" close to each other; and

3. the aircraft remained appropriately separated but some other potential hazard to safety existed (such as the entry of an unauthorised aircraft into controlled airspace or the failure of Airservices' facilities).

All things being equal, the first of these possibilities is regarded as the most serious and the last, the least.

The second dimension is based on the principle of defence in depth — the famous Swiss cheese model (Reason 1997). Safety in hazardous systems depends on multiple barriers or defences against hazards, so that if one defence fails, disaster may still be averted if the other defences remain in place. Accidents only occur when all defences fail simultaneously (when all the holes in the cheese line up). In the present context, the following defences stand in the way of accidental collision between two passenger aircraft. First, the aircraft should be following paths designed by ATC to keep them separated. Second, if they accidentally deviate from these paths in such a way as to reduce separation from each other, ATC, which is monitoring their progress, will advise of the error. Third, if air traffic controllers fail to notice or respond to such a deviation, pilots may become aware of the proximity of other aircraft by other means, such as radar, or even visually. Finally, if all else fails, the aircraft collision avoidance system will sound a warning to pilots when aircraft appear to be on a collision course (assuming the aircraft are equipped with such a system). If an accident is prevented by one of the early defences in the sequence,

14 Airservices Australia, *ESIR business rules*, Airservices Australia, Canberra, 12 December 2005, pp 42-44.

this is less serious than if the last line of defence had to be activated. Most serious of all is when all defences fail and a collision was avoided simply by luck.[15]

The two dimensions by which Airservices assesses the significance of incidents are set out in Table 2.

TABLE 2: Incident significance matrix

Proximity	Defences	
	One or more failed	Worked as expected
Dangerous	1A	1B
Breakdown of separation	2A	2B
No breakdown of separation	3A	3B

This matrix serves to prioritise incident reports. Notice that the "defence in depth" dimension discussed above is collapsed into two categories: did one or more of the defences fail (A),[16] or did the defences work as expected (B)? "A"s are more troubling than "B"s, and "1"s (especially "1A") are enough make your hair stand on end, according to Airservices' staff.

The number of cases in each category in the sample week identified above is given in Table 3.[17]

TABLE 3: Incident significance matrix for sample week

Proximity	Defences	
	One or more failed	Worked as expected
Dangerous	0	0
Breakdown of separation	0	2
No breakdown of separation	10	92

---

15 This second dimension is widely recognised in the aviation industry. Macrae has coined an interesting term to describe what is at stake: "organisational risk resilience" (see Chapter 5 of this book).
    As Brooker (2005) notes: "… the most important incidents to air traffic management system safety are surely those in which only the [final] Alert layer (eg TCAS) prevents collision."
16 The A classification also includes cases where the control system was "significantly disrupted". This amounts to a failure of the defence system and has been collapsed here in order to simplify the presentation.
17 The category "other" is missing data and has been eliminated from the table.

The table shows that there were no cases where aircraft were in dangerous proximity and only two cases in which a breakdown of separation occurred. In these two cases, the system defences operated as expected to restore separation. Of the cases where there was no breakdown of separation, there were 10 in which system defences failed to perform as expected. It is clear from this description that the Airservices prioritisation system functions effectively in directing attention to those matters requiring the most urgent consideration.

It must be stressed that the prioritisation discussed above reflects Airservices' concerns. An emergency landing necessitated by a mechanical failure, though a matter of great concern to passengers and aircraft operators, will nevertheless be classified as 3B (the lowest priority) as far as Airservices is concerned. The reason is clear. The system of priorities described here is designed to assist Airservices in providing separation services as safely as possible; it is not designed to deal with all of the hazards that confront an airline operator. Major airlines will have different systems of prioritisation, as will the Australian Transport Safety Bureau, whose concern is to avoid accidents of all types. The priorities that Airservices has designed for itself are a thoughtful attempt to use its incident reporting system as efficiently as possible to learn from incidents in such a way as to maximise the safety of the separation services that it provides.

This discussion highlights a distinction between collision avoidance for which the air navigation service provider normally has responsibility, and other aspects of flight safety for which the airline or perhaps the pilot has some responsibility. This distinction has been noted in other parts of the world. It has been argued in Europe that compartmentalising safety in this way detracts from overall passenger safety and that, in years to come, the two will need to be united (Kirwan & Perrin 2004). Be this as it may, it is clear that the reporting system used by Airservices is designed to maximise safety in matters for which it is responsible.

Things never stand still, however, and the system of prioritisation described above has been supplemented by a second system. The perception at Airservices was that the system described above did not focus sufficiently on the defences for which Airservices was responsible. Accordingly, it has developed a way of focusing even more tightly on matters that are within its control. The new system does not classify all incidents, only those that are attributable to Airservices. For this reason, it supplements rather than replaces the earlier system. It consists of the following four categories, in increasing order of severity:[18]

1. errors or failures by air traffic controllers that are identified and rectified by the person responsible or by some other air traffic controller before they have any significant impact on aircraft (rectified by ATC);

---

18   AA Safety Management Group, *Review of safety severity incidents 2*, Airservices Australia, Canberra, 2006, p 14. The numbering used above is the reverse of that used in the original document.

2. errors or failures by ATC that are identified by ATC but can only be remedied by requiring significant corrective action on the part of an aircraft, such as a go around or a change of course (rectified by ATC, but not effectively);

3. ATC errors that are not identified by air traffic controllers, and are identified by other parties such as pilots or other air navigation service providers. Airservices describes these as errors that "bleed out" or escape its system (rectified by pilots/other industry participants); and

4. failures by ATC that are not identified by pilots or any other party and in which an accident is avoided only by the aircraft's last line of defence (its collision alert system) or simply by luck (providence/airborne defence).

The supplementary classification represents a philosophical advance on the original one, in two respects. The original classification was influenced by whether the outcome resulted in a near collision. To some extent, whether the failure of a defence results in a near collision or only a breakdown of separation is a matter of chance and there is no logical reason to give a higher priority to near collisions.

Second, the original classification reduces the defence failure dimension to two categories and does not specify whether the failure was attributable to ATC. The supplementary system focuses on errors by ATC and treats errors that are allowed to "bleed out" or escape from Airservices as most significant. Classifying errors in this way will enable Airservices to understand why it detects some errors more quickly than others, and to learn from this how to recover from errors as quickly and with as little disturbance as possible. Recent thinking on accident prevention has emphasised that, despite the best attempts to eliminate errors, people will nevertheless make them. What is important, therefore, is to design systems so that they are not disabled by errors or, to put it another way, to design systems that are as resilient as possible. It will be recalled that a commitment to resilience in the face of error, that is, a commitment to rapid recovery in the face of error, is one of the five characteristics of an HRO identified by Weick.[19] The supplementary system contributes to Airservices' performance in this respect.

It is evident, then, that Airservices has applied itself to the issue of classifying and prioritising incident reports in a quite remarkable way. Few other organisations can match the analytic power that has been applied to the question of how to extract maximum value from an incident reporting system.[20]

---

19 Chapter 1. See also Hollnagel, Woods & Leveson (2006).
20 A petroleum company that I have studied identifies "high potential incidents" (HPIs) as ones which could have resulted in at least one fatality if one additional defence had failed. It then applies more rigorous incident investigation procedures to its HPIs.

The wider context

Let us consider briefly the implications of this discussion for other contexts. The first and most important implication is that systems for reporting and prioritising incidents must be tailor-made for the particular context. The two systems of prioritisation described above have served the needs of Airservices, but they will not necessarily be appropriate for other players in the aviation industry, let alone other industries. The failure of aircraft components, such as the blow out of a door, is a matter of great importance to the airlines themselves, but these failures are not prioritised in the Airservices classification systems. Organisations in other industries that seek to learn from the Airservices model will need to put considerable effort into identifying what they want reported and devising their own priorities.

There is a particular aspect of the supplementary Airservices' reporting system that limits its applicability in other contexts, namely, its exclusive focus on error. There are certainly some contexts where this sharp focus may be useful. For instance, the errors made by surgeons during operations may have increasingly severe consequences the longer they go undetected, and systems that encourage early detection and correction may well be appropriate in this context (Rosenthal & Sutcliffe 2002). But, in other contexts, incidents are not always the result of errors by frontline operators. In particular, when flight safety is viewed from the airlines' point of view, error is not the only source of incidents. Helmrich attributes incidents experienced by pilots to two sources: crew errors and threats. He defines a threat as "an event or error that is not caused by the crew, and increases operational complexity of a flight, requiring crew attention and management if safety margins are to be preserved" (Helmrich 2006, p 29). The most prevalent threats for airlines (according to his research) are set out in Table 4.

TABLE 4: Types of threats experienced by airlines

Threats	Percentage of flights
Adverse weather	61%
ATC[21]	56%
Environmental operational pressures	36%
Aircraft malfunctions	33%
Airline operational pressures	18%

Chapter

3

---

21 Notice that things that are errors from an ATC point of view are threats from a pilot's point of view.

Based on this analysis, many airlines do not just focus on error management, but on *threat* and error management.[22]

In keeping with a concern about threats, some airlines operate a hazard reporting system independently of their incident reporting systems. Qantas, for instance, operates a "safety observation report" system in which users are invited to report hazards or hazardous situations, such as poorly worded operational documents.[23] Poorly worded documents can contribute to misunderstanding and hence errors. Thus, a hazard reporting system is, among other things, a line of defence against errors; it can facilitate error avoidance, not merely error recovery.

The Airservices reporting system is not designed to encourage the reporting of hazards of this nature. Its philosophy is that such hazards will be revealed in the analysis of errors to which they may give rise, and that a good incident reporting system is sufficient to highlight hazards of this nature.[24] Of course, not all hazards reveal themselves in this way and Airservices also maintains a quite distinct process for hazard identification that is independent of any reporting system. This will be discussed in Chapter 4.

Using incident reports as an indicator of performance

Airservices' experience in using incident reports as an indicator of performance is worth outlining at this point. For several years, it used the number of ATC-attributable incidents per 100,000 aircraft movements[25] as a safety indicator, and set itself the target of a 2.5% annual reduction for each air traffic controller subgroup. However, in many cases, targets were not met. Indeed, the 2005/06 annual report notes that, in the most recent five-year period, the number of incidents reported by tower controllers had increased by 300%, while reporting by another subgroup of controllers had increased by 170%. These results forced the organisation to reconsider its performance measurement strategy. It noted that:

> "This surge in reporting is viewed by the organisation not as a decline in operating standards but as a reflection of an organisational culture which recognises that submission of information about the smallest deviations can assist in identifying strategies to prevent high-risk occurrences. We therefore see the positive cultural driver as a

---

22 Dodd, B, "New developments in data analysis in an airline", in the proceedings of *Emerging Approaches in Safety Analysis*, Canberra, 25-26 October 2005.
23 Ibid.
24 It would, of course, be open to controllers to report poorly worded documents through the event reporting system.
25 Technically, jurisdiction tracks.

major factor in two traffic segments failing to meet the target for the 2005-2006 financial year."[26]

Airservices had recognised its mistake. Generally speaking, an organisation that seeks to encourage reporting cannot at the same time treat the number of such reports as a performance indicator that is to be driven downwards. Clearly, Airservices needed to devise a more appropriate indicator. Accordingly, it chose to base a new set of performance indicators on the four-part classification of air traffic controller errors identified above. The principal indicator was the number of type 4 incidents, that is, where the ATC error had been detected either by an aircraft warning system or it had not been picked up at all, and an accident had been avoided only by good luck. Airservices set itself the goal of zero incidents of this type, although it recognised that this would be difficult to achieve. It subsequently reported that it had four such incidents in 2005/06.

One of the features of this indicator is that type 4 incidents are likely to be reported by pilots into airline reporting systems, as well as being reported by air traffic controllers into the Airservices reporting system. Any underreporting by air traffic controllers will therefore be obvious as soon as the information is shared. Consequently, the number of such reports is likely to be a reflection of the actual number of such incidents, rather than simply a measure of the propensity to report. It is only if incident reports are relatively immune to variations in reporting practices in this way that they can serve as reasonably robust performance indicators.

A second feature of this new indicator is that is a measure of the number of ATC errors that have escaped the system entirely. Thus, Airservices can improve its performance with respect to this indicator, not only by reducing the number of errors, but also by improving its capacity to detect and recover from errors before they escape. This will drive precisely the organisational behaviour that Airservices wants.

There has been much talk in other industries about the way that certain safety indicators, such as lost-time injuries, focus attention on relatively minor hazards (trip hazards, for example), while systematically diverting attention from catastrophic hazards, such as fire and explosion. The oil and gas industry, in particular, is feeling its way towards indicators that more effectively measure how well the risk of explosion is being managed.[27] Airservices is an example of an organisation that has identified the risks about which it is most concerned and has now constructed a system of performance indicators to address these risks.

---

26 Airservices Australia, *Annual report 2005-2006*, Airservices Australia, Canberra, 2006, p 26.
27 *The Report of the BP US Refineries Independent Safety Review Panel* (Baker Report), US Chemical Safety and Hazard Investigation Board, Washington, January 2007.

Responding to reports

A reporting system facilitates organisational learning only if the organisation has developed ways of responding to reports. Too often, reports end up in databases and may be used for trend analysis, without any attempt being made to evaluate individual reports and to learn from them. Airservices has a well-developed system for responding to individual reports and extracting the greatest possible value from them.

Reports are made electronically and, once submitted, they are immediately visible, not only to the local line manager, but also to head office in Canberra and to external organisations such as the Australian Transport Safety Bureau, the Civil Aviation Safety Authority, and any airline concerned. There are protocols with these various external organisations to ensure whatever degree of confidentiality is appropriate, but this is a far more open reporting system than exists in many organisations where a key concern is often to protect the organisation from any legal liability for errors (Hopkins 2006b). The wide distribution of Airservices' incident reports ensures that as many pairs of eyes as possible are able to scrutinise the incident and maximises the chance that appropriate lessons will be learned. The existence of multiple watchers, it will be recalled, is a recurrent theme in the HRO theory.

Once a formal incident report has been entered into the system, there are two sets of responses, one local and one corporate. I deal with these in turn.

The local response

A safety panel of senior local area staff meet once a week to review incidents that have occurred during the week, as well as other safety-related issues. These meetings can involve quite spirited discussion about whether the response to date has been adequate, and they invariably give rise to further action items.

Apart from this, incident reports go to a line manager who must decide whether a formal investigation is required. If the manager decides that no investigation is required, he or she must provide a written justification.[28] This is a vital safeguard, forcing line managers to respond in a conscientious fashion. In too many other reporting systems, managers have the easy way out of dismissing reports without providing any justification. This has led directly to disaster on more than one occasion (Hopkins 2000b). Any decision not to proceed to an investigation is reviewed by a local area safety manager, providing further assurances of conscientious decision-making.

If the matter is to be investigated, the line manager must appoint a trained investigator to carry out this task. The investigator compiles a written report. Until

---

28   Airservices Australia, *ESIR business rules*, issue 5, Airservices Australia, Canberra, p 13.

recently, the investigator was also responsible for formulating recommendations. If the line manager accepted these recommendations, they went into a corrective action database and were tracked until closed. This outcome was also monitored by the local area safety manager.[29]

An interesting development in this process occurred when head office monitoring revealed that too many investigator recommendations were being rejected as impractical by line managers. In response to this discovery, Airservices decided to change the process. In the modified system, investigators make findings about causes but they do not make recommendations. The findings go to the safety manager. This individual meets with the line manager to develop agreed recommendations that are seen by the line manager to be practical to implement.

This focus on what is practical increases the likelihood that at least something will be done, but it has the disadvantage that more fundamental and more costly system enhancements may be discounted. Investigators who are examining why an air traffic controller has made an error often discover that the root cause is located in the computer software governing ATC displays. Changes to this software are time-consuming and must be carefully risk assessed. The result is that there is a long queue of system enhancements waiting to be carried out, and three-year delays are not uncommon. Faced with these constraints, safety managers may fall back on recommendations for more training as the only practical way forward. This leads to a certain level of disillusionment among investigators. They know that the best response to hazards is to remove them; merely providing air traffic controllers with additional training in how to deal with hazards is second best. By no means all investigations lead to second-best outcomes in this way. Moreover, it should be observed that it is the quality of Airservices' incident investigations that brings these issues to light. Nevertheless, this is one area in which, as Airservices acknowledges, there is room for improvement.

The head office response

There is a second and quite distinct response to incident reports, at the corporate level, designed to ensure that the highest level of the organisation engages with what is happening at the front line. High reliability organisations, it will be recalled from Chapter 1, "are attentive to the front line, where the real work gets done".

Each day, a duty officer examines all electronic reports as they come in to the corporate head office, and selects the most significant incidents. The selection criteria used are roughly the criteria identified above. Very early the next morning, the officer finalises the list of significant incidents for inclusion in a "daily operations

---

29 Reports are called system action improvement reports (SAIR) and the database is called SAIR2000.

safety report". He or she checks not only the main incident reporting system, but also several other Airservices' reporting systems, for anything that may be worth drawing to the attention of top management. The scanning process also extends to media reports. In this way, the organisation casts the net as widely as possible. The resultant list may contain a dozen or so items. The list is delivered to the corporate safety manager by 7.30 am each morning. He studies it closely and then presents the report at 8.30 am to an "executive morning briefing". This meeting is usually attended by the Airservices CEO and most of the general managers who report directly to him. The executive group will highlight anything requiring follow-up and this is duly attended to by the safety management group. The daily operations safety report also contains information on the status of matters previously highlighted for follow-up in this way. Finally, the report contains a "safety issue list" which is designed to keep unresolved safety issues in the consciousness of executive group members. For instance, one of the issues discussed on the day I observed the process was an ongoing concern about the integration of civilian and military ATC at an aerodrome that services both civilian and military aircraft. There had been several incident reports highlighting problems at the interface of these two systems and the executive group wanted the matter resolved as quickly as possible. The CEO undertook to raise it with the Chief of the Air Force with whom he happened to be meeting that day. The incident illustrates how the system that Airservices has designed for itself escalates issues to the very top of the organisation, thus maximising the likelihood of decisive action.

The procedures involving senior management appear to duplicate the local investigative response to some extent. But they also ensure that corporate officers in Canberra remain in daily contact with frontline issues and they minimise the risk that critical matters will somehow be lost in the system.

Example: the response to a report of job overload

The response to one particular report demonstrates the reporting system in action. The report (as it happens, an event rather than an incident report) concerned an occasion of significant job overload.

In order to set the scene, it is first necessary to observe that two of the greatest threats to ATC safety are air traffic controller fatigue and air traffic controller overload. However, air traffic controllers and their managers are well aware of these threats and manage them carefully.

Supervisors monitor workloads, but air traffic controllers don't wait for supervisors to intervene. They know best if the number of aircraft in their sector is becoming difficult to manage and they can request that the sector be divided into two, represented on two different screens, and another air traffic controller brought in to share the load. Supervisors generally endorse these requests and the staffing arrangements at the Melbourne ATC centre are generally such that there are additional air traffic controllers on hand.

Fatigue is the other great enemy. Air traffic controllers are encouraged to call in sick if they are fatigued, for example, if they have had a bad night. There is basically no limit to the amount of paid leave that can be taken in this way, except that days cannot be taken consecutively. One air traffic controller told me that he had taken a total of 20 days off in one year because of bad nights caused by a new baby. Furthermore, supervisors routinely check on air traffic controllers for signs of fatigue or other problems. Perhaps once a month, a supervisor may decide that an air traffic controller is too tired to be working and needs to be replaced, always on full pay. Shift length is designed with fatigue in mind and varies from eight hours for various overlapping daytime shifts down to six hours for the midnight to dawn shift. Even so, there is considerable debate about whether fatigue is being properly managed.[30] Resource constraints have meant that there are not enough air traffic controllers to cover all shifts adequately, and they are frequently called in to work overtime. This has exacerbated the fatigue problem. There is a worldwide shortage of air traffic controllers and Airservices has not yet found a way to respond to this shortage.

Supervisors are also attuned to any medical issues that air traffic controllers may have. One air traffic controller who had just been diagnosed with cancer was taken off the job, on full pay, because of concern that his condition might distract him. In short, there is a high level of scrutiny of fitness for work — higher even than exists for airline pilots.

Against this background, let us now consider a report made by an air traffic controller following a midnight to dawn shift (the "doggo shift"). The report noted "traffic levels and complexity on doggo approaching unsafe capacity" and went on to provide details. The sector concerned was traversed by international aircraft destined to arrive at capital cities in south eastern Australia at daybreak, and traffic congestion in the sector was greatest at around 4 am. The work was complex because aircraft were not following fixed routes but were being allowed to follow flexible tracks[31] in order to take advantage of tailwinds. The sector was managed by three air traffic controllers in accordance with minimum staff guidelines but, at about 4 am, one of the air traffic controllers, who had been unwell, declared himself unfit for work and left for home. There was apparently no possibility of

Chapter

3

---

30 While this study was underway, Airservices conducted a fit for duty audit, focusing mainly on air traffic controllers' experiences of fatigue.

31 A non-fixed air traffic route calculated on a daily basis to provide the most efficient operational flight conditions between specific cities.

rostering additional staff at such short notice and this left two air traffic controllers to carry an exceptionally heavy workload, which they did without a break, until traffic began to ease some time after 5 am.

A report of this incident was filed at 5.30 am and was identified in head office in Canberra as a matter of concern, requiring follow-up. Accordingly, an investigation was carried out, resulting in a 24-page review document.[32] The investigation canvassed in some detail the way in which flexible tracks had increased the workload, and it recommended that air traffic controllers should be able to modify flexible tracks and fix aircraft in particular tracks where overload was becoming a problem, for whatever reason.

There are several things about this event report and the response to it that are worthy of note. First, the report concerns overload of frontline workers. Fatigue and job overload are frequently identified as contributory factors in accident investigations in many industries and are clearly matters worthy of report. However, there are few organisations where an experience of job overload would be deemed an appropriate matter to enter into an electronic reporting system. Second, the period of overload passed without mishap, although air traffic controllers recognised that the situation was unsafe and therefore reportable. This demonstrated a high level of risk awareness. Third, the report did not just disappear into a database. Head office identified it as a matter of high priority, and resources were devoted to investigating it and exploring possible mitigation strategies. This account shows the Airservices reporting system operating at its best.

Monitoring safety performance

The databases maintained by Airservices provide it with the means to monitor all kinds of safety trends. In recent years, Airservices has been examining trends in breakdown of separation incidents and closely studying the reasons for these incidents. This research effort provides a glimpse of an organisation that is actively learning from its errors.

The research was initiated in 2003, following a serious breakdown of separation incident. Airservices' safety staff examined data going back over three years to determine how and why the system's defences were failing. Of 160 breakdowns that had occurred in this period, they found that the great majority had been identified and rectified by air traffic controllers themselves. However, in 18 cases, the breakdown of separation had been picked up by the pilot, while in two cases, the

---

32 Almond, S, *Review of event report 2005*, document number 1452, Airservices Australia, Canberra.

last line of defence, an aircraft collision avoidance system, had been activated. In a sense, therefore, the system of defences was working reasonably well, although reliance on the last line of defence is never a satisfactory state of affairs.

The review then discovered that the incidents fell into two categories, which it called controlled and uncontrolled breakdowns. A controlled breakdown was one in which an air traffic controller was carefully monitoring an aircraft, perhaps inserting it in a landing sequence, and slightly misjudged the situation, so that two aircraft might end up 4.8 miles apart rather than the standard 5 miles. In these cases, the "rate of decay" of the situation was low and air traffic controllers rapidly recovered from such errors, perhaps by asking one aircraft to slow down. On the other hand, uncontrolled breakdowns were those in which air traffic controllers were caught unaware and "the rate of decay of the situation was high". The review team found that more than half of the breakdown of separation incidents were of this more serious, uncontrolled type and that air traffic controllers did not recover from these situations well. The report made a number of recommendations to deal with the problem.

Eighteen months later, safety staff carried out a follow-up review. The follow-up showed that the initial review had had a dramatic impact on thinking within the organisation. Moreover, there had been a sharp drop in the number of uncontrolled breakdowns.

A further 12 months on, the figures showed two unexplained monthly "spikes" and another review was commissioned. It was concluded that the spikes were probably due to improved reporting of minor, that is, controlled, breakdowns and that the proportion of uncontrolled breakdowns had continued to decline. However, examination of the circumstances of uncontrolled breakdowns suggested that a number of them had occurred because air traffic controllers had been distracted by non-routine events, such as aircraft radio failures and unusual weather events. Further follow-up action was taken.

This account shows how an incident reporting system, and associated incident investigations, can be used to great effect. It reveals an organisation that is energetically reviewing its errors, prioritising them, studying their causes, learning how to reduce their number and to recover from them more efficiently, implementing this learning, and, finally, using its reporting system to evaluate how effective that learning has been. This is a learning organisation in action.

Monitoring the effects of organisational change

Incident reporting systems can also be used to evaluate the impact of organisational change. Airservices provides an example of this that is worth describing.

It was noted in Chapter 2 that Airservices carried out a major organisational restructure in 2006. Best practice dictates that major organisational changes, particularly those that involve staff reductions, should be subjected to management of change procedures, that is, they should be examined to determine the impact that they may have on safety. It must be said that relatively few organisations measure up to this requirement.[33] Airservices, however, conducted a safety assessment to ensure that the restructure was in no way detrimental to safety. This included a demonstration that all safety functions in the old structure were carried over into the new. But it also included a series of hazard identification workshops where the new functional groups had to pinpoint hazards associated with the new structure. The hazards identified by staff included reduced accountability for safety, ineffective interface arrangements, documentation not being amended, and so on. These hazards were logged and controls were established to deal with them.[34] In this way, Airservices sought to minimise any potentially detrimental effects on safety resulting from the restructure.

Safety assessments such as the one described above can never provide a once and for all guarantee of safety. A risk-aware organisation that has carried out an organisational restructure will be concerned that uncontrolled hazards remain, and it will therefore be alert to warnings of trouble. This is where Airservices has used its reporting system to good effect:

- it carried out a trend analysis on incidents such as facility failures and loss of separation assurance to identify any possible impact of the changes on ATC performance;

- it improved the availability of its confidential reporting system so that staff could identify concerns that may have arisen about the new structure;

- it monitored the level of reporting to ensure that there was no negative impact on the established reporting culture; and

- it reviewed the rate of closure of investigation recommendations.

These monitoring activities revealed no changes in incident rates. However, two issues did emerge. First, reports were not being made as promptly as they were previously. This was raised with relevant managers and immediately resolved.[35] Second, resource limitations under the new structure were hampering the

---

33 A notable example was the 25% operating budget cut that BP imposed on all of its business units without careful attention to the safety consequences. This cut was implicated in the 2005 Texas City Refinery explosion. See Baker Report, fn 28.
34 The hazard logging system will be dealt with in Chapter 4.
35 Interview, 30 April 2007.

implementation of recommendations arising from incident investigations.[36] This was drawn to the attention of management.

In summary, intelligent use was made of the incident reporting system to pick up warnings about possible detrimental effects on safety from the new organisational structure. Here again we see a risk-aware organisation worrying about the possibility of failure and mobilising its resources to deal with this possibility. What is especially significant about this example is that it concerns safety risks associated with organisational change — not something that most organisations deal with well.

Conclusion

Airservices operates a highly developed reporting system that is designed to identify and respond to warnings of danger. It has decided what it wants reported and it has gone to great lengths to develop a reporting culture, that is, to ensure that people in fact report what they are supposed to. The organisation has put thought into prioritising these reports, and it has structured itself to bring the most significant events to the attention of its most senior managers, including its CEO, on a daily basis. Finally, it has a system for carefully investigating the most significant incidents in order to learn from them.

Airservices is an organisation that worries about the possibility of things going wrong. It exhibits the chronic unease that has been identified as one of the crucial characteristics of HROs. Reason puts it well:

> "If eternal vigilance is the price of liberty, then chronic unease is the price of safety. Studies of [HROs] … indicate that people who operate and manage them tend to assume that each day will be a bad day and act accordingly. But this is not an easy state to sustain, particularly when the thing about which one is uneasy has either not happened, or happened a long time ago, and perhaps to another organisation." (Reason 1997, p 37)

Importantly, chronic unease is not just a state of mind. It manifests as a set of practices which are aimed at detecting problems and rectifying them before they culminate in disasters.[37] Moreover, Airservices' practices ensure that its most senior managers are kept abreast of whatever bad news there may be at the workface.

---

36 Airservices Australia, *Operational restructure, all phases, safety assessment report*, Airservices Australia, Canberra, 8 June 2006, p 42.

37 Not everyone appears to recognise that chronic unease is a desirable state. Consultants employed by Airservices noted the sense of chronic unease felt by Airservices' staff and then spoke about the need for strategies to dissipate this unease. Dyson, L & Searles, B, "Ensuring a safety and high reliability culture", in *Feedback report to Airservices Australia*, 2005, pp 12, 18, 160.

Finally, it needs to be stressed that any organisation seeking to develop its capacity to hunt out and correct errors must devote considerable resources to the task. It is not sufficient to issue an instruction to staff to report and then to assume that they will. The Airservices experience suggests that it takes a dedicated and active central safety management group to make this happen. Moreover, learning from these reports is not automatic. Again, it requires an active safety management group to ensure that the organisation really does learn from its errors. When this research was carried out, there were about 90 people (in an organisation of 3,000) who were specifically concerned with safety. They were at various geographical locations but they reported to the safety management group, headed by a general manager who himself reported directly to the CEO. This is precisely the kind of structure needed to drive the systems described above.

This chapter has provided a description of how one organisation has gone about designing and implementing a system to capture warnings and learn from them. It is a case study of what it means to be a learning organisation which, as was shown in Chapter 1, is the central feature of the HRO ideal. Other organisations that aspire to the HRO ideal have much to learn from Airservices. This does not mean that Airservices' practices can or should be slavishly followed. Each organisation must work out for itself what the relevant warning signs are and what the most appropriate strategy is for capturing and learning from them. However, the Airservices case is useful in identifying some of the issues to be addressed.

CHAPTER 4

RISK MANAGEMENT: FROM HAZARD LOGS TO BOW TIES

Max Bice and Jan Hayes

Introduction

Bow tie diagrams are becoming increasingly common as a risk assessment tool, with their use recommended or endorsed in industries as diverse as mining, offshore oil and gas, petrochemical manufacturing, and aviation.[1-4] Despite this, very little has been published about the details of the practical aspects of how to use this tool and its strengths and weaknesses.

This chapter describes our experience in using bow ties and, in particular, the application of this method within Airservices Australia (Australia's air navigation service provider). We hope that other organisations considering using this method will find useful tips — or at least some food for thought — in the following description of our experience.

Airservices, like other high-hazard organisations, uses risk assessment as one way of continually improving safety performance. The generic steps of hazard identification, risk assessment and risk control are well known and have been applied in various forms for more than a decade. In 2005, Airservices concluded that its existing risk management system would soon be reaching the limits of useability for "operational risk". Spawned out of a major project to upgrade the national air traffic control (ATC) system in the mid-1990s, the risk database (known as HAZLOG) was great for managing project safety risks but not ideal for managing operational risks. The different levels and layers of risk information were difficult to present using traditional approaches. Risk interfaces between ATC operations and engineering

---

1 See, for example, Joy, J & Griffiths, D, *National minerals industry safety and health risk assessment guideline*, version 6, Minerals Council of Australia, Minerals Industry Safety and Health Centre (University of Queensland), Brisbane, 2007.

2 Visser (1998); UK Health and Safety Executive, RR637 — *Optimising hazard management by workforce engagement and supervision*, HSE Books, Norwich, UK, 2008.

3 See, for example, Victorian WorkCover Authority, *Major hazard facilities regulations — Guidance note GN-14 safety assessment,* Victorian WorkCover Authority, Melbourne, 2006.

4 See, for example, Federal Aviation Administration and Eurocontrol, *Air traffic management safety techniques and toolbox,* issue 1, FAA, Washington, 2005.

were difficult to analyse, and the data tended to be specific to the discipline being studied.

An example perhaps best illustrates the issues. Consider a project that includes an upgrade to the software that takes radar data and displays the location of aircraft on each air traffic controller's screen. One of the risks associated with this project might be the failure of the new software to correctly display the data. The project might include a range of measures to reduce this risk, including software testing prior to installation on the live system, doing the upgrade at night (when traffic volumes are less), and having a contingency plan that enables a return to the old version of the software. This type of risk is easy to manage in a risk database using a series of linked lists. In the early days, this risk would have been captured in the engineering risk register as it has its roots in engineering.

In an operational context, however, this risk needs to be considered more broadly if decisions are to be made about the overall acceptability of the risk and those controls that are most important. A software bug is just one of a number of reasons why the system may not correctly display aircraft. Other possible causes relate to hardware failure and a range of human errors. Each potential cause has numerous risk controls in place. In addition, air traffic controllers are trained to detect such system errors and to respond appropriately. Ultimately, the concern is not the display error itself, but the potential for this to lead to aircraft to come into close proximity with each other or with a fixed obstacle. For the purposes of the software upgrade project, all other aspects that are not impacted can generally be assumed to be constant. For managing operational risk, all of this rich complexity needs to be addressed for the best risk management strategies to be developed. The relationship between the engineering systems and the delivery of ATC instructions needs to be clearly understood. All of those involved in analysing the risks and controls need to have the same mental model. The method that Airservices chose to address these issues is known as a "bow tie".

A bow tie is a diagrammatic representation of a specific hazardous event, the causes and consequences of the event, and all of the controls that are in place to prevent, mitigate and recover from the event. The event is shown in the middle of the diagram, the causes fan out on the left, and the consequences fan out on the right — hence, the generic name "bow tie".[5] The method has been used for some years in the chemical and the oil and gas industries, but we believe that this is the first time this method has been applied to service delivery in an air navigation service provider and that it is one of the broadest applications of the method in aviation generally.

---

5   They are sometimes called butterfly diagrams for the same reason.

Before we describe Airservices' bow tie experiences in detail, we would first like to make some general points about the development of bow ties and the strengths and weaknesses of this approach compared with other risk management tools and methods.

Moving on from simple hazard registers

Many organisations use a risk or hazard register system to manage information about monitoring current risks and the actions required to reduce them. A typical datasheet from such a system is shown in Figure 1.

Although there are many individual idiosyncrasies, these systems are all very similar in concept and intent. A separate sheet is used to record details for each hazard or scenario. Usually, a multidisciplined group representing engineering, maintenance and operations develops the list of hazards and completes the details for each one. In practice, the paper-based form shown in Figure 1 is often the input form for a database application. The causes of the hazard, along with the current risk controls (or reduction measures), are noted first. Sometimes risk controls are separated into those that act to prevent the hazard from developing and those that limit the impact of the hazard should it occur.

An assessment is made of the current risk level (typically, using a risk matrix). Depending on the result, additional risk controls may be preferred or necessary, and the risk is reassessed assuming those controls are put in place until the level of risk is judged to be as low as reasonably practicable.

This type of qualitative risk assessment is used by many organisations and can be an effective way of ensuring that risks are addressed. It is especially strong in two specific applications — for projects and for managing short-term operational risk issues.

For projects, matrix-based assessments allow an "apples with apples" comparison of various project options and, if the risk assessment is started early, the explicit consideration of risk during project development improves the project design and minimises the potential for late identification of safety-related problems (usually requiring more expensive solutions). A database allows the effective management of safety actions as part of project governance. Airservices uses a system like this for project risk, and the intention is for that to continue in conjunction with the work on bow tie diagrams.

Some organisations effectively use a hazard register for prioritising work in order to address short- to medium-term risk issues as they arise. Staff are encouraged to proactively identify hazards, and items are added to the database from across the organisation. A system owner manages the use of the system, and actions are

Hazard Register Sheet	
Project:	Date:
Hazard:	Hazard #:
Identified causes:	
Current risk controls:	
Consequence: Frequency:	Matrix rating:
Potential additional risk controls:	
Consequence: Frequency:	Revised matrix rating:
Comments:	

FIGURE 1: Example of a hazard register sheet

forwarded electronically for approval and implementation. At least one of the major international oil companies uses their hazard register in this way. Clearly, some well-understood and strictly applied guidelines are required about what is reported into this system rather than the site incident reporting and investigation system.

Having highlighted some of the ways in which this type of risk management works well, there are also a number of limitations associated with managing risks in this way. Using a simple hazard register:

- does not easily allow causes to be linked with specific risk controls (although, to some extent, this can be achieved by numbering the lists in the database);
- does not easily show which risk controls apply to more than one cause (unless items are repeated in numbered lists);
- does not usually allow for more than one outcome (although these can be treated as separate scenarios and given separate sheets in the register);
- does not show which causes are the biggest contributors to risk (unless this is added as a note);
- encourages risk reduction by adding extra controls, rather than improving existing risk controls; and
- draws the focus to assessing the level of risk for each perceived hazard, often at the expense of properly assessing the effectiveness of controls in managing the risk.

For these reasons, matrix-based hazard identification and risk assessment workshops are less effective as a management tool for baseline operational risks. This is because baseline risks are often complex, with well-developed risk control strategies already in place. A typical scenario from a baseline risk assessment for a chemical plant might be a leak of a flammable or toxic chemical in a specific part of the plant. Such a scenario can have 20 to 30 identified causes. Some of the causes may have 10 or more risk controls. There may be up to to 10 credible outcomes and, again, more than 10 risk controls aimed at mitigation and recovery from the leak. If this information is stored in a standard hazard register format such as Figure 1, the information soon becomes a blur of lists from which it is difficult to draw any overall meaning.

Occasionally, people attempt to summarise the information, but in these cases transparency and reproducibility of data may be quite low and it may be difficult for those not involved in the original work to learn from and use the results. For example, a typical control that often comes up in workshops is "training". However, unless the training program explicitly addresses the identified causes, it is difficult for those not directly involved in the training program to understand whether or not the training control is or will be adequate.

One technique that is used by organisations to address these issues and to show the operational risk baseline (or base case) is bow tie diagrams. In one sense, a bow tie is simply a diagrammatic representation of information that has been stored in database form for many years. Airservices found, however, that as it started to prepare the bow ties, a required discipline was involved. Showing the information in a fixed structure taught managers and staff new things about the risk management strategies that the organisation had adopted.

Moving to bow tie diagrams

The generic representation of a bow tie diagram is shown in Figure 2.

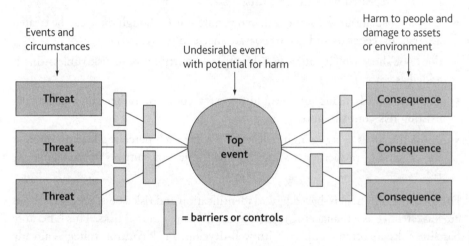

FIGURE 2: Generic bow tie diagram[6]

The exercise of producing a bow tie diagram is one of formalising existing organisational knowledge about safety in a way that can be shared. A bow tie shows how systems operate in real scenarios, and hence should pay no heed to interdisciplinary or interdepartmental divisions. The results can be surprising when what is common knowledge in different parts of the organisation is drawn up in a concrete form on one page, as in the following example.

Providing a system that doesn't work

One possible cause of a chemical release from process plant is the inadequate preparation of equipment that needs to be opened to the atmosphere for maintenance work. In a workshop discussion about preparing equipment containing hazardous chemicals for maintenance, the key barriers identified to prevent a spill were first operating and maintenance procedures, and second the drain and venting system. Plant operations personnel said that there was *always* a 10 litre chemical spill when one particular piece of equipment was prepared for

6   Adapted from Visser (1998).

maintenance work because the configuration of the piping prevented liquids from draining from the system. The engineers who had designed the drainage system were unaware of the problem.

Bow ties also promote clearer thinking about hazards, causes and controls. Consider the following real scenario from the minerals processing industry.

Hazard or failure of a control?

Plant operators are required to manually add the contents of drums of acid to an open tank, based on regular pH tests. The activity is tricky from a manual handling perspective and requires the work to be done on an elevated platform in full protective clothing. The activity sometimes occurs at night. There is a light in the area but the area is dusty and sometimes the light becomes significantly dimmed by accumulated dust. The risk assessment work done for this part of the plant had identified one hazard as "lack of lighting". This hazard was risk assessed using a matrix, with the conclusion that the risk was moderately high and improvements in the lighting arrangements were justified. In fact, a much better risk reduction action would have been to change the acid dosing arrangements. Defining "lack of lighting" as a hazard focused attention for risk control on the issue of lighting, rather than problems with the design of the task of adding acid to the tank. A much better approach would be to define the hazard as "acid spill during dosing", with lighting as one of the risk controls.

Chapter

4

It is quite common in qualitative risk management schemes to find hazards recorded in the database that are more usefully considered as failures of controls. In one sense, this doesn't matter provided the issue is addressed but, as shown by the example above, this can limit discussion about the best solution by focusing on a single control, rather than the broader risk issue. While there are many advantages to using a database as a recording and data storage tool, the tool itself does not provide guidance about the quality of the information recorded (in the sense that the information is all simple text). As alluded to before, another commonly recorded hazard is "lack of training" (or something similar). Again, this is failure of a control, rather than a hazard in its own right. In a safety context, training is about providing the skills and knowledge for avoiding or responding to a hazard. Problems with training are most usefully considered in that context, not as a separate hazard.

In bow tie analysis, issues are more clearly defined as hazards, causes, controls, or escalation factors. While there is some flexibility, if an issue is incorrectly defined, it soon becomes clear that it is not possible to make the appropriate connections with other parts of the diagram and the classification needs to be reconsidered. As described in the example above, this distinction is important when determining the best strategies for risk control.

Preparing bow ties

The following section describes the steps in producing a bow tie diagram. The terminology used to describe the various components of the bow tie is determined specifically as a result of the commercial software package that Airservices chose to use to record, produce and maintain its bow tie diagrams. What we call threats in this section could also be called causes. What we call threat barriers and recovery preparedness measures could be called risk controls. While it does not make a great deal of difference as to which terms are used, selecting a single set of terms and defining what those terms mean exactly in your risk management system is important to ensure that all contributors to, and users of, the data have a common understanding.

The first stage in preparing a bow tie diagram is to identify a hazard and the associated "top event". Consistent with AS/NZS 4360, a hazard is defined as a source of potential harm.[7] Many of the activities that Airservices undertakes can be described as sources of potential harm if they are not adequately controlled. The top event is the specific undesirable event that has the potential to cause harm. For chemical plant bow ties, the hazard is usually a specific flammable or toxic chemical, and the top event is usually a spill or leak from a specific inventory at a specific location. For Airservices' bow ties, the top events are:

- an aircraft in unsafe proximity to another aircraft in the air;
- incorrect presence of an aircraft, a vehicle or a person within the runway strip;
- an aircraft on the ground in unsafe proximity to a ground obstacle;
- an aircraft in unsafe proximity to terrain; and
- an aircraft in an unsafe environment (for example, bad weather or turbulence).

Later in this chapter, we describe how the final version of this list was determined. Some people believe that top events are somehow uniquely defined. We do not concur with this view. The types of potential accidents and incidents that are treated by this method occur as a sequence of failures that may have occurred over

---

7   Standards Australia and Standards New Zealand, AS/NZS 4360:2004 — *Risk management*, Standards Australia and Standards New Zealand, Sydney and Wellington, 2004.

a long period of time. Any point in that sequence could be chosen as the centre of the bow tie.

Some organisations define top events as the point at which control has been lost. According to this way of thinking about the structure of a bow tie, barriers on the left of the bow tie are designed to make sure that control is not lost and those on the right are designed to recover control in the event that those on the left fail. In our thinking about risk barriers, we are heavily influenced by the Reason (1997) "Swiss cheese" model and the message it brings about the role of latent failures in the system. In this way of thinking, "control" may be lost long before a leak occurs (or aircraft are in unsafe proximity) due to latent failures. We prefer to see the choice of top event as one which is based on useful groupings of common barriers, or high-level undesirable outcomes. For example, in ATC, an aircraft coming into unsafe proximity with another aircraft or the ground is an undesirable outcome, whereas for an engineering system, the top event may be associated with the engineering system no longer performing its intended function. In an operational sense, the undesirable outcome of the engineering system may not necessarily lead to the aircraft coming into unsafe proximity, as there are other controls available to the air traffic controller. Nevertheless, from an engineer's perspective, the integrity of the system function is paramount; hence, the engineers' bow ties are different to the ATC bow ties — but they do connect.

The second stage in the process is to identify threats. Threats are events or conditions that have the potential to *directly* cause the top event. The directness is important, as this is a good test to determine whether the threat is truly a threat or perhaps a failed control. For example, will air traffic controller fatigue cause two aircraft to come into close proximity, or will it defeat air traffic controller skill and cause an error of instruction to a pilot? Clearly, the latter is true, so air traffic controller error is the threat rather than fatigue. Threats may also be events, such as the failure of a specific piece of equipment, a malicious act, or an external event such as windshear or bad weather. They may also be conditions, such as high pressure or low temperature, with the potential to cause loss of inventory.

When identifying threats, it is important to define which modes of activity/ operation must be considered (normal operations, maintenance activities, etc).

The third stage in the process is identifying barriers. A barrier is a protective measure that is established to prevent the threat causing the top event. Barriers are best described as "real things that exist or real things that are done". Hence, barriers can be of different types — physical systems or procedures. It is useful to classify barriers by type in order to review the breadth of the overall risk control strategy. Generally speaking, engineering controls are more reliable than procedures due to the potential for human error when applying a procedure. The chance of a

Chapter

4

person making a mistake is generally greater than the probability of a well-designed engineering system failing. Having said that, almost all physical engineering controls rely on procedures in some way (for example, for maintenance) and many procedures rely on engineering systems, so any general rule that separates the two is necessarily a simplification. Strategies for risk control are covered in more detail below.

Barriers that are management system procedures should be linked to specific reference documents as the bow ties are prepared. This helps to ensure that the procedures cited really are relevant to the specific threat. It also makes for easier links at a later stage to systems for management of change, that is, if a change to the procedure is planned, it is easy to track which hazards and threats are potentially impacted.

The fourth stage in the process is to identify the consequences of the top event. These are the possible outcomes that could occur as a result of the top event being realised. Outcomes should be carried to the final conclusion (that is, for a process plant, consequences might be injuries, fatalities or damage to other equipment rather than fire or explosion). Depending on why a bow tie is being prepared, this step may be done in a preliminary form much earlier in the process. In some cases, the scope of the study may be defined by a particular type of consequence, for example, the potential for multiple fatalities in Australian offshore oil and gas industry safety cases.

Once the consequences have been developed, the next step is to identify recovery measures. A recovery measure, like a barrier, is a protective measure that is established to stop, limit or recover from the chain of consequences that have arisen from the top event. It is normal that many bow ties for one organisation or site will have similar consequences and recovery measures, and hence the right-hand sides of the bow ties may be the same or similar.

The last stage in the bow tie method that we have adopted is the definition of the escalation factors and the associated controls. Escalation factors are conditions that lead to increased risk by eliminating or reducing the effectiveness of the barriers or recovery measures. Escalation factor controls are measures that are established to prevent or mitigate the effects of escalation factors. The escalation factors and their controls are where some of the most valuable information comes from regarding the integrity of the risk management effort — and often where traditional methods tend to stop short.

The real advantage of bow ties over database lists is the rigour imposed on the discussion by the structure of the drawings, that is, the positioning of the information. Importantly, everyone involved in the development has the same mental model of what is being analysed, which provides better understanding of the threats and controls. Producing a diagram showing the barriers makes it much less likely that barriers will be missed or that barriers that are not effective will be shown without comment from the group. The following example illustrates the types of issues that may arise regarding the effectiveness of risk controls that are in place.

Risk controls may not be as effective as you think

In a workshop discussion, a maintenance error had been identified as one potential cause of leakage from a process vessel that was normally filled with liquid LPG. The discussion then moved to specifically what maintenance-related activities take place in this part of the plant, how these might cause a release of LPG, and hence what barriers were in place to prevent such an error. This led to a detailed discussion about how the equipment was prepared for maintenance, that is, the vessel was emptied of all LPG so that it could be safely opened to the atmosphere.

The procedure for preparing the equipment consists of two general steps: drain all liquid LPG, then introduce nitrogen to remove LPG vapour before opening the equipment to the atmosphere. Changes to plant operation meant that this equipment was now opened up for maintenance much more frequently than the designers had originally intended. Operators had found that liquid draining was slow, so they had informally started the practice of introducing warm nitrogen into the partially drained vessel to speed up the drainage process (by vaporising the liquid LPG). This seemed an expeditious way to achieve the necessary operational outcome and was not in contravention of the procedure (although not strictly in compliance with it).

As the engineers in the workshop knew, this is a potentially dangerous practice. Liquid LPG, especially with a nitrogen atmosphere, can generate very cold temperatures to the point where the mechanical integrity of the steel vessel could be in danger.

The cross-discipline discussion of what everyone assumed to be a routine activity highlighted that, not only were the existing risk controls ineffective, but that a new hazard had also been introduced by what the plant operators had seen to be an insignificant change in their work practices.

Chapter

4

Sometimes it is useful to record ideas for new/additional risk controls (either barriers or recovery measures) when bow tie diagrams are initially prepared. Similarly, comments on control effectiveness should be recorded for input into future risk management activities.

Analysing controls and how they can fail: escalation factors

Once the diagrams exist, they become a useful tool (and source of information) for analysing overall risk control strategies. Most organisations have a good knowledge of the individual procedures and systems that have been put in place to manage risk. Often, there is much less understanding (if any) about the *overall* risk control strategy that is inherent in the decisions that have been made about the details. This includes considerations such as the degree of diversity among the controls in place and the extent to which the system relies on one or two items that appear repeatedly on the bow ties. In reliability jargon, this is looking qualitatively at issues that impact on the potential for common mode failure.

The graphical nature of bow tie diagrams makes it immediately apparent if there are significant gaps in the overall risk control strategy, that is, if threats have been identified that have few or no risk controls. Apart from this simple assessment, there are two other important characteristics of the risk controls as a group.

1. **Types of controls:** there are basically three types of risk controls:

- hardware-based systems or engineering controls;
- specific procedures; and
- administrative systems (such as permit to work or controller licensing).

2. **Hierarchy of controls:** this is sometimes blurred with the type of control (for example, in an OHS sense) but is actually a different property of any given control. It relates to where the control sits in the accident prevention sequence, that is, the timing of when the control operates to reduce the risk. Controls may be classified as:

- elimination — operates before the threat and is intended to eliminate the threat in the first instance;
- prevention — operates after the threat but before the top event and is intended to prevent the threat from leading to the top event;
- reduction — operates after the top event but before the consequence and is intended to reduce the consequences flowing from the top event; or
- mitigation — operates after the consequence and is intended to mitigate the undesirable outcome once it has occurred.

Figure 3 illustrates the classification of controls based on when they operate. Note that, for the purposes of drawing the bow tie, controls are only shown immediately left or right of the top event, as is typical of the bow tie software programs currently available.

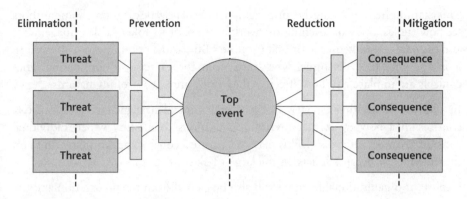

FIGURE 3: Control classification

An effective risk control strategy will have diversity in both types of control and classification, as the following example illustrates.

Moving further up the hierarchy of controls

A small chemical plant was located on the same site as a larger facility with a different owner but it shared some utilities with the larger plant, including the site flare system. On several occasions each year, it was necessary for maintenance staff at the small plant to work on their flare header. This required physically breaking the piping to block off their header to ensure that no gas could enter their flare system from the larger plant. While this would always be done with the small plant shut down, the larger facility would still be operational. There was some risk involved in the activity of opening the live flare piping to block off the header to the small plant. Since the flare system provides the safe venting route for many parts of the process, the risk was that there would be some kind of process upset in the larger plant which resulted in gas being directed to the flare system when the line was open.

Over a period of some years, the maintenance staff at the small plant had developed a range of risk control measures associated with this activity, including full protective clothing for the people doing the work, independent observers with a gas detector, and a fire extinguisher standing by. These controls were all on the right-hand side of the bow tie, since that was the only part of the hazard that was within the control of the maintenance department.

This scenario was discussed in a bow tie workshop at a time when the operations manager had chosen to sit in. On hearing of this significant risk, he undertook to raise the issue of work coordination with management of the larger facility in order to develop risk controls aimed at eliminating or preventing the hazard, that is, focusing on the left-hand side of the bow tie.

This example highlights another important benefit of bow tie diagrams. Some authors see bow ties as a way of teaching the workforce about its role in risk management, and they are certainly useful for that purpose.[8] But, as the example above illustrates, it is not only field personnel who learn from the exercise of considering what controls are in place and how effective they really are in controlling hazards.

In addition to inviting a review of the overall control strategy, laying out *all* risk controls in a bow tie format invites organisations to identify which individual controls are most important. This may be because a control appears many times on the drawing, or because it acts on the largest risk contributors.

Important organisational learning will also be gained from the preparation and use of bow ties. The structure of bow ties and the links between specific threats and barriers mean that bow ties can be an important repository of corporate memory for design decisions and operational experiences. They also provide a useful tool for incident investigation and audits.

Figure 4 is a simple example of a bow tie. In this example, there are three threats which could lead to the dog escaping from the backyard. With the first threat line of "gate left open", there are three barriers intended to prevent the dog from escaping via the gate:

1. installing an automatic closer on the gate;
2. checking that the gate is locked after entry/exit; and
3. installing a gate latch.

Barriers 1 and 3 are termed "engineering barriers" as they are physical things that operate to secure the gate once it has been opened. Barrier 2 is termed a "procedural barrier" as it relies on a human to operate. This illustrates a key point: barriers are *real things that exist or real things that are done* to block the progress of a threat. Hence, there is value in describing the barriers in an active sense. Merely referring to the existence of a procedural document can undermine the integrity of the analysis, as procedures sit on shelves. The action that is carried out is the real risk management activity, whereas the document enshrines that activity in the management system.

If the dog were to escape from the yard, there are three potential outcomes:

1. the dog bites a person;
2. the dog gets hit by a car; or
3. the dog waits in the front yard.

---

8   See UK Health and Safety Executive, RR637 — *Optimising hazard management by workforce engagement and supervision*, HSE Books, Norwich, UK, 2008, which focuses strongly on the use of bow ties in teaching field personnel.

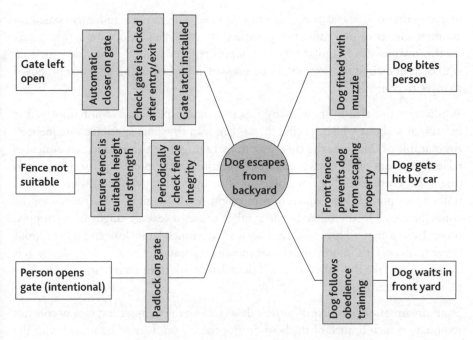

FIGURE 4: Simple bow tie: dog escapes

Following the top consequence line, an engineering control is applied, that is, the use of a dog muzzle. This control is not effective until the dog escapes from the front yard and attempts to bite someone; hence, it appears on the right-hand side or downstream of the top event. This information is important and will be discussed later when the hierarchy of controls is discussed.

What hasn't been shown in Figure 4 is the next layer of information, that is, how each of the controls might fail (escalation factors) and the controls that are put in place to manage the escalation factors. For example, an escalation factor for the automatic closer mentioned earlier might be that the closer fails to operate properly. An appropriate control for this would be a regular inspection or maintenance program to ensure that the closer operates effectively when it is required. The control of "checking the gate is locked after entry/exit" could fail if it is simply not done. Perhaps the installation of an audible buzzer that sounds when the gate is unlocked would serve as a reminder to lock the gate.

Bow ties and as low as reasonably practicable

Like the hazard register system described above, a bow tie diagram does not, of itself, make any finding about whether the risk being addressed has been reduced to a level that is as low as reasonably practicable.[9] This requires judgment based on another rule set or procedure being applied. Many organisations use a risk matrix for this purpose (in a similar way to a hazard register system). The risk associated with each branch of the bow tie can be assessed, both before and after any proposed changes to controls.

While bow ties clearly show many linkages, one aspect that is not displayed is information about which specific threats can lead to which specific consequences. An example of this from the chemical industry might be threats and consequences related to a leak of flammable gas from a section of the process plant. One threat might be corrosion. The credible leak size associated with corrosion may be limited to a pinhole size, which in turn might result in only the least severe of the consequences. On the other hand, another cause of leakage might be a dropped object from a crane. This could credibly lead to a much larger leak and more serious consequences. This information is not shown on a standard bow tie but, clearly, it is important to take this into account if the relative risk from each branch of the bow tie is to be determined.

Some organisations adopt qualitative rule sets about the number and type of controls required on each branch of the bow tie, depending on the risk associated with the branch (as determined by risk matrix evaluation or similar) and the rules regarding overall control strategies. Such a rule set consists of a number of steps, such as:

- rank the risk associated with the top event, that is, the bow tie as a whole (using a risk matrix);
- rank each branch of the bow tie;
- based on the overall level of risk associated with the top event and the contribution of the branch to that risk, assess the adequacy of the number and type of controls on each branch;
- review all bow ties together to identify which controls occur most frequently and hence are most important; and
- review the overall distribution of types of controls — do procedural or hardware controls dominate? Are there gaps in the hierarchy of controls?

It is also common for organisations to use a method like this to extract a list of critical controls from the bow ties that can then be subject to a higher degree of monitoring via other parts of the safety management system (for example, training, testing, inspections, auditing, etc).

---

9   For details on as low as reasonably practicable (ALARP), see UK Health and Safety Executive, *Reducing risks, protecting people: HSE's decision-making process*, HSE, Norwich, UK, 2001. For more information on risk matrices, see Standards Australia, *Risk management guidelines: companion to AS/NZS 4360:2004*, Standards Australia, Sydney, 2004.

An important point here is that risk acceptance in bow ties can be more explicitly focused on the effectiveness of controls and the diversity of controls used to manage the risk. An organisation may develop control-based risk acceptance criteria that require increasing diversity of control types and control classifications as the risk increases. For example, where there is the potential for high-consequence outcomes, an organisation may require a minimum of four procedural controls and two independent engineering controls, and a mixture of elimination, prevention, reduction and mitigation controls.

In addition, control effectiveness may be scored on a scale, and a weighting applied to engineering controls that reflects their value over procedural controls. The higher the risk, the higher the control score required for acceptance within the above diversity requirement.

Chapter

4

Bow ties and quantitative techniques

Some project work within Airservices (for example, assessing changes to airspace classifications) uses quantitative risk assessment techniques for evaluating safety risk. The risk of aircraft collision is modelled mathematically, taking into account such issues as aviation traffic patterns and schedules, aviation traffic type, the flight threats of individual flights, the probability of error on the part of both the pilot and the air traffic controller, and the potential for failure of the relevant ATC and aircraft systems. At its best, this type of modelling can identify complex system interactions that may otherwise go unnoticed, but the highly technical nature of the modelling means that the results are sometimes perceived to emerge from a "black box" by those not directly involved. The bow tie method will not replace this type of risk modelling as it is not a quantitative technique and does not use the logic gates required in an event tree or a fault tree. To say that a bow tie is a combination of an event tree and a fault tree is not correct, and such a statement does an injustice to each technique. Each has its own useful purpose.

Quantitative risk analysis (QRA) modelling, no matter how complex the calculations, ultimately produces a result in the form of a risk index or indices. This makes for simple comparison with numerical risk criteria (for example, limits on individual risk per annum, and so on) and hence can provide clear and unambiguous input to decisions about whether risk in a specific situation is as low as reasonably practicable. Demonstration of this with bow ties is messy and complex (as described above), but in many cases the neat numerical results of a QRA can hide from non-specialists (including senior management) the uncertainties and messiness in the analysis that produced the results.

Having said that, high-quality QRA modelling can answer some risk management questions that bow ties will not address. Design questions, such as the potential for structural failure due to fire events on an offshore oil and gas platform or the necessary reliability of a critical process control system, are best addressed using appropriate numerical modelling techniques. These are specialist fields that produce specialist results, and one of the problems with QRA is its lack of transparency for non-specialists. Bow ties are useful in recording the results of such design decisions and showing how such technical systems fit into the overall risk control strategy of the operational facility, but they do not replace quantitative techniques completely.

Pitfalls

A niggling issue with bow ties relates to the finished physical size of the drawings when printed or plotted. Some users maintain that it is best to limit the size of the diagrams to those that can be printed legibly at A3 size. This necessarily means that bow ties are either highly simplified, or that the threats and barriers related to one top event are divided into groupings of similar issues (sometimes called pathways) and displayed on a series of separate drawings. Simplifying the data on the bow ties in any major way may compromise their main purpose (that is, to show diagrammatically the links between specific threats, barriers, etc). Segmenting the drawing also carries some of the same risk as it spreads the complete risk picture across several pages. As such, Airservices decided to produce detailed drawings at whatever natural size is required and to plot those on the facilities used for project drawings. Many of the drawings, when fully expanded, are the size of a large poster (that is, A1 and A0). Fortunately, the software allows for each branch to be collapsed, enabling individual branches to be printed at A4 or A3 size for review and analysis.

A more detailed look at Airservices' experience

Against this background, we can now take a more detailed look at Airservices' experience. According to one senior manager:

> "We had a lot of data, but felt there was a gap in information. We needed a better management system to help us see more clearly how well we were managing our risks. It was time to embark on a journey of risk system research and workshops with those who would challenge our concepts and ideas."

The problem was, as noted in the introduction to this chapter, that the existing hazard register system did not capture operational risk in a holistic way. Airservices needed a more integrated view of risk management that captured interfacing hazards between the business groups. It became apparent that managing the risk information was going to be a more difficult exercise than before. This exercise required more sophistication to collect the risk information than was available in the software tool at that time. No longer was each business unit to be treated as an island, but rather as an integrated unit managing risk within the system as a whole, that is, air traffic controllers, engineers, technicians and firefighters interacting with the infrastructure through defined processes and procedures. The organisation needed a new method and presentational technique to portray the operational risk situations. This was the genesis of the bow tie project.

Establishing the bow tie project

The aim of the project was to establish a top-down operational safety risk baseline using a model that was easily understood by, and useful to, managers and staff. Use of the model needed to demonstrate value by improving the visibility of operational requirements, procedures and practices. People needed to be able to see their contribution to managing risks in their work areas; they needed context for their efforts — a tool that would allow them to think of risk management as part of their normal day-to-day work rather than a "bolt-on" activity.

Chapter

4

The project team decided to conduct the work in two phases.

Phase 1 focused on establishing a framework and structure for assembly of the risk baseline information. Without an appropriate structure in which to construct the "risk picture", the organisation would be no better off than if it were using the existing system and a lot of valuable time and effort would be wasted.

Phase 2 of the project integrated the existing risk management data from the old system into the new system (that had been selected and tested in phase 1) and developed the new system to an operational stage.

Phase 1: generating a high-level industry bow tie

The public expectation in relation to aviation safety is reflected in government policy across the world, with Australia being no different. Section 9 of the *Air Services Act 1995* states that:

> "In exercising its powers and performing its functions, AA [Airservices Australia] must regard the safety of air navigation as the most important consideration."

While the safety of air navigation is Airservices' most important consideration, it is not the only consideration. The organisation must stay in business and provide an air traffic management environment that allows the aviation industry to prosper and grow. This can best be achieved by working with the various government agencies, airlines, airport owners and general aviation associations. All of these respective organisations have the opportunity to "get it right" and build on Australia's good aviation safety record. To "get it right" requires an understanding of our own and each others contribution to safety. All organisations and players can generate causes that could ultimately lead to an aviation accident, and all manage controls that are intended to prevent accidents. There are literally many thousands of causes and controls requiring ongoing management and maintenance. Airservices operates as part of the overall Australian airways system. One of the key learnings from the exercise of preparing bow ties was a better understanding of the organisation's role in risk management in relation to other stakeholders. Day-to-day activities in many areas include interactions with many other organisations and individuals that impact on risks. Some examples are:

- staff operate facilities that are owned and maintained by others, for example, runway lighting is operated by ATC tower staff based on environmental conditions, but the lighting belongs to the airport owners;

- airline policies can impact overall system environmental factors, for example, airline schedules (developed by each airline based on individual commercial considerations) have a direct impact on aircraft traffic levels and hence air traffic controller workload;

- airline policies can directly affect the potential for air traffic controller error, for example, aircraft call signs are fixed by airlines and similar call signs can increase the potential for communication errors between pilots and air traffic controllers;

- the Bureau of Meteorology provides forecasts that pilots use in planning their flights. Unforecast weather can have a significant impact on the safety of flight; and

- the buoyant Australian resources sector has led to a high demand for pilots (driven by the mining and related industries). During a period when demand for pilots is high, this could mean that there are more flights being undertaken by licensed, but less experienced, pilots.

An organisation must be cognisant of the level of influence and control that it has over a particular risk and be in a position to partition risk ownership. Airservices not only has to treat risks for which it is responsible in a reasonable and practicable way, but it should also communicate, consult and work with risk owners who are external to the organisation in order to reduce external sources of risk. This demonstrates due diligence in addressing risks and may also assist in reducing risks to Airservices' operations.

The project team determined that terms were required to address direct risk and indirect risk and to declare a general delineation between risks for which Airservices has full control and risks for which it does not. For example, the ATC system is vulnerable to the effects of pilot behaviour which may involve errors and/or violations — intended or otherwise. External stakeholder action (for example, political, regulatory, supplier) may elevate existing risks or create new risks. Where such external factors exist or arise, Airservices can seek to influence behaviour and/or decision-making but cannot necessarily control the factors that create the risk.

To support the top-down approach, the following definitions were developed:

- **direct risks:** those risks involved with Airservices' operations and activities where the causes lie within the control of Airservices; and

- **indirect risks:** those risks involved with Airservices' operations and activities where the causes lie outside the control of Airservices.

Visualising the interactions between these causes and controls is a significant challenge, let alone managing the information.

To help this visualisation, we have used the bow tie method to present a high-level picture of the aviation industry (see Figure 5).

Chapter

4

Advantages of using the bow tie method

Although simple bow tie diagrams were initially being drawn, this type of analysis was showing clear advantages. This method was providing a simple (but not simplistic) diagrammatic representation of the risk scenarios; the causal pathways, outcomes and controls were displayed in a manner that emphasised the linkages between them, showing the relative importance of the risk controls and helping to identify vulnerable pathways. In addition to identifying the internal business unit interfaces, the bow tie method was helping to show the interfaces with external agencies and where these agencies impact on Airservices' risk baseline.

The development of bow ties was providing useful information about Airservices' risk baseline. For example, even in the initial bow ties, it could be clearly seen that, in the ATC environment:

- there was limited protection from cognitive failure — if an air traffic controller makes an error which he/she does not detect, there is a real possibility that the error will be passed on to the pilot or another air traffic controller. These areas present potential opportunities for the development of engineering controls to support the air traffic controller, and provide diversity in the types of controls being applied (the principal of defence in depth);

- there was heavy reliance on procedures and rules rather than engineering controls — mapping the causal pathways showed that there were many procedures but few "hard" (engineering) controls between the causes and top events. In these areas, Airservices had the opportunity to further explore the vulnerabilities of the procedures and rules, and implement improvements that block those

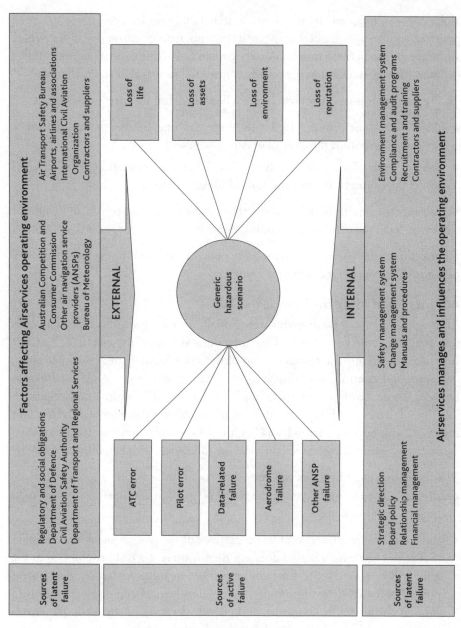

FIGURE 5: Industry-wide bow tie

vulnerabilities. This may require procedural design changes to effectively eliminate the causes of those vulnerabilities — but *that* is safety improvement;

- there was heavy reliance on training to prevent failure in the first instance — training appeared in most causal pathways because training is essential in the application of procedures. While training is provided to prevent failure in the first instance, humans have natural performance variations. Training fulfils an important role in enhancing the skills of humans to apply specific procedures (for example, risk controls) and the techniques to detect and correct errors before they lead to a problem, particularly where there are few or no engineering controls. Training for air traffic controllers and technical staff should explicitly address the connection between causes and controls. In fact, all staff should understand their own contribution to safety;

- some of the main sources of failure are also key components of recovery — while human performance variation (threat) might lead to a hazardous (top) event, the people involved are often those who recover the situation or play a key role in the recovery mechanism; and

- a single failure can initiate threats on multiple pathways — as Airservices' systems and processes are highly integrated, the cause and effect relationships quickly become very complex.

Opportunities for the enhancement or reduction of risk controls

The project identified that the clear depiction of controls and the way in which they are linked to various causes in the bow ties provides Airservices with the ability to significantly enhance its current risk management processes. In the first instance, it provides an indication of the number of controls currently in place for a particular cause.

Simplistically, if there are few or no controls attached to a pathway, this may indicate the need for further analysis to identify new controls. Conversely, if there are many controls, further analysis may allow for the consolidation or removal of some of the controls (as shown in Figure 6).

At a more detailed level, identifying the controls and their specific links to causes and pathways within the bow tie provides the foundation for a more comprehensive analysis aimed at identifying: the amount of risk associated with a particular pathway; the number and type of controls required to reduce the risk to a tolerable level; and the effectiveness of each control in reducing the risk. This provides an ability to clearly identify whether the number of controls and the mix of control types effectively manages the risk associated with a particular pathway, whether control improvement is required, or whether control reduction may be possible (to better deploy resources elsewhere).

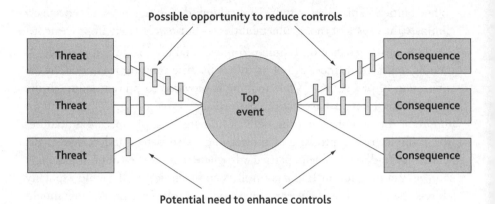

FIGURE 6: Possible control changes

For example, engineering controls such as system alerts that manifest as warnings on ATC screens (for example, short-term conflict alerts) can be, if designed appropriately, more reliable than controls that depend on people following procedures. The introduction of a conflict alert in airspace without surveillance (for example, the flight plan conflict function) may enhance the mix of control types by introducing a "hard" engineering risk control. This could strengthen the effectiveness and diversity of the control measures for managing the risk of aircraft collision. Such an enhancement may also provide opportunities for the removal of less effective ATC procedural risk controls which could increase capacity in some ATC areas.

However, this type of action does come with a caution. Increasing the number of alerts and alarms can of itself increase risk, as it might desensitise the air traffic controller to valid alarms through the presentation of false or spurious alarms. Hence, any proposed changes to existing controls, or the introduction of new controls, should be properly assessed to ensure that no new threats are inadvertently introduced.

All of this raises the question of how many controls are necessary, and to what quality are they sufficient, to say that a risk has been reduced as far as reasonably practicable. The traditional method of deciding this issue is simply to ask a group of knowledgeable people whether they think the system of controls is adequate using a risk matrix for guidance. Airservices is considering replacing this with a rule of thumb tailored to the bow tie method. The system of controls for an identified top event might consist of a specified minimum number of engineering and/or procedural controls to the left of the top event and a similar specification to the right. Of course, this rule will need to be circumscribed in some way. It will not apply to the most trivial of risks, nor will the most severe risks be dealt with in this way. But for those risks to which it is applied, it will provide a more transparent method of judging adequacy.

Assurance process

Findings from the risk baseline work could assist both safety management and audit in redefining the internal audit program, and help to ensure that the audit program is appropriately risk-based.

While the audit program must seek to ensure compliance with legislative requirements, there would be substantial benefit in using the bow tie method to target specific pathways in order to assess the effectiveness of controls. The bow tie method could provide further assurance to the Airservices board, committees, CEO and executives that identified risks are both accurate and complete, and that controls were appropriate and managed effectively to mitigate the risk to as low as reasonably practicable.

Chapter

4

With the completion of phase 1 of bow tie implementation, it was clear that the bow tie method had significant potential benefits — not only in presenting and understanding risk information, but also for use in investigations and audits. If Airservices was to capitalise on the bow tie "adventure" of phase 1, it needed to establish phase 2 and use bow tie in "earnest".

Phase 2 of bow tie implementation

With the inception of phase 2, the plan was to expand on and enhance under-standing of the bow tie methodology and develop key aspects for implementation into Airservices' safety management system. The learning from phase 1 would be put into practice with the translation of existing risk information into bow ties. Converting spreadsheets of data into bow ties would be no mean feat, as the existing risk management system contained over 5,000 recorded hazards and many more controls in hundreds of hazard registers.

There was still a major limitation to managing the data in the new format because there was no suitable software tool in the organisation to effectively support the information to be captured within the bow ties. Without such a tool, the project would be going no further. A database was required which had a graphical engine to support the presentation of bow tie diagrams, and which would allow the user to move between the database and the diagrams. Evaluation of "off the shelf" software applications that specifically supported bow tie risk assessment and management was required to determine a suitable application for installation within the Airservices desktop environment.

Once a suitable application was identified, the refinement and further development of the hazardous (top) events established in phase 1 commenced in earnest. Although identified independently, it was found that the hazardous events were similar to accident categories identified by Eurocontrol (the European Organisation for the Safety of Air Navigation) in the development of the integrated risk picture for air traffic management. This is illustrated in Table 1.

Interestingly, the Airservices' hazardous events were one step to the left (if presented in a bow tie diagram) of the Eurocontrol accident categories. This was quite deliberate from Airservices' perspective. The aim was to focus attention not just on the final disastrous accident, but on the prior events that needed to be avoided. So, for instance, in the first line of the table, Airservices sees unsafe proximity as the hazardous event to be avoided, not just midair collision. Moving the focus of the bow tie diagram one step to the left directed attention to defences that would prevent unsafe incidents, not just catastrophic accidents.

The high-level bow ties that were developed with the hazardous events described in Table 1 were used as models to be populated by real data from the current risk management system (HAZLOG). The data that had been captured and developed over the last nine years logically fitted mostly into the left-hand side of the hazardous events.

TABLE 1: Eurocontrol accident categories and Airservices hazardous events

Eurocontrol accident categories	Airservices hazardous events
1. Midair collision	1. An aircraft in unsafe proximity to another aircraft in the air
2. Runway collision	2. Incorrect presence of an aircraft, a vehicle or a person within the runway strip
3. Taxiway collision	3. An aircraft on the ground in unsafe proximity to a ground obstacle
4. Controlled flight into terrain	4. An aircraft in unsafe proximity to terrain
5. Wake turbulence accident	5. An aircraft in an unsafe environment

Conclusion

In many ways, the most difficult part of safety and risk management is for everyone involved in operations to understand how their day-to-day activities connect to the safety of the system as a whole. This applies to managers, operations and maintenance personnel, and engineers.

Bow ties make that connection in a clear and graphical way. They allow individuals and departments to see how their activities directly impact on safety, and effectively move the focus of risk management from hazards to controls — moving from analysis to action.

A review of the relatively small amount of published material on the subject of bow tie diagrams shows significant variation in what a number of authors see as the role and purpose of bow tie diagrams, but a key and common theme is communication:

> "[a bow tie diagram is] ... a helpful representation of the overall picture of an unwanted event."[10]

> "The primary objective of bow tie analysis is to give safety experts a means to communicate with operational experts regarding safety findings, so that these operational experts can identify preventative and recovery measures for hazards, while the safety experts keep a neutral position."[11]

> "The bow tie diagram is a graphical way to present the complex interactions [between equipment, people and the surrounding environment] and the actions that can be taken to stop the development of major incidents." (Visser 1998)

For Airservices to move to a bow tie approach to risk assessment has required considerable resources. However, the results show promise for a significant return on investment in terms of the detailed understanding that has been gained about risk control strategies and how they might be improved.

Although it is early days in the operational use of bow ties, the potential benefits are acknowledged across the board. The challenge is to harness the simplicity of this method without complicating it. Ongoing training of operational staff is essential if they are all to come on the journey and enhance the management of risk at Airservices.

---

10   Joy & Griffiths, op cit.
11   Federal Aviation Administration and Eurocontrol, op cit.

PART 2

Other studies

INTRODUCTION TO PART 2

Part 1 of this book focused on one organisation, Airservices Australia. Part 2 deals with several different organisations operating in hazardous industries. Given the discussion in Chapter 1, it would be foolish to claim that all of these organisations are high reliability organisations (HROs). But they are all organisations that aspire to HRO functioning, simply because the consequences of failure are so great, and they are therefore all organisations from which there is something to learn. The chapters in Part 2 take up many of the themes developed in Part 1, so it is appropriate to introduce them here by drawing some of the connections.

Chapter 5 is written by Carl Macrae and is based on his PhD from East Anglia University. Some of the fieldwork for his PhD was carried out while he was a visiting fellow at the Australian National University, working with me. The chapter is an analysis of airline incident reporting and investigation systems. This complements the previous discussion of Airservices' reporting system. The major airlines prescribe, to some extent, what they want their employees to report, just as Airservices did, and while their lists overlap with Airservices' list, they are by no means identical. This difference is an important reminder that organisations must put considerable effort into deciding exactly what they want reported.

Macrae argues that airlines do not try to assess the significance of incidents by using the traditional risk matrix. Rather, as in the case of Airservices, they treat incidents as telling them something about the state of the risk control system. Put simply, the fewer the barriers between the incident and some major event, the more serious the incident is judged to be. Macrae defines a new term, "risk resilience", by which he means the capacity of the organisation to prevent small incidents becoming major ones.

Macrae also challenges the universal applicability of the well-known Swiss cheese model of defence in depth. That model is based on the idea that there are hazards that must be contained. It applies very well to the chemical and petrochemical industries, where the goal is to "keep the stuff in the pipes". However, defences in the airline industry are not about keeping hazards at bay; they are designed to ensure that organisational processes do not break down. If Macrae is correct in his analysis, we need to replace Swiss cheese with some creative new image that better describes the situation that the airlines confront.

Macrae's risk managers display all of the characteristics of mindfulness that Weick sees as the hallmark of an HRO: they are on the lookout for discrepancies and patterns of anomalies, and they devote considerable effort to uncovering and examining small things that would otherwise pass unnoticed. Moreover, the very fact that airlines employ people whose full-time job is to think about the significance of small incidents is again a characteristic of HROs.

Chapter 6 is based on some of Jan Hayes' PhD fieldwork in a United Kingdom nuclear power station. She provides an interesting account of the strengths and weaknesses of the incident reporting system in use at the power station. The chapter begins with a discussion of the distinction between the safety triangle and Reason's Swiss cheese model. The former is relatively atheoretical and suggests no real accident prevention strategy — other than trying to reduce the number of minor incidents. On the other hand, the Swiss cheese model is based on a theory of accident prevention and treats small incidents as clues about the way the safety system may be failing.

Hayes argues that the nuclear power station makes good use of its data to fix specific problems, but that it does not treat incidents as clues about the way the organisation may be failing — and hence fails to extract maximum value from its incident reporting system. She demonstrates, too, that attempts to prioritise incidents using the standard risk matrix yield unsatisfactory results for the reason identified in earlier chapters, namely, that, strictly speaking, risk assessment can only be applied to a hypothetical event, not a small incident that has actually occurred.

Chapter 7 is written by a former senior executive of the DuPont chemical company, Richard Angiullo. I came know Angiullo when we formed part of a team reviewing safety in a large petroleum company. I was fascinated by his stories and prevailed upon him to write them down. This chapter is the result. It is a very personal account, based both on his career at Dupont and on consultancy work since his retirement.

DuPont is best known for its behaviour-based safety program, STOP (Safety Training Observation Program), that has been marketed around the world. Critics have often pointed out that this program misses the big picture; in particular, it misses major hazards (Wokutch & VanSandt, 2000). There is, however, a second DuPont concept that goes a long way to filling this gap, namely, operational discipline. Angiullo's chapter introduces this idea.

The chapter is partially structured as a comparison between the nuclear and chemical industries, and Angiullo argues that United States nuclear power stations exhibit far more operational discipline than chemical and petrochemical facilities.

As one reads the chapter, it becomes clear that operational discipline is precisely what we find in HROs. Let me develop this point. According to Anguillo, one of the features of companies with good operational discipline is a good incident reporting system, where people feel some real pressure to report (as was described in the case of Airservices). Operational discipline also requires the participation of frontline workers in decision-making and senior management sensitivity to their experiences — a characteristic of HROs. Moreover, workers are constantly reminded to challenge unworkable procedures rather than to find "workarounds" (Bourrier, 1998). Finally, there is a strong emphasis on the need for management to provide the necessary resources to make all this happen. Although Anguillo's chapter is not informed by HRO theory, it is clear that his concept of operational discipline highlights many of the things to which HRO theory draws attention.

One other feature of Anguillo's discussion deserves mention. It is the idea that the more safety-critical a procedure is, the more detailed the instructions that cover it must be. There is an assumption here that it is possible to specify completely the behaviour required of operators in the most safety-critical situations. Hayes offers a contrasting view in the following chapter.

Chapter 8 is again based on PhD fieldwork by Jan Hayes. Safety research is often focused on the behaviour of frontline workers. Seldom does it look at the decision-making by people at the level of shift managers. This is Hayes' level of interest, and the research question concerns how such people balance safety and production in highly hazardous operations. In particular, how do they decide whether to stop operations in the interest of safety?

Her findings challenge some of the current thinking in this area. For a start, such managers don't think of themselves as balancing safety and production. Instead, they have a rather more black and white concept of what they are doing: "If it's not safe, we stop." This of course raises the question of what they mean by "safe". Hayes shows that, for many of these decision-makers, the system is safe if it is operating normally and, in particular, with all its safety systems and protective barriers functioning as intended. Where these systems are not functioning as intended, safety is degraded, and if a critical system goes down, managers may decide that the system is categorically unsafe and must be shut down.

Hayes argues further that the decisions of these managers are not and cannot be entirely determined by rules. Rules may define the outer limits of operation, but within those limits there may be times when managers determine that the system is unsafe and needs to be shut down. These decisions are made on the basis of professional judgment, which can never be entirely codified.

Finally, and somewhat ironically, Hayes finds that managers who are faced with uncertainty about what to do will often resolve this uncertainty by creating a rule for themselves — a line in the sand. For example, if a particular safety system is down but the operating system as a whole is still reasonably well defended, managers may decide to continue operation, conditionally: "If it's not fixed in half an hour, we'll stop production." In this way, what is essentially a risk management problem is converted into a matter of compliance with a self-imposed rule.

In summary, the operational managers that Hayes studied are not engaged in risk assessment and risk management as conventionally understood and taught. Her work broadens our understanding of what risk management can mean in practice.

Chapter 9, by Kate Branford, is based on her honours thesis. It is about accident analysis methods, as applied in aviation. Her starting point is that accident analyses based on the Reason model of organisational failures are intended to be blame-free. She argues that, in general, such analyses succeed in shifting blame away from frontline operators (such as pilots), but that they can easily be read as allocating blame to those responsible for the organisational failures. She shows that, following the crash of a Singapore Airlines plane at Taiwan airport in 2000, the Taiwanese authorities were so fearful that a Reason-style analysis would be seen as blaming them that they declined to carry out such an analysis. Indeed, they developed a unique style of analysis that had the effect of pointing the finger of blame at the pilots. Branford concludes that the human tendency to blame is so strong that it can only be defeated by extending the causal analysis beyond the organisations in question into political and social realms. She shows in this case that the poor runway lighting and other airport deficiencies that contributed to the accident can be attributed to the fact that Taiwan was not a member of the United Nations — itself a consequence of the UN's one-China policy. Such an extension of the analysis does not lead to any additional insights into how the accident might have been prevented, but it serves to diffuse blame to such an extent that it no longer interferes with the objectives of accident analyses.

Chapter 10 develops this theme, and is based on Branford's PhD work. It discusses an alternative to the Reason model, known as AcciMap analysis, which systematically identifies factors beyond the organisation in which the accident took place. AcciMaps are diagrams that show how a wide range of factors combine to produce the accident of interest. They have been used to good effect by various accident analysts, but most of these analyses have not laid out the logic of AcciMaps in any detail. This chapter sets out the logic of the approach and provides guidelines to help analysts who are seeking to use the AcciMap method. Coincidentally, the Australian Transport Safety Bureau has recently produced an important parallel document describing its own approach to AcciMap analysis (ATSB 2008).

Branford's PhD was funded by the Defence Science and Technology Organisation (DSTO), and the thesis was jointly supervised by myself and Dr Neelam Naikar from DSTO. Naikar and I had previously worked together developing AcciMaps for a number of Australian Air Force F111 aircraft crashes, and this collaboration paved the way for Branford's PhD work. Chapter 10 was written by Branford, but she requested that her supervisors be included as authors in recognition of their contribution to the thesis.

An important part of the logic of AcciMaps is what can be called "counterfactual analysis", that is, imagining things to be other than they were. If something is to be regarded as a cause, we need to be able to argue that, had it been different, the outcome would have been different. For instance, suppose it is agreed that, if Taiwan airport had had better lighting, the accident would not have occurred. Then, and only then, can we include poor lighting as one of the causes of the accident.

Chapter 11 demonstrates what can happen when accident analyses fail to apply this logic. It is based on an honours thesis written by Madeleine Rowland in which she examines the findings of the coronial inquiry into the bushfires that ravaged Canberra in 2003. The coroner identified a series of alleged failures by government officials and made negative findings against these individuals that changed their lives forever. It turns out, however, that the action or inaction by these individuals made very little difference to the outcome, and they should never have been blamed for the massive damage done by the fires. Had the coroner applied her mind to drawing the causal connections in the way that is required in AcciMaps, she would not have come to the conclusions that she did.

CHAPTER 5

FROM RISK TO RESILIENCE: ASSESSING FLIGHT SAFETY INCIDENTS IN AIRLINES

Carl Macrae[1]

Introduction

Analysing and learning from errors is a common risk management strategy in many organisations that strive to achieve high levels of safety in the face of serious risks, such as commercial airlines, nuclear power stations, and chemical processing plants. Learning from errors is a particularly fascinating risk management strategy as it explicitly aims to turn moments of risk into opportunities to improve safety. In doing so, it confronts some of the key challenges and paradoxes of managing risk in inherently risky domains. How can "safety" be defined and assessed in organisations where catastrophic risks are ever present? How can minor errors in routine operations be analysed to identify the sources of serious but rare accidents? And how can errors and other failure events be used as a resource for organising and building high levels of safety? These are all key practical and theoretical problems that are central to understanding how risk is managed in modern organisations.

This chapter argues that many of these difficult questions can be resolved by examining the fundamental assumptions, beliefs and analytical tactics that support processes of risk management. As such, the chapter focuses on the analytical and interpretive challenges that errors and failure events present to risk managers — how errors and failure events can be interpreted, how risk and safety information should be analysed and acted on, and how these processes are influenced by risk managers' beliefs and assumptions.

One arena in which these analytical and interpretive challenges come to the fore is the risk management of flight safety in commercial airlines. Incident reporting and investigation systems are well established in many airlines and aviation regulators. The efforts that go into analysing and learning from minor safety incidents are widely acknowledged as a key driver of the high levels of safety achieved in the airline industry (Reason 1997; Perrow 1999). To explore how risk managers use

1   This research was funded by the Economic and Social Research Council and a collaborative industry partner. I am grateful to the many practitioners who gave up so much of their time during the course of this research, and to Andrew Hopkins for his helpful comments on earlier drafts of this chapter.

errors to improve safety, this chapter presents a detailed analysis of the analytical and interpretive practices employed in airline safety incident reporting systems. It draws on an in-depth qualitative study of the beliefs and practices of flight safety managers in several airlines and regulators, both in the United Kingdom and Australia. The key aim of this chapter is to characterise the beliefs, assumptions and analytical tactics that allow risk managers to turn moments of risk into sources of resilience.

This chapter is structured as follows. First, some of the relevant theories and ideas are presented. This is followed by a discussion of the structure and practical arrangements of incident reporting and investigation systems (IRISs) in airlines. Next, the findings from the qualitative study are presented, along with a discussion of their implications in terms of current literature. This analysis is organised according to three core components of risk management: identifying risks, assessing risks, and resolving risks. Conclusions are then drawn regarding current theory and practices of risk management.

Errors, risk and high reliability

Risk management has been elevated to the top of many organisational and regulatory agendas in recent years, in part in an effort to prevent costly organisational accidents (Hutter 2005; Power 2007). Human errors, technical failures, procedural inadequacies and managerial oversights can severely disrupt an organisation's operations. And as organisations have become more complex and interconnected, the potential consequences of these events are increasingly severe and dramatic (Perrow 1999). Seemingly minor errors and failures can rapidly escalate into catastrophic accidents (Reason 1990, 1997). A wide range of prescriptive models and normative blueprints of risk management have been developed (IRM 2002; ILGRA 1996; Cabinet Office 2002; COSO 2004). However, these formal models rarely recognise or address the key analytical and interpretive problems involved in assessing errors and managing risk. Many of these problems have come to light following major accidents, and relate to how information on risk is collected, analysed, interpreted, communicated and understood in organisations — and how these interpretive processes can fail.

Following major accidents, it is commonly found that key risks remained misunderstood or entirely unnoticed for lengthy periods of time prior to the event. Turner argues that major organisational accidents result from the gradual accumulation of events and circumstances that are at odds with the culturally accepted models and norms within an organisation (Turner 1976, 1978, 1994). He characterises organisational accidents as a sudden and shocking discovery of this "collective neglect" (Turner 1976, p 385) that results in massive "cultural collapse" (Turner & Pidgeon 1997, p 72) — a dramatic failure of current beliefs and activities. Vaughan's work built on this approach, examining how weak signals of anomaly and deviance from accepted standards can be readily normalised in organisations (Vaughan 1996), and the ways in which organisational structures and hierarchies inevitably create patterns of secrecy and "systematic censorship" (Vaughan 1996, p 257) as information gets filtered and differentially distributed throughout organisations (Vaughan 1990). Likewise, Hopkins' (2005) concepts of risk denial and risk blindness refer to similarly insidious processes of ignoring or missing emerging signs of risks.

Organisations that achieve high levels of safety and reliability in extremely risky and trying conditions demonstrate a range of organisational processes that appear to counteract the risk of slipping into collective neglect, normalised deviance, and risk blindness. These high reliability organisations (HROs) seem particularly adept at identifying and responding to anomalies, errors and surprises. Weick, Sutcliffe and Obstfeld argue that the distinguishing characteristics of HROs are essentially interpretive — they support processes that allow weak signs of unexpected problems to be readily noticed in order to "enlarge what is known about what was noticed" (Weick, Sutcliffe & Obstfeld 1999, p 91). This framework centres on the organisational detection of unexpected events (Weick & Sutcliffe 2001). Organisational members seek to identify and explore events that challenge their expectations by focusing on moments of surprise: where events conflict in some way with prior assumptions and models. These disruptions act as sites around which networks of specialist personnel temporarily coalesce to understand, act on and resolve problems (Rochlin 1989). These processes of interpretation aim to reduce pockets of ignorance and avoid cultural blind spots (Weick & Sutcliffe 2001; Turner & Pidgeon 1997; Hopkins 2005).

Research on HROs has proven to be one of the most fertile areas in the field of risk and safety management, in large part due to its relentless focus on the ground-level practices and cognitive processes of workers. However, it remains somewhat removed from broader considerations of risk and its management. Indeed, even though risk management frameworks are now widely used in many organisations, and even though the management of risk has risen high up the regulatory and managerial agenda in recent years, the concept of risk and methods of risk management have barely been considered from a high-reliability perspective. In analysing the ground-level assumptions, beliefs and analytical tactics that support processes of risk management, this chapter in part intends to do just that. Incident reporting and investigation systems provide a key arena in which concepts of risk and the processes of interpreting and learning from errors intersect, particularly in safety-critical domains such as commercial aviation.

In addressing these issues, this chapter draws on the author's extensive fieldwork in the airline industry in which a community of 26 airline flight safety risk managers

Chapter

5

were studied over a period of three years. A primary responsibility of these risk managers was to analyse and manage flight safety incident reports. Ten of these risk managers were based at a large UK airline (where much of the research was conducted). The rest were based at three smaller UK airlines, a large Australian airline, and both the UK and the Australian air safety agencies. Repeated rounds of in-depth interviews were conducted, along with extended periods of participant observation in which the risk managers were observed while analysing and investigating incidents, attending meetings, and working with their colleagues (Macrae 2007). By drawing on these data, this chapter develops a detailed picture of the core beliefs and assumptions of flight safety risk managers, and how these influence how they interpret incidents, apply the concept of risk, and use safety-relevant information to address problems. Before analysing these practices, it is important to understand the basic structure and arrangements of most aviation IRISs (which have themselves often been used as the model for systems developed in other industries). This is examined next.

Incident reporting and investigation systems

Incident reporting and investigation systems are used to collect short reports of operational errors and mishaps from frontline personnel (such as human errors, technical malfunctions and procedural failures) in order to identify, investigate and address any underlying organisational risks (Van der Schaaf, Lucas & Hale 1991; Reason 1997). This represents a risk management strategy that aims to identify risks early, when they are small and when warning signs are still weak. As such, they have been used for many years in safety-critical industries such as the airline, nuclear power and chemical processing industries (O'Leary & Chappell 1996; Phimister et al 2003), and they are currently being developed in other settings such as healthcare (Barach & Small 2000) and banking (Muermann & Oktem 2002).

A typical IRIS in a large airline can receive tens of thousands of incident reports a year from pilots, cabin crew, engineers and ground crew. Incident reporting and investigation systems are typically managed by an independent oversight unit. Risk managers in this unit receive reports directly from operational personnel in order to encourage personnel to report events that they may be reluctant to report via their immediate line managers. Reporting requirements are typically broad. In airlines, it is a requirement that certain types of incident are reported (such as problems with de-icing aircraft or alerts registered by fire warning systems), along with any other event that may have implications for flight safety. The incidents reported relate only to a subset of the total number of those that may actually occur in an organisation. What is reported depends on a variety of factors, such as the ease of reporting, the fear of disciplinary action, and how worthwhile reporting is perceived to be (Pidgeon & O'Leary 2000).

Once received, incident reports are entered into a database and management information system. On initial receipt, each incident report is reviewed by a risk manager to assess its risk and to determine an appropriate response. Assessments of risk are often assigned on a simple risk matrix according to the severity and likelihood of potential harm (see Table 1). Such tables are widely used in risk management to prioritise action and record risk exposure (Reason 1997). Assessing the risk of incidents nonetheless depends heavily on the professional judgment, experience and expertise of risk managers (this is explored in detail below). Each report provides only a short and technical account of what are often complex and unique operational events. Risk managers require extensive operational knowledge to understand and assess these incidents (most have lengthy operational experience and are drawn from operational positions).

Risks are responded to in a number of ways through the IRIS. Risk managers can request additional information or clarification regarding an event by electronically forwarding a report and their request to the relevant specialist or manager. This may involve an engineer checking a piece of equipment, a manager debriefing flight crew members, or a specialist reviewing a local procedure. Due to the limited information provided by initial reports, any incident that is considered problematic must be followed up in order to make a fuller assessment of the event. From these initial enquiries, complex and lengthy investigations may result involving a range of people from around the organisation. These may last from a few days to several months, and in a large airline, several hundred can be ongoing at any one time.

A second and equally important component of risk management in an IRIS is communicating and reporting on safety events and distributing safety information throughout the organisation. Typically, IRIS risk managers give regular briefings to senior management that highlight recent significant incidents. They circulate regular newsletters to frontline personnel that communicate noteworthy events, lessons learnt and action taken. And they have significant input into the framing of

Chapter

5

TABLE 1: Generalised example of a simple risk matrix used in IRIS

Probability of occurrence	Severity of outcome		
	Low	Medium	High
High	C Medium	B High	A Extreme
Medium	D Low	C Medium	B High
Low	E Minimal	D Low	C Medium

discussions at board-level committee meetings by preparing the focus and content of board papers for review. Nonetheless, with no executive authority, IRIS risk managers cannot direct or control change. An IRIS provides a system of oversight. The responsibility for risk management lies with operational departments, and it is the personnel in these departments who are accountable for the risk management decisions and actions that they take. Much of this risk management activity is nonetheless coordinated, recorded and reported on by IRIS risk managers.

Having set the scene, the analytical and interpretive processes of IRIS risk managers will now be examined. First, the beliefs and analytical tactics underlying the initial identification of risks are examined. This stage of identifying previously unknown risks is critical to risk management, but is often assumed rather than explored in formal models of risk management. The chapter then goes on to examine how risks are understood and assessed by risk managers, and how risks are acted on and communicated within organisations.

Identifying risks: interpretive vigilance

Risk identification concerns how risks come to be noticed and initially known about in organisations, and is a crucial stage of risk management. If risks are not known about, they cannot be managed. The IRIS risk managers who participated in this study aimed to maintain a high degree of alertness and sensitivity to early, weak signs of previously unknown risks. The interpretive processes and analytical tactics used to achieve this can be described and characterised as "interpretive vigilance". The risk managers aimed to interpret and analyse incident reports in a close, detailed and attentive manner. They identified risks by remaining vigilant to potential flaws and gaps in their own interpretation, knowledge and assumptions about the safety of current operations.

A distinct set of assumptions and beliefs shaped and supported the processes of interpretive vigilance. The IRIS risk managers viewed their role as one of maintaining knowledge and awareness of all risks facing their organisation. A core assumption — and aspiration — was that signs of new and emerging risks could be discovered by piecing together small cues in apparently inconsequential minor events. A core belief was that their job was to identify risks "early" to avoid being "caught out" and surprised by problems that had gone unnoticed for some time:

> "The ones that trouble you are the ones that come out of left-field and
> you think, how did we get caught out like that? ... You've not done
> your job by flagging this back earlier." (Participant S3-1)

Discovering that a problem had not been noticed or fully understood for some period of time was considered a serious failure — both of organisational safety and the risk managers' own ability to monitor it. However, while being caught out was considered a highly unacceptable failure on their part ("it means we have been derelict" (S3-8)), it was also considered inevitable. The risk managers frequently discussed their own experiences of missing and misinterpreting early signs of risks. Knowledge of risk was assumed to be always partial and incomplete. Dealing with a continuous stream of incident reports reinforced this assumption:

> "We do our hazard identification and risk analysis and think we've cracked it. And then things happen: events." (S5-6)

Incident reports continually exposed the risk managers to information about unexpected and previously unrecognised problems. As such, their interpretations and assessments of risk were seen as being continually open to change: "… your judgment of risk is dependent on what's happened in the past, *it's not a fixed entity*" (S3-2). It was widely acknowledged that near-identical incidents could be interpreted in very different ways at different times "because your knowledge has moved — and hopefully expanded" (S3-3). As discussed below, these assumptions present a significant challenge to formal models of risk assessment (typified by the risk matrix described previously).

This set of fundamental assumptions underpinned the risk identification strategy used in the IRIS. Risks were identified by discovering and enlarging small disruptions to current beliefs about organisational activities. In their analysis work, the risk managers sought to disrupt and challenge what was currently taken for granted and assumed about safety. They used incidents to test their existing knowledge in order to find where it was wanting. Four distinct analytical tactics were used to identify where operational safety — and knowledge of it — may be weaker than previously believed. Each of these is examined in turn.

1. **Making patterns:** the IRIS risk managers suspected that a risk may be emerging if they could make some sort of pattern in reported events. Patterns suggested to them that there was some common, underlying problem of which they were currently unaware. Patterns were sometimes easy to make, especially when they involved the repetition of similar events. One example concerned marshallers at the newly-opened terminal of a foreign airport who were consistently guiding aircraft extremely close to a building while parking. It was found that these events were recurring on the same stands every time, and further investigation revealed that the stop lines for the type of aircraft involved had simply not been painted. Identifying this simple pattern of repetition was taken as a strong indication of a problem, not only regarding the specific operational circumstances, but also relating to broader processes of risk management in the area. In this instance, it led to a wide-ranging review as it was realised that, while the airline had rigorous processes for assessing the safety of new destinations, it did not have any formal

process to assess new extensions (such as this new terminal) at current destinations. Identifying these repeating events therefore allowed the risk managers to identify a previously unknown risk. More generally, "repeaters" suggested to them that there was a problem in that area that had not been adequately addressed.

Patterns were not always easy to make. In many cases, the IRIS risk managers had to more creatively piece together possible relationships between events. For instance, when reviewing an event in which a flight crew member had been slow to disconnect the autothrottle (resulting in a relatively insignificant eight knot speed exceedence for the flap setting), a risk manager connected this failure with a set of apparently diverse events. He thought it looked like "a distraction-type one" (S4-1), and related it to a recent event where crew members had nosed out onto a live runway, and another where crew members had forgotten to switch the altimeter out of take-off mode for the cruise stage of the flight. Later, another event was added to the pattern, when a crew member reported flying a manoeuvre too slowly for the flap setting they were on, wondering aloud whether there was an underlying risk that connected these superficially disparate events:

> "This is pilot handling, so is it part of a big picture, are we building up
> a risk? Is this something we need in the sims [simulators], or training
> — or a route check?" (S4-1)

The crew member wondered whether these various events indicated that they were "building up a risk" around inattentive pilot handling and crew "distraction", and they wanted to find out more. The links between these events were not obvious. Whether an event was part of a "big picture" was not always self-evident and, as in this case, depended on the risk managers actively *building* the big picture that they suspected it might then fit into. In this case, identifying the pattern resulted in significant efforts being put into emphasising to flight crews the importance of monitoring for minor distractions and disruptions to performance, both through simulator training and within each fleet, including, for instance, "they've launched a 'flap selection awareness drive', of all things" (S4-4).

Further, the patterns that the risk managers made were based on small numbers of events. They were extremely liberal with the terms "trend" and "spate" because they wanted to find and fix problems early. Two events could make a trend, three or four a spate. Their analysis was largely based on "extrapolating" (S3-1) and enlarging small trends which were necessarily based on little evidence, as one explained:

> "… you can't back it up with enough data. The bigger the trend the
> better, but the database won't always tell you that because it is three
> examples that lead you to a conclusion." (S6-5)

Making patterns — and so identifying risks — was therefore an interpretive rather than a statistical exercise. It was based on the construction and interpretation of a feasible pattern of failure; one that pointed to an underlying, common and systematic organisational weakness.

2. Drawing connections: seeing a connection, no matter how weak, between an incident and a broader safety issue or a past major accident led the IRIS risk managers to doubt the safety of the operational area concerned. Past accidents and broader safety issues (such as industry-wide problems identified by safety agencies or ongoing safety investigations) provided frames of reference that the risk managers used to interpret otherwise minor and equivocal events. References to past accidents while reviewing incidents were profligate. An incident could be "like Taipei" (S2-1), or was "Tenerife all over again" (S4-3), or "stinks of Milan" (S4-4) — all references to past major air accidents. These connections were made on the basis of *any* perceived similarity between the organisational processes that underlay the accident, and those implicated in the incident. For instance, in one incident, a crew member reported that they had nearly used the full length of the runway to land. It had been raining, and there had been some confusion over the functioning of the windscreen wipers. As a result, they had inadvertently left the autothrottle engaged and failed to select idle reverse thrust, as they had been briefed for. The risk managers immediately deemed this "a bit of a QF1" (S4-1), referring to the flight code of another airline's aircraft that had overrun a runway in a heavy rainstorm under similar, though far from identical, conditions several years previously.

Relating incidents such as this to the broader frame provided by a past major event led the risk managers to question aspects of operations more broadly, and more seriously, than the incidents on their own would reasonably have justified. Equally, ongoing "issues" that served as frames of reference arose from various sources. Sometimes they emerged from particular accident enquiries. This included the "runway incursion" issue, where a recent accident investigation had highlighted the risk in the industry of aircraft accidentally moving across active runways without permission. Sometimes issues emerged from analysis work or special reports produced by safety agencies or regulators. Further, issues could arise from investigations or analyses conducted within the risk managers' own organisation. This was particularly the case for ongoing investigations, or problems that the risk managers couldn't seem to get to the bottom of or resolve. Connecting an otherwise minor event and a past accident was one way that the risk managers enlarged their concerns beyond the immediate incident reported, even though connecting just one incident to another past accident was acknowledged to be a "tenuous link" (S4-4). Tenuous though they may have been, such connections provided a key basis for identifying suspect areas of safety. Connecting various minor events to a central "issue" extended the boundary of the risk managers' suspicions; it was the means

Chapter

5

by which they enlarged areas of ignorance and "generalised" individual errors to the broader systems involved.

3. Recognising novelty: the IRIS risk managers developed doubts about the adequacy of operational processes — or their knowledge of them — if an event was perceived to suggest some new or previously unrecognised aspect of organisational failure. Recognising new ways that organisational activity might break down was a key indicator of potential ignorance. It involved identifying signs of new and previously unheard of forms of organisational weakness — either by seeing new forms of failure or by seeing new implications of known failures, such as novel ways that they might occur and develop:

> "It could be either a new kind of condition or a condition you have had for a while, but you will suddenly see it as a major link in a chain … a new link in a chain that gives us an unease." (S4-7)

Recognising novelty was a simple and direct way of exposing the limits of current knowledge. The process was as much about reflecting on the risk managers' own knowledge as it was about examining organisational processes. Where making patterns and drawing connections involved a "big picture", recognising novelty was about identifying where they had *no* picture. Signs of novelty suggested to the risk managers that their knowledge of the specific organisational processes surrounding a particular event was lacking.

Signs of novelty were typically both subtle and specific, relating to some slightly different or new aspect of operational failure. One example concerned the momentary "sticking" of flight controls. On investigation, this turned out to have resulted from de-icing fluid dehydrating and accumulating in crevices of the aircraft, re-hydrating on warm, humid days, and then freezing at high altitude — later discovered to be an industry-wide problem (Wastnage 2005). While problems with flight controls were on their own clearly considered a "bad thing", these events also signalled a pressing gap in organisational knowledge that had gone unnoticed. As one risk manager commented: "… the audits say: de-icing procedures — all in place and complied to" (S5-6). By recognising signs of novelty, incident reporting was uniquely valuable for discovering new aspects and variations of organisational risk. As such, the IRIS risk managers uncovered latent organisational risks by identifying novelty and overturning their previously accepted beliefs of operational normality.

4. Sensing discrepancy: the risk managers suspected that their knowledge of operations may be inadequate when they identified any apparent inconsistency in organisational processes or their understanding of them. These inconsistencies and discrepancies were where things didn't seem to properly match up or fit together. There were often subtle signs, and their precise nature or cause was rarely immediately obvious to the risk managers. These were "the little niggling things" (S2-1) that they sensed in events, the things that "irked" them. It was where it seemed that there was "something not quite right" (S3-3), but they didn't know exactly what. A simple example, for instance, concerned a report that described an apparent mismatch between the ECAM (electronic centralised aircraft monitoring) warning drill and the MEL (mandatory equipment list) procedures for dealing with a fuel pump pressure warning prior to take-off:

> "Anytime we see a disagreement between ECAM and MEL it's very worrying, as the manufacturers write both. And generally the crew follow the ECAM. So we definitely need to understand this." (S4-6)

Such discrepancies worried the risk managers, and they consequently wanted to understand them further. Further, the risk managers became suspicious when they perceived any slight discrepancy between what they would have expected to happen and what was reported in incidents (Weick & Sutcliffe 2001). On one occasion, a risk manager reviewed an incident in which a take-off had been aborted at low speed due to an engine overspeed warning — signalling that one of the compressor fans in the jet engine was spinning too fast and reducing thrust. The flight crew contacted the engineering control centre, and were advised to check the engine with a stationary engine run and, as that was clear, to depart as planned. While rejected take-offs were considered part of normal operations, the risk manager was unsure about the advice given to the flight crew. He wasn't certain, but "thought they would have done other checks before restarting" (S4-3) with that particular type of warning. He decided to have "a dig around" (S4-3) and, when he made a few phone calls, found out that the power plant engineers "weren't happy" (S4-3) either, and believed that further maintenance checks would have been appropriate. Picking up on small discrepancies between the way that the risk managers believed things should be and the way that they occurred in incidents allowed them, through these moments of ignorance, to identify risks. The risk managers developed suspicions based on identifying where their expectations were challenged or violated by events, even in the weakest of ways.

Implications: knowledge, ignorance and early warning signs

Practices of risk identification in an IRIS can be described as involving processes of interpretive vigilance. This represents an approach to risk management that is based on a deep appreciation of the limits to knowledge, and that employs interpretive tactics that aim to find gaps and inadequacies in current knowledge of risk. Primarily, this indicates a core but relatively underexplored issue — that risk management is crucially concerned with acquiring and maintaining *knowledge* of the challenges and threats that face an organisation. Managing risk is a process of developing and revising current knowledge in the face of irreducible uncertainty

Chapter

5

(Wildavsky 1988). Risk management models typically specify the infrastructures of information collection and manipulation that can support this. But studying risk management practice highlights the intuitive, generative, creative — and fallible — sociocognitive processes that seem essential to interpreting and making sense of ambiguous risk events in organisations.

For the IRIS risk managers, identifying risks was largely an interpretive rather than a statistical process. It involved piecing together the limited, ambiguous and fragile information available on incidents within broader frames of reference and bodies of knowledge. The comprehension of data by connecting concrete "cues" with more abstract "frames" is a classic process of sensemaking (Weick 1995) and knowing (Cook & Brown 1999). Viewing risk identification as an interpretive process in this way leads to several important insights. First, the available knowledge and frames of reference are as important as the information and data collected. While most effort is focused on the collection of relevant risk data, this may only be half of the story. In the IRIS risk managers' case, detailed knowledge of operational processes, organisational goals, previous problems and past accidents was of particular importance in identifying new risks. How such knowledge is used, shared and represented in risk management (often in the form of stories about past events (Orr 1996; Weick 1987)) would seem a critical issue that requires closer attention. Further, these findings reinforce the argument that these forms of detailed, practical knowledge may easily be lost in efforts to systematise and standardise risk management processes (Power 2007).

Moreover, the continual changes and developments in knowledge — and the resulting changes in how incidents are interpreted and risks assessed — present a considerable challenge to current formal models of risk assessment. Judging events according to the standard risk matrix implies that each event carries an intrinsic level of risk, determined by the likelihood and severity of the adverse consequences that could result. In contrast, changes in the risk managers' knowledge were acknowledged to dramatically alter the risk attributed to an event. That is, the risk of an event was not an inherent quality of the event itself, but rather was dependent on the assumptions, information, knowledge and, ultimately, imagination of the risk managers who were analysing it.

Similarly, a second important implication is that "warning signs" of organisational problems (Kiesler & Sproull 1982; Sheaffer, Richardson & Rosenblatt 1998) are not self-evidently warning signs, but must be actively constructed. The processes involved in constructing warning signs are central to understanding risk management practice in organisations (Vaughan 1996; Turner 1978). For the IRIS risk managers, warning signs were constructed by forming a tentative belief that current knowledge was in some way inadequate or incomplete. That is, risk management was an interpretive process of testing and identifying the limits of current knowledge. Incidents were used to interrogate the unknown (Wildavsky 1988), to test assumptions (Turner & Pidgeon 1997), to challenge expectations (Weick & Sutcliffe 2001), and to become aware of ignorance (Smithson 1989). Practices of risk identification were organised around finding areas of organisational ignorance, that is, where knowledge of operational processes was poor or confused. This broader framing of ignorance seems central to explaining risk management practice, in contrast to the narrow definition of uncertainty that is typically deployed in risk management models that focus exclusively on the probability of future adverse consequences. Further exploration of the nature and purpose of different forms of ignorance (Smithson 1989) in risk management practice would seem a valuable research endeavour.

Assessing risks: organisational risk resilience

Risk assessment in the IRIS required determining the level of threat that an incident posed to flight safety. Assessments of risk were based on a set of assumptions and beliefs concerning the nature of risk and the drivers of safety in complex organisations operating in risky environments. These beliefs and assumptions framed how the risk managers interpreted incidents. This interpretive framework can be characterised as one in which safety was viewed as the organisational capacity for "risk resilience". This had two key components. First, safety was understood in organisational terms, that is, as an organisational capacity to prevent minor mishaps developing into major operational breakdowns. Second, risk was understood as weaknesses and gaps in this capacity for risk resilience. The IRIS risk managers assessed risk by analysing whether organisational defences could adequately control and contain operational failures.

The core assumption was that the potential for catastrophic consequences always existed in airline operations. Human error and technical failures were considered inevitable and entirely normal features of organisational activity: all aspects of operations were "fallible and frangible" (S3-5). The IRIS provided risk managers with reports of these operational failures every day. Significantly, there was a pervasive and fundamental belief that major accidents could result from a unique combination of these otherwise banal and minor failures. One risk manager explained this with reference to another airline's recent accident:

> "The classic one is … the causes of the Paris Concorde accident. And it's fascinating, the number of factors that led to that accident, fascinating. And any one of them would have stopped that accident, and yet they happen every single day — every one of them." (S6-5)

The assumption was that every minor event had the potential, however remote, to develop into a serious accident. As such, assessing risk on the basis of "worst case" potential outcomes (as many risk assessment guidelines recommend) was considered impractical because, taken to the extreme, "every incident would be a catastrophe" (S5-12). In practice, risk assessment in the IRIS was directed at assessing the underlying organisational capacity to prevent minor mishaps escalating into major breakdowns. Simply put, the risk managers were literally interested in: "What are the things that stop this being a catastrophe?" (S3-2)

The risk managers were also concerned with how resilient operations were, that is, how effective risk controls and safety defences were at correcting or containing small failures. These assessments were not simply about analysing how well an error or failure event had been caught by controls. Of central importance was analysing what defensive capacity remained beyond the defences that were called on: what processes were in place to capture the event if it developed further.

A key principle underlying risk assessment was that numerous diverse defences should remain in any situation, protecting operations against the *potential* for an event to escalate further. That is, operational safety required not simply resilience to actual failure, but resilience to the *risk* of failure. An example that highlighted this perspective was recounted by one risk manager: a hypothetical "worst case" scenario in which a flight crew member received a warning from the ground proximity warning system (GPWS) to urgently pull up and away from terrain:

> "The GPWS is the classic really, that's a worst-case, if you get a real one you've lost it really, it's one circuit breaker left to protect you. You are down to tight stuff." (S2-1)

While a safety system might do as it was designed to and catch the problem, situations such as these were nonetheless considered "as bad as it gets" (S2-1). With no further defences remaining, this type of failure would leave operations entirely unprotected and exposed to potential catastrophe. In light of this, incidents were used to assess the underlying organisational capacity for resilience to risk, rather than to simply assess the actual adverse impact of an incident, or to try and predict the likelihood and extent of the harm that it could have led to.

Assessments of risk resilience drew together a range of subtle judgments regarding the efficacy and adequacy of safety defences and risk controls. These judgments focused on the organisational nature of defences. Safety defences or risk controls were viewed as properties of practical work routines that provided capabilities to deal with failures. Work routines involved the interaction of social and technical elements: people operating, managing and maintaining technologies. Defences and controls were not viewed as simple mechanisms, but as organisational processes that hinged on the cognisance and competence of personnel in relation to technical systems. In assessing the effectiveness and quality of defensive processes, a number of key attributes and qualities of organisational processes were routinely attended to. These organisational attributes were core properties of risk resilience, and perceived deficiencies in these attributes were interpreted as signs of degrading risk resilience.

These assessments of the quality of organisational risk resilience were made along a broad spectrum, but tended to fall into three key distinguishable groups. First, assessments were often made that defensive processes were adequate and currently acceptable — for the time being. This broadly represented a "normal" and unproblematic state, and a close approximation to relative "safety". Second, assessments were sometimes made that risk resilience was reduced and existed in a somewhat deteriorated state. This was where defensive processes were considered less robust or extensive than they could have been. Operations remain protected, but in a less than optimal condition. Third, assessments were occasionally made that risk resilience was entirely degraded. Here, a state was deemed to exist where appropriate defences were deficient or absent, providing little or only weak protection against the potential for minor failures to escalate into major ones.

These assessment processes were conducted with little reference to the formal criteria of the risk matrix, that is, the two axes of the severity and frequency of events. Instead, the IRIS risk managers described the process as one of drawing on their expertise, prior knowledge and judgment regarding the resilience of the systems involved, then recording their assessment by simply selecting an appropriate risk category on the ordinal scale A to E provided by the risk matrix. Making this selection was important as it provided the formal record of a risk level that was circulated to others within the airline, including operational departments and senior executives. In broad terms, events that were not considered of immediate relevance to safety management were recorded in the E category — a category that required no further action. The three levels of assessment described above broadly fitted the D, C and B risk categories, respectively representing acceptable, reduced and degraded risk resilience. The A-level risk category was viewed as so uniquely severe that it was used only in extraordinary circumstances. The risk managers viewed it as a last resort, and aimed to avoid using it in order to preserve its shock value in their organisation. So, as discussed in more detail below, risk was assessed both in relation to assessments of risk and in relation to managing organisational responses to risk.

Implications: resilience, defences and organisational control

Practices of risk assessment in the IRIS can be usefully theorised and characterised in terms of the concept of organisational risk resilience. This represented a set of assumptions and a framework for interpreting organisational events, and distinguishing where organisational processes were acceptably safe and where they were exposed to potential breakdowns. In practice, risk assessment involved assessing the quality and extent of organisational control. Importantly, risk was not routinely assessed by predicting the likely consequences of individual incidents (as models of risk management typically specify (IRM 2002)). Instead, risk assessment was more of a diagnostic activity. It involved diagnosing where organisational processes did not provide adequate protection against failures, and then assessing the severity of this degradation.

These findings are in line with research that increasingly focuses on understanding resilience in organisations (Reason 1997; Weick, Sutcliffe & Obstfeld 1999; Sutcliffe & Vogus 2003). In essence, resilience has been conceived of as the ability to flexibly "bounce back" (Wildavsky 1988, p 77; Weick & Sutcliffe 2001, p 14) and to learn from errors and failures as they occur. But, defined in this way, the concept of resilience is rather narrow and is wedded to a purely reactive and retrospective model of risk management. This makes little sense when considering safety-critical, well-defended and proactively managed HROs in which a range of defences, safeguards, procedures, backup systems and protocols are designed in advance to catch possible failures. What is focused on in these organisations is resilience to *risk*. As indicated by the IRIS risk managers, in practice, their ideas of risk and resilience were heavily integrated and bound up together. Organisational safety was not construed simply as an ability to bounce back from adverse incidents as they happened, or merely to recover from harm once it struck. Instead, safety was viewed as the ability to defend against the potential — or the risk — of the minor mishaps and performance fluctuations of normal operations escalating into major breakdowns of organisational processes. Safety was only considered to be acceptable when this potential or risk was adequately defended against — in short, where there was *risk resilience*. This study of risk management practice provides an outline of how the concept of resilience can be better defined by explicitly integrating it with notions of risk. It also implies that research on organisational resilience should more closely examine the question, resilience *to what* — actual errors and events, possible failures and mishaps, or the risk of minor incidents escalating into catastrophe? Current research largely leaves this question open.

One of the most notable developments of existing theory from this study of practice centres on the ideas of safety defences or barriers and risk controls (Hollnagel 2004; Reason 1997; Svenson 1991). Studying practice suggests that the way safety defences, risk controls — and operational hazards — are currently defined may be somewhat problematic. In most accounts, it is assumed that defences are designed to keep "bad" things "out". Like the concentric fortifications of a castle, safety barriers stop hazards (such as fire or explosions) from coming into contact with valuable and fragile assets (such as people or property) (Reason 1997). These are the assumptions that "barrier" theories of safety (Hollnagel 2004; Svenson 1991), as well as basic models of risk management, are based on. Accidents happen when hazards penetrate system defences and cause damage. But, in the IRIS study, defences were not viewed as a barrier that separates an asset from a hazard. In fact, the traditional notion of "hazard" barely featured. Threats were viewed instead as the possibility of organisational processes breaking down, and by weaknesses in the capability for effective control. That is, defences were conceived of as keeping organisational activity within safe, known and manageable confines. Defences didn't stop a hazard getting "in". They stopped operations getting "out", that is, out of control and out of the normal safe range of activity (Reason & Hobbs 2003). The risk was organisational processes themselves becoming unwieldy or fragile. This represents a subtle but important shift in emphasis regarding the nature of safety defences and risk controls. These may be better defined and assessed in terms of the degree to which they constitute and control effective organisational processes.

Resolving risks: participative networks

Resolving risks requires taking action to fully investigate, understand and address the underlying problems implicated by an incident. As an oversight mechanism, the IRIS did not provide direct authority to mandate or enforce action. Instead, the risk managers worked to resolve risks by coordinating investigations, managing awareness of risks, and creating ownership and accountability for resolving risks in their organisation. As such, the IRIS supported a distributed and decentralised approach to acting on and resolving risks. These processes can be characterised as the creation of "participative networks" around risks. The risk managers initiated, coordinated and monitored the participation of personnel from around the organisation (and often from other organisations) in examining and resolving risks.

A central belief of the risk managers was that their ultimate goal was to generate action to resolve risks and improve safety. Incidents were used by the risk managers to provoke and trigger deeper investigation of risks, to focus organisational resources on problems and, essentially, to effect organisational change. Assessments of risk were therefore used to drive action and get things done, as the risk managers commonly explained:

> "The purpose you do [risk assessments] is ... because you want to understand the appropriate corporate response. It helps you focus your resources on the appropriate areas to bring about the change that will hopefully get rid of that problem." (S3-7)

While organisational action was the aim, the risk managers had no direct control or authority over this action. In the IRIS, getting organisational action was about influencing and guiding the action of others. In practice, the risk managers worked to achieve this in two ways. First, they publicised signs of potential risks in their organisation. The risk managers kept directors, managers, supervisors and operational specialists informed of significant incidents by distributing regular (typically weekly) briefings and producing papers for review at board level. These were intended to make sure that people who should know about serious incidents did:

> "It means it gets to people. With the best will in the world, the director wouldn't have time to go in to [the IRIS database] to search himself, and so someone would be doing it for him. So if they aren't telling him the good stuff, then we are." (S4-1)

Second, the risk managers constantly posed questions about the adequacy of organisational processes by requesting investigations and further information regarding incidents from operational specialists around the organisation.

In posing questions and publicising incidents, the risk managers aimed to direct attention and manage awareness of risks in their organisation. The aim was straightforward: to "flag it up, and say these are the things you should be looking at today" (S6-1). The risk managers were setting and continually revising a risk agenda, that is, what people should be aware of, attending to, and acting on. Equally, the risk managers aimed to provoke enquiry and action in order to make risks visible to those responsible for resolving them:

> "[We] don't take the decisions, we invite the departments to — to take ownership of safety ... It is making them accountable, and it is their decision." (S5-6)

By creating awareness of current risks in their organisation — and an audit trail — the risk managers made the ownership of risks visible, as much as the risks themselves. They aimed to ensure widespread participation in risk management. By distributing signs and questions regarding risks, incidents were used to engage networks of diverse specialists and personnel in the investigation and management of risks. The risk managers contacted personnel who were relevant to resolving a risk, often bringing together a range of people from different operational areas and forming a temporary and distributed team. Incident reports provided a focus around which reflection and action were organised.

The extent of intervention required by the IRIS risk managers in resolving a risk was determined according to three criteria. These criteria were used to evaluate how worthwhile and beneficial it would be to act on a risk — in simple terms, the risk management *value* of action. Judgments of the potential value of acting on a risk were based on three factors. First, the risk managers considered the potential safety benefits that would accrue in terms of strengthened resilience and greater knowledge of risks in their organisation. Second, the risk managers considered the extent to which current organisational activity was already addressing risks, and whether a risk needed to be addressed with greater fervour. And third, the risk managers considered the practicality of addressing risks and achieving actual improvements, that is, whether the organisational issues could be resolved directly or whether alternative courses of action needed to be taken through, for instance, international agencies. These criteria determined the extent to which the risk managers aimed to encourage participative investigation, analysis and action around a risk.

Implications: organising culture, learning and expertise

Practices of risk resolution in the IRIS were characterised in terms of participative networks. Risks were responded to by initiating and shaping distributed processes of investigation and action, and the need for this action was evaluated in terms of what it might achieve. Primarily, these findings demonstrate that the IRIS not only provided a mechanism to monitor and analyse organisational risks — it equally provided an important means by which organisational culture and practice were constituted and fashioned.

In practice, incidents were actively used for organisational purposes. They were used as points around which diverse operational specialists were connected and brought together to manage risks. They facilitated communication about risks that otherwise may not have taken place. And they provided small, concrete cues that acted as focal points for line personnel, operational specialists and managers to reflect on, and enquire into, the adequacy of operational processes and their assumptions about them. In a real sense, incident reports were used to direct and ground the ongoing reflection and learning that seem critical to maintaining effective and informed cultures of safety (Reason 1997; Pidgeon & O'Leary 1994). As such, the IRIS directly addressed some of the most insidious organisational risks that allow the causes of disaster to incubate and remain latent (Turner & Pidgeon 1997; Reason 1997; Vaughan 1996).

The analysis also points to how a small group of risk managers led broader processes of organisational learning. The risk managers chose many of the issues that were explored by operational specialists and they shaped the nature of the ensuing investigations. They linked their processes of interpreting incidents with the reflection and learning of personnel from around the organisation. In this sense, processes of risk management involved the bridging of individual and organisational learning (Holmqvist 2003).

Further, assessments of risk were inextricably tied up with judgments of how those risks could be acted on and resolved — and by whom. The practical interplay between processes of risk assessment and risk evaluation has received limited empirical scrutiny to date (Wilpert & Fahlbruch 2002; Hutter & Lloyd-Bostock 1990). However, in the IRIS study, interpreting risk was heavily oriented to acting,

Chapter

5

and was structured by a set of criteria that evaluated the level of achievable action and the likely value of the results. While, in many domains, risks have traditionally been evaluated in purely negative terms — stopping the unacceptable and preventing the intolerable — risks were evaluated by the IRIS risk managers as sources of potential gains and valuable improvements to organisational processes. One important implication of this is how judgments of risk were used in practice as an interpretive tool. Risk assessments were constructed for the purpose of directing attention, focusing resources and getting action. Like Smith's (1988) definition of managerial "problems", assessments of risk were applied in order to generate and direct organisational action (Power 2003).

Practically, these findings reaffirm the importance of social skills in risk management (Weick & Roberts 1993; Weick, Sutcliffe & Obstfeld 1999). For instance, the practical ability to frame and pose appropriate questions to shape the enquiry of others seems a key, if easily overlooked, skill. The IRIS created organisational spaces and forums in which this collective reflection and participative learning could legitimately unfold. Further examination of how participative engagement in risk management unfolds (Hutter 2001), and how these social processes are supported, would seem a valuable area for future research.

Conclusion

This chapter has examined some of the key interpretive processes and analytical tactics that are used by airline flight safety risk managers to assess, interpret and learn from errors and failure events. As already indicated, analysing and learning from errors is a particularly fascinating risk management strategy because it directly confronts some of the most problematic issues in risk management — how to define safety in risky environments, how to analyse minor errors to identify major risks, and how to use moments of risk to create organisational resilience. In attempting to address these questions, the study presented in this chapter raises some interesting implications for how we understand safety and risk in the context of HROs.

Past research has highlighted how effectively HROs deal with errors and failure events. Indeed, one of the defining characteristics of an HRO is how it is "activated" by errors — how personnel come together around problems in order to understand and resolve them (Rochlin 1989). What has not been considered in any great detail is how organisations cope when they face the occurrence of large numbers of minor errors and failures — a fairly common situation for many organisations. How to deal with this is one of the key challenges in incident reporting systems, and risk management more broadly. The findings presented in this chapter suggest that what becomes important in this situation is how risk managers think about and define risk and safety. The perspective observed here, where the risk managers viewed safety as resilience to risk, provided one way of sorting the important from the less important when faced with a large number of incidents. In situations where predicting future consequences is tricky, risk managers can distinguish between incidents that should be attended to, and those that can be safely ignored, by analysing the strength of the underlying organisational processes involved (Reason 1997). Moreover, while HROs are viewed as being activated by disruptive and unexpected events (Weick & Sutcliffe 2001), the findings in this chapter imply that, in many cases, a lot of work and analysis goes into identifying and uncovering what it is that is unexpected. Expectations and beliefs are not always challenged in obvious ways by single, simple events. Risk managers are required to actively piece together, interpret and interrogate the errors they encounter in order to determine why these events may be surprising and what risks they may warn of. As previously indicated, warnings are not so much there for the taking but must be actively constructed and uncovered through vigilant interpretive work. Further, the findings of this chapter suggest that risk managers can directly counter and address many organisational risks simply by distributing information appropriately, communicating effectively, and managing both awareness of and accountability for risks. Through these processes, risk managers can help to prevent cultural blind spots, collective neglect and risk blindness from forming (Turner 1976; Hopkins 2005). What is more, by centrally coordinating investigations and setting and continually revising a safety agenda for the organisation, risk managers are able to directly manage and increase what has been termed "the processes of enlarging what is known about what is noticed that are central to maintaining resilience and high reliability" (Weick & Sutcliffe 2001). That is, risk managers play a critical part in coordinating the organisational production and circulation of knowledge — and counteracting the emergence of organisational ignorance (Smithson 1989).

Exploring the beliefs, assumptions and interpretive processes involved in analysing safety incident reports raises a range of implications for how we understand risk, safety and high reliability. Taken together, one overriding implication is that, when viewed from the perspective of practitioners, risk management can involve a far more subtle and nuanced analytical approach than is often presented in formal models of risk analysis that typically focus on predicting the extent of future harm. In practice, risks may be defined and assessed in ways that both extend and contradict current normative models of risk management. From the perspective of the risk managers studied here, risk management involved an ongoing process of discovering the limits of knowledge in their organisation, identifying weaknesses in the capacity for organisational control, and then choosing how best to draw attention to these issues and organise resources around them. The analytical processes described in this chapter in terms of interpretive vigilance, risk resilience and participative networks present three intertwined and complementary tactics for moving from risk to resilience.

Chapter

5

CHAPTER 6

INCIDENT REPORTING: A NUCLEAR INDUSTRY CASE STUDY

Jan Hayes

Introduction

Learning from incidents is a key feature of the safety strategy of high reliability organisations (HROs). Such organisations operate complex, high-hazard technologies in an environment where overall failures in safety performance are not tolerated. High reliability organisations try to use data collected about small incidents to improve their safety performance, but what can be learned from such information and how can it be used to improve future performance?

Many organisations learn by trial and error. An example might be a recruitment campaign based on a particular remuneration package. The package may have been developed based on research about what other organisations are doing, carefully targeted at the demographic that the organisation wishes to attract. Based on the response, the organisation may change the package for the next recruitment program by offering more, less or different items to take account of the outcome of its initial program, especially if the original recruitment targets were not met. To some extent, the same learning method is used to improve safety performance. While most organisations would now be aware of the potential for back problems and would have put systems in place aimed at effectively managing manual handling, an increase in manual handling injuries would trigger a review of such systems. In both of these examples, the trigger for change is "error" or an undesired outcome.

Incident reporting has its origins in this type of trial and error learning — measuring undesired outcomes so that changes can be made to improve performance. This is analogous to automatic feedback control used in the process and manufacturing industries. The desired outcome is specified and the actual outcome for a specific set of inputs is measured. Any deviation from the desired outcome is corrected by making changes to the system inputs.

High reliability organisations operate in an environment that requires a different strategy. Accidents must be prevented before they occur *in all cases*; specifically, no deviation from the required outcome is acceptable. In the language of process control, what is required is feed forward control. In this type of control scheme, measurements of the system are made and used to predict the future performance of the key parameter. If the predicted performance is not as desired, changes are made to ensure that deviations are corrected before they impact on the overall result. The challenge for HROs is to understand the relationship between the current organisational performance and their future safety performance — what factors need to be measured, recorded or observed, and how should they be changed in order to meet the overall safety performance target?

This chapter describes two ways of thinking about the relationship between reported incidents and the expected future safety performance of the organisation based on two well-known ways of thinking about safety performance improvement — the safety triangle and the Swiss cheese model. The incident reporting system in use at a nuclear power station is also described and considered in relation to those models. Finally, comparisons are drawn with the Airservices Australia incident reporting system described in Chapter 3.

The Bird safety triangle

In the process industries, thinking about the role of incidents in safety performance improvement has been heavily influenced by the well-known safety triangle (see Figure 1), taken from the work of Frank Bird in the 1960s and 1970s.[1]

FIGURE 1: Safety triangle (Bird 1975)

---

1   Also known as the Bird pyramid, the iceberg theory, and other variations on these.

The original research suggests that, for every 600 incidents without damage or injury, there will be 30 incidents where some property damage occurs, 10 minor injuries, and one serious injury. Bird's monograph from 1975 defined "incident" as "an undesired event that could (or does) downgrade the efficiency of the business operation". Incidents could be related to safety, quality, the environment, production or security — the common factor is a loss of some kind compared with the desired performance of the business. The key to improved overall business performance becomes "loss control" — a strategy of eliminating or controlling all incidents which downgrade the performance of the business.

Bird puts forward the case that there is a direct link between the number of small incidents and the number of serious accidents.[2] The ratios developed above (originally published in 1969) were based on raw data from almost 300 companies in 21 industrial groups with 1,750,000 employees. Bird emphasises that the exact ratios that he found were specific to the time and circumstances of the organisations being reviewed (Bird & Germain 1986). The general point that he made to his industrial readers was that they did not have to wait for an injury or death to occur before acting to improve safety. Plenty of information was available to them to target their efforts and resources in appropriate ways. All they had to do was take more notice of the near misses already occurring in their workplace. This was an important advance in safety thinking.

If this relationship is correct, an effective strategy to reduce the potential for injury is to reduce the number of incidents. The role of incident reporting and analysis in accident prevention becomes one of ensuring that the identified incidents are followed up and fixed to prevent recurrence, thereby reducing the number of incidents and hence the overall number of injuries. While this was not Bird's intent (as is clear from reading the original published work), the safety triangle can be seen to imply that any reduction in small incidents is equally useful in preventing serious accidents.

Organisational error and the Swiss cheese model

The ideas behind the safety triangle were radical 30 years ago, but safety research has moved on. An organisational view of accidents that is consistent with HRO thinking takes a very different view of the role of incident reporting in safety performance improvement.

The Swiss cheese model (see Figure 2) conceptualises accidents as a complex chain of small failures that build up over time. The immediate trigger for any accident

---

2 Other research has questioned the exact ratios between serious and less serious events, but the basic idea retains currency. See, for example, Kjellen (2000).

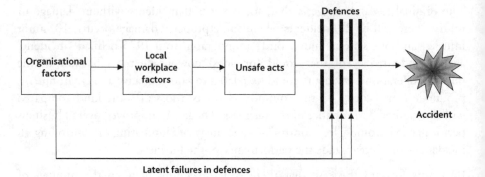

FIGURE 2: Swiss cheese model (Reason 1997)

is an unsafe act of some kind, but a well-functioning organisation minimises accidents in two ways. First, unsafe acts by individuals are seen as a function of organisational factors (such as policies and procedures) which, in turn, determine the local workplace factors (such as shift patterns, physical working arrangements, and specific procedures). Improvements in organisational and local workplace factors reduce the number of unsafe acts that occur. Second, HROs have many organisational defences in place so that any given unsafe act leads to an accident only if all of the defences fail in that specific case. Safety improvements can be made by strengthening defences. The layers of defences are seen as being like slices of Swiss cheese. If all the holes in the Swiss cheese line up, then an unsafe act will result in an accident.

In the Swiss cheese model, it is accepted that no organisation is ever perfect (Swiss cheese always has holes). Small incidents are valued for the information that they collectively contain about the overall state of the organisational system. Like the safety triangle, the Swiss cheese model suggests that it is useful to pay attention to small events in order to prevent larger events (specifically, accidents). Unlike the safety triangle, the Swiss cheese model also emphasises the role of latent conditions in the system (such as gaps and failures in defences). It links general organisational conditions to specific failures in defences and specific unsafe acts.

Implications for incident reporting systems

The issues described above might seem rather theoretical and somewhat removed from the day-to-day business of incident reporting, but the two models have different implications for how incident reporting systems are designed, how the data are used, and how such systems are likely to be perceived by the organisation at large.

At its best, an incident reporting system based on the safety triangle approach to safety performance improvement can mobilise organisational resources to fix a broad range of small safety issues. Employees are likely to get quick and concrete feedback on reports that have been raised, thus encouraging further reporting. On the other hand, because of the presumed fixed ratio between incidents and injuries, the ultimate goal in safety performance improvement is to *reduce* the number of incidents and hence reduce the number of injuries. This provides management with a fine balancing act of encouraging incident reporting while promoting the organisational goal of fewer incidents. If this is not managed carefully, the potential certainly exists for reporting rates to drop, giving a false indication that the number of incidents is falling.

There is another way in which framing the incident reporting system as primarily about getting problems fixed can stymie the best efforts to collect useful data about safety trends. Consider the following real process plant example relating to the reliability of the plant's instrument air system.[3] In this plant, the original design included a backup nitrogen supply to the instrument air system. The purpose of the nitrogen was to provide a backup source of pressure to operate plant instrumentation in an emergency, for example, to allow a controlled shutdown of the plant on loss of site instrument air supply due to a power failure. Due to a gradually increased demand on the system as more instruments were added over the years, the instrument air system became unable to supply the necessary pressure under many normal operating conditions. The nitrogen supply cut in regularly and therefore use of nitrogen to supplement the instrument air became normal practice. Long-term use of nitrogen as the prime medium for the pneumatic instruments had some very real safety issues.[4] A new hazard had been introduced into the system that the designers had not foreseen, even though there had been warnings of the developing problem and some operational staff were aware of the implications.

In this case, when the issue first arose, it was reported into the site incident reporting system. The site had a relatively good reporting culture, with the emphasis on problem solving. Fixing the issue of the instrument air capacity was neither simple nor cheap (requiring a new air compressor to be installed), and so the initial report was not acted on. Operational staff raised no further reports, despite the increasing use of nitrogen, because as far as they were concerned the problem was well known. After all, they had already reported it. A new compressor was eventually justified and installed, but this could have been done much earlier (and the hazard associated

---

3   Thanks to John Muller for this example.
4   This was an old facility with pneumatic controllers (which, at times, vent the motive gas as part of their operation). As they were located in a restricted space behind the control room panels, there was a significant risk of asphyxiation of maintenance personnel who might be working in the area if nitrogen were used instead of instrument air to drive the controllers on a continuous basis.

with the overloaded system eliminated) if repeat incidents had been formally reported. If an incident reporting system is to be useful for trend analysis, then those who are contributing reports must be encouraged to take the time to report all small incidents, even if they are the same, or very similar to, ones that have been reported previously.

While some reports might indicate that immediate action is required to correct a specific problem or fault, others are useful primarily for bringing forward an issue that requires further monitoring before a decision on any required action can sensibly be taken. For operational staff, this may mean that there is little observable action following a specific incident that they have reported, as the reports are analysed in the longer term as part of a search for overall trends. Technical improvement actions (such as upgrading the instrument air system in the example described above) may well be removed in time and scope from any given particular report raised. This emphasises the need for feedback and acknowledgment to reporters so that they are aware that all reports are important, even if they are not acted on immediately.

In the hands of engineers and other technical staff, the implications of the ratios shown in the safety triangle have sometimes been taken a step further. If the relationship between the tiers in the triangle is a fixed ratio, then the number of injuries can be addressed by reducing the number of incidents — irrespective of what those incidents actually involve. This is perhaps why in the 1980s and early 1990s many chemical and oil companies put enormous effort into managing a large number of small incidents, many of which were not even indirectly related to process safety.[5] Taken to extremes, safety triangle thinking about safety improvements can be akin to the old story of the drunk looking for his lost keys under the lamp post (because that is where the light is).

In contrast to the Bird approach, the strength of an incident reporting system based on HRO thinking is the focus on analysis and trending of incidents as an important adjunct to immediate action. Significant analysis and trending is required before any firm conclusions can be drawn about possible workplace or organisational weaknesses. This implies that sufficient skilled resources are available to do this work, and a detailed and widely varying set of incident reports is seen as the raw material for a rich understanding of the social, as well as technical, aspects of organisational safety performance. High reliability organisations consider the reports to be good news — specific data to work on in a system acknowledged as less than perfect. The Airservices system described in Chapter 3 is based on this type of approach. Employees are motivated to report incidents and data are collected and analysed for overall trends.

---

5   A typical example was the huge focus on minor accidents in company cars for which one major oil company was notorious. Hale (2001) makes a similar point.

In summary, the Bird approach seeks to minimise the chances of an accident by minimising smaller incidents. On the other hand, the Swiss cheese model suggests that the key to reducing the chance of an accident is to maximise incident reports and thereby identify and seek to strengthen systemic weaknesses.

The rest of this chapter reviews the operational experience feedback system and the associated action tracking system in use in a nuclear power station, and draws some conclusions about the way this organisation thinks about incident reporting. The author spent two months at the nuclear power station as part of her PhD research during late 2006. The station (which has a generation capacity of 980 MW) is part of the United Kingdom power grid. The workforce at the site (employees and contractors) numbers approximately 650.

Initial reporting

What constitutes an incident?

All organisations have difficulty specifying in exact terms the types of things that should be reported into their incident reporting systems. Some cases are clear, for example, where there has been an injury. But when it comes to collecting data about occurrences that could have led to an undesired outcome (but did not), things become more difficult. In the Airservices example discussed in Chapter 3, guidance is given to employees about what specific occurrences should be reported. For process industry cases like the nuclear power station, such a list would be prohibitively long due to the range of possible accidents that could occur and the large number of precursors to each one.

Some organisations ask employees to focus on the potential outcome and to report any event or occurrence that, given other circumstances, could or might have resulted in an injury or fatality. This sounds straightforward in theory, but in practice is significantly open to interpretation, either too broadly[6] or too narrowly.[7]

The nuclear power station's definition of things that should be reported via the incident reporting system covers "any actual unplanned deviation from normal operating conditions, procedures or practices that results in loss such as injury, occupational illness, fire or explosion, property damage or plant trips costing over £500, environmental discharges or any near-miss events that could have potentially resulted in such a loss". This owes much to the 1960s research described above. In fact, reports are made on a form known as a loss control report, echoing the language used in the early research.

---

6   On the basis that almost every minor anomaly, in combination with a large number of other failures, could lead to an undesired outcome.

7   Most failures are not catastrophic unless they occur in combination with others.

In practice, reporting at the nuclear power station is resulting in a wide range of types of events being reported (currently averaging over 2,000 events per year and rising). In one sample week, reports included:

- equipment failures with possible safety implications (for example, the failure of a cooling water pump);
- procedural breaches with possible safety implications (for example, a fire door being left open);
- incidents in which someone was (or could have been) injured or exposed to radiation (for example, a routine radiological survey showing very low-level contamination in a recreation room);
- observed conditions directly creating a hazard (for example, potholes in the approach road that may be a hazard to cyclists); and
- observed shortcomings in safety systems (for example, poor coverage of the emergency public address system in one area).

Given that approximately 650 people work at this site, the number of reports averages more than three per person per year. This is impressive and equals the best reported rate for the chemical industry (Phimister et al 2003; Kjellen 2000, p 158). Reports are not confined to technical staff. The last two examples listed above were issues raised by administrative staff. These were taken just as seriously as other more technically-based incidents because it was well recognised that, given the nature of the facility, any personnel could be impacted by serious events and hence all personnel have a role in safety assurance.

What are near misses?

It is also interesting to note the range of types of incidents being reported. Phimister and his colleagues (2003) have reviewed the types of occurrences reported in their research on the use of near-miss reporting systems at 20 Fortune 500 United States chemical and pharmaceutical companies. They found that, in practice, near misses tend to be reported only if they are actual "events" (rather than a condition) or if they involve challenging the last barrier. The example that they give is the theoretical case of a mechanic working on a platform at the top of a distillation column. The platform and guardrail arrangement is such that the mechanic needs to lean well over the rail into a precarious position to do the required work. They found that a significant proportion of their interviewees would not have reported such a condition as a near miss, unless the mechanic involved had done the work under these conditions and slipped. Most interviewees would not have reported the existence of the unsafe physical arrangement as a near miss because it was not a specific event and no specific person had been (almost) hurt. As the researchers point out, this is a significant lost opportunity for their research subjects to identify safety improvements.

The reports made at the nuclear power station, on the other hand, cover a broad range of incident types. Some are specific events and others are conditions — things that, in the terms of the Swiss cheese model, might be seen as latent failures in the system. These can be seen as more important than the events that are reported, since latent conditions are difficult to find unless and until they are highlighted by poor performance in relation to a real incident.

Another example of a type of incident that must be reported at the nuclear power station is the case of a pressure safety valve (PSV) lifting on high pressure equipment. Pressure safety valves are designed to relieve pressure safely so that equipment is not damaged, but they are a backup device that is called into play only if the process control instrumentation has failed or if there has been some other malfunction of the system. If a PSV lifts, either the device itself has malfunctioned or several other defences against high pressure have failed. This is important information regarding process safety performance, but it is not normal practice to record the fact that a PSV has lifted as a safety incident. Since there has been no hazardous outcome, it may not be seen as a near miss (unless it is designed to relieve to the atmosphere and there has been a controlled spill/release which normally would be reported).

The term "near miss" used in the work described above is common in the process industries to describe the occurrences that should be reported. It is a hangover from the safety triangle thinking described at the beginning of this chapter and, while many organisations in the process industries have attempted to expand the working definition of the things that they would like to see reported, the term remains in common usage. For HROs, the challenge is to identify relevant events or conditions that may be far removed in time and geography from the ultimate accident that the organisation is seeking to avoid. To use the term "near" focuses attention on events that are close precursors to the undesired event, rather than latent conditions. It may be a coincidence, but the nuclear power station emphasises the term "operational experience feedback" rather than "near miss", which results in the reporting of a broader range of incidents than is normally included in near-miss reporting systems.

Occupational health and safety versus nuclear safety

The incident reporting system described in Chapter 3 addresses the potential for aircraft accidents only. Occupational health and safety issues associated with providing the air traffic control service (for example, electrocution or falls from height while working on field equipment) are not included (but are covered by other systems). At the nuclear power station, all losses or potential losses are reported via the operational experience feedback system. While a large proportion of the reports are safety-related, the system also covers environmental and security concerns (and, in other cases, the potential "loss" was financial). A large proportion of the reported safety-related incidents have no direct relevance to nuclear safety. No distinction is made at the reporting stage between occurrences that have the potential to impact nuclear safety and those related to other forms of safety (or loss more generally). Historically, this is undoubtedly the case due to the theoretical thinking behind the system, but there are practical reasons why the choice not to make a distinction is sensible in the context of nuclear power station operations.

The nuclear power station is a large industrial site involving many potentially hazardous facilities and activities that are not related to the nuclear reactors themselves. Conventional plant safety is a major issue for the site and is recognised and managed as such. Also, management is well aware that the overall safety performance must be exemplary, not only to protect the welfare of its employees and contractors, but also because the political environment surrounding nuclear power generation is such that accidents will not be tolerated. Any injuries or deaths, even those that have nothing to do with the nuclear aspects of the plant, will result in public outcry and more regulatory pressure on the organisation.

In addition to protecting reputation, there are other reasons for the nuclear power station to be interested in data about non-nuclear incidents. The Swiss cheese model illustrates how consideration of the causes of all incidents could be relevant to preventing nuclear safety incidents. In this model, both latent failures and active failures are caused by workplace and organisational factors. Loss incidents of all types may indicate weaknesses in these broader areas that have the potential to impact nuclear safety. An example of this is a single breach of the site permit to work system. A group of contractors conducting routine maintenance on conventional (non-nuclear) equipment had not completed the necessary paperwork to close out the job or notified the control room operator that they had finished and that the equipment was cleared to go back into service. The control room operator realised later in the day that the job seemed to have been left in this open-ended state and contacted the contractors to ask them to formally complete the job. He also raised a report to record the incident. Since permit to work is a key operational system in ensuring the safety of conventional and nuclear plant, this report could be an important indication of potential problems with the system. It is also worth noting that the control room operator acted as an effective "barrier" in preventing the error of the contractors from propagating through the system. He was not tempted to start the equipment without the formal maintenance clearance. Many readers will no doubt recognise shades of Piper Alpha in this small incident (Cullen 1990). In that case, confusion over open permits led to unserviceable equipment being put back into operation. The resultant hydrocarbon leak ultimately escalated to loss of the entire oil platform and 167 lives.

There is a good argument for an HRO to record and analyse all loss control incidents, rather than just those directly related to the specific high-hazard activity or technology that puts the organisation into the category of an aspiring HRO. Of course, this does not have to be one single database, provided the overall trends are reviewed from the collected data.

Action and investigation

Immediate action

In theoretical terms, the occurrences reported at the nuclear power station represent a jumble of loss-related information that needs to be put into some kind of order by safety department personnel. In HRO terms, the volume of information is a good thing, although organisations that operate on a model that puts a higher value on efficiency might see such a system as inefficient and wasteful of resources and effort. Three full-time people (an engineer and two technicians) are employed in the safety department to manage the reporting system. Their role is much greater than simply data entry and management. They are organisational generalists with an excellent knowledge of who does what at the site and how to make things happen. They are well respected by most people in the organisation (from field personnel to senior management), and they have successfully "sold" the usefulness of the concept of operational experience feedback. The success of the system is in no small part due to the skills and enthusiasm of the safety department personnel.

What follows is a description of the sequence of events when dealing with a loss control report.

Any report must be delivered immediately to the shift manager on duty (the person directly responsible for the day-to-day operation of the station). He screens each report to identify any issues that require immediate action from the operational staff. Again, this might seem inefficient (why does the shift manager need to know immediately about potholes in the approach road when he is managing the operation of two nuclear reactors?), but the few minutes it takes for the shift manager to read each new report is seen at the power station as time well spent. This procedure ensures that the short-term implications of each report are understood and any urgent problems that could impact nuclear safety are acted on immediately.

As each report is passed to the safety department, the causes of each incident are allocated by choosing relevant factors from a set of standard codes issued by the World Association of Nuclear Operators. The codes cover a broad range of physical and behavioural causes, such as lack of appropriate equipment inspection, incorrect procedure, or lack of procedure. A single safety department technician allocates the cause codes to the three to 10 reports received each day. An important part of the technician's role is the informal and early identification of trends based on the reports coming across her desk. More formal trend analysis of causes is also completed at regular intervals. Although many structured methods are used in the process industries for developing incident causes (CCPS 2003), the selection of causes for a given incident remains somewhat idiosyncratic. At the nuclear power station, this part of the data is given much less attention than the details of the incident itself and the developed action items. A set of cause codes related to management issues is available, but these codes are rarely used. The technician reported that she felt it was beyond her skills and her role to allocate organisational causes to reports.

For simple cases, the person who initially raised the report often identifies the immediate actions required to fix the problem. Safety department personnel review these for appropriateness, and develop remedial and preventive actions in consultation with those involved. More complex or significant events may be referred to a more formal investigation (of which there are three distinct types).

Senior management on site takes this system very seriously. Apart from the costs associated with administering the system (three full-time staff), reports are discussed at the weekly operations experience meeting, which gives them a high profile. All heads of department are required to attend (or send a delegate), plus safety department personnel. Attendance is recorded, tracked and published. The meeting is chaired by the deputy site manager, and information circulated in advance by the safety department is reviewed. Agenda items include the status of all action items that are due, a review of the action plan developed for each new report received over the past week (typically over 50), plus results of any investigation reports released and a review of incidents at other sites.

The discussion at the meeting is by exception. It is assumed that attendees understand, and are in agreement with, the printed material unless they specifically state otherwise. The circulated information is simply too lengthy to be read on the spot and some preparation by attendees is necessary for the meeting to fulfil its intended function. The level of discussion observed in these meetings over several weeks indicated that many people had read the information and thought about the immediate implications for their areas and/or had completed the actions assigned to them. Importantly, the deputy site manager made it clear that he had read the information and was in a position to ask probing questions of those present.

The meeting was very much about taking action and complying with internally imposed deadlines. With the amount of material that needed to be covered in the time available (nominally 60 minutes), there was little time for reflection.

Prioritising incidents and actions

Many aspects of the reporting system are highly proceduralised. The initial reports are made on a four-page form. Regular meetings are held with fixed agendas, and attendees review a large number of database printouts. But there is one significant aspect of the system that is not proceduralised. There is no specific recorded rule set about how incidents or action items are to be prioritised. This is done based on the experience and judgment of the various people involved. Like many organisations, safety department personnel at the nuclear power station had attempted to use a risk matrix for this purpose. The reporting form includes a simple 3 × 3 risk matrix that asks the report originators to rank their reports according to two scales — loss/severity (including potential) and probability of recurrence. The experience of the safety department personnel was that the priorities based on these data were often not appropriate.

The first issue is that report originators tend to rank incidents relative to the most serious things that can happen in their own part of the business, rather than in the business as a whole. An example of this was the report of a leak in the roof of the visitors centre. The visitors centre (located well away from the secure area surrounding the nuclear power station itself) aims to provide information to interested members of the public about the power station, the nuclear fuel cycle, and the nature reserve on the associated company-owned land. Staff had previously put in a maintenance work order to have the roof repaired, but no action was taken as the maintenance department had given the work a low priority. After several weeks, with winter (and more rain) coming on, staff members decided to raise an incident report about the leaking roof because it was a safety hazard. The tool that they were expected to use to prioritise the work was the risk matrix. On the consequence scale, in their view, there was the potential for someone to be seriously injured by slipping on the wet floor (rating 2 out of 3). On the probability of recurrence scale, they saw the situation as "frequent" (rating 3 out of 3) because the roof leaks whenever it rains. On this basis, the leaking roof scored 6 out of a possible 9 points for significance, making it potentially one of the most significant safety issues on the site and a very high priority to fix. This is not a realistic assessment of the situation.

Some readers will have spotted a flaw in this argument that illustrates the other problem with using a matrix to rank events that have actually occurred or conditions that continuously exist. Risk matrices work only if the consequence and frequency assessments are referring to the same scenario. In this case, the consequence of "serious injury" does not belong with the probability of "frequent" (which is the assessed probability of recurrence for the leak, not the injury). This makes ranking most reports very difficult, as they usually have no direct adverse safety outcome (only the potential for one).

Another example of this might be a faulty self-closer on a fire door that results in it being constantly left open. The scenario of the failed door alone would result in a risk matrix ranking of high on the frequency scale but low on the consequence scale. On the other hand, the real problem posed by the failed door is a reduced level of defences which may then not be available when called on to act. For the scenario of fire escalation due to the failed door, the frequency would (hopefully) be very low, but the consequence of the scenario may be high, for example, the significant escalation of a fire.

In practice, it makes more sense to assess the significance of reports based on the type of outcome that the scenario relates to (injury, fatality, environmental impact, multiple fatalities, etc) and the number of other defences in place. Action items can then be prioritised based on the report significance and the associated cost. This is similar to the approach used by Airservices as described in Chapter 3.

What is normal activity?

At the nuclear power station, as with all industrial facilities, there are a large number of support staff whose day-to-day job is to address operational problems as they arise or to anticipate future issues and plan how they will be addressed. This raises the issue of how much of their day-to-day activity should be recorded in a system like operational experience feedback.

Again using the frame that the system is about stimulating action, some people had adopted the view that issues should only be reported if the other work management system was not resulting in the issue being fixed. This is the case of the leaking roof described above.

It could be argued that this is a valid use of the reporting system. Perhaps the lack of action from maintenance is a symptom of an inappropriate prioritisation system or of a resourcing problem. On the other hand, if all "repair" items are raised only as work orders for maintenance and not recorded as incidents, then a rich source of information about safety issues is lost (unless the maintenance records are also analysed for trends). In practice, significant equipment failures that warranted technical investigation rather than simply repair were reported into the operational experience feedback system so that the range of action items (one being the repair managed under the maintenance work order) could be tracked.

Incident reporting also creates a significant workload for the operations support engineering group. This group exists essentially to troubleshoot day-to-day operations and to provide engineering and physics support to the operations department. The group has a work plan based on known issues that need technical resolution. These may have been identified from routine observations of reactor and plant performance or from technical knowledge of the system (for example, developing the refuelling pattern based on measurements of fuel rod performance). An annual review of past incidents also plays a part in setting the work program. As a result of the increasing reporting, more investigative actions were being placed on this group. Tension was developing at the site as the group was allocated many new follow-up actions, with deadlines determined at the operational experience meetings described above. This system certainly gave the manager of this group incentive to attend in order to keep some control over the priorities and workload of his staff.

While this kind of bottom-up input to technical programs is important, to some extent the system was in danger of becoming a victim of its own success. One of the safety department personnel mentioned that, on some days, it felt as if they were managing the workload of all of the support staff at the nuclear power station.

This raises important issues about the range of sources that present useful information for organisational learning. However sophisticated the incident reporting system is, there are bound to be other useful records for an organisation that thinks carefully about how it manages its work.

Preventing recurrence

Learning some specific lessons

While it is important to manage the specific responses to incidents and events, once the data have been collected and the immediate problems fixed, the information remains useful. It provides an important source of specific information about past events that can prevent repeat events. This is well understood at the nuclear power station. Summary incident data are widely available on the company intranet and the safety department personnel encourage use of the information in planning and analysis by offering to search the data and provide customised information packs for any subject.

The name of the system (operational experience feedback) gives a strong indication of the way that it has been designed to be used. Many individuals and departments take advantage of the vast store of data contained in the system in various ways.

Each plant operational shift and each maintenance group has at least one nominated operational experience feedback communicator. These communicators generally act as a liaison between the safety department and their specific work groups. They ensure that their co-workers are aware of any new reports, investigation findings or actions that are especially relevant. They are experts on finding their way around the large amount of information available via the company intranet and helping their workmates to find any information in the system that is relevant to specific tasks at hand.

Shift managers pay particular attention to reports that relate specifically to unexpected operating anomalies with the reactors and associated plant. These would normally be reported by the shift that was on duty when the issue arose. Personnel on other shifts (especially shift managers and other control room personnel) are interested in finding out what has occurred. In especially interesting cases, the details are referred to the simulator engineer who can set up a new case on the simulator of the reactor control scheme so that people can experience in real time how the scenario developed and experiment in a safe way with various responses.

Engineering department personnel use incident data as part of the input to their annual review of each engineering system. These reviews require them to look at the overall performance of each system over the past year and to develop an action plan for the coming year. Incident data (along with maintenance records) provide an important historical basis for these decisions.

Unfortunately, not all departments are so enlightened. It was reported to the author that a contracts manager had requested data on reports that mentioned a specific contractor as part of his preparation for their annual review. Far from planning to praise the staff employed by the contractor for reporting potential loss incidents (involving themselves and others), the manager was planning to criticise them for having any incidents that needed reporting. Needless to say, if contractors are managed in such a way, the safety department is unlikely to receive further reports from them unless there is a serious incident where reporting cannot be avoided.

Safety department personnel also do some quarterly trend analysis work based on the allocated causes of incidents, although the nuclear power station is only in the early stages of assessing how this information could be used for improvements.

Impact of regulations

Apart from internal organisational drivers to reduce loss, the nuclear power station is also subject to a strict safety regulatory regime that includes a requirement for an incident reporting system. The site operates under a licence issued by the UK Health and Safety Executive. One of the licence requirements is that the company establish and implement adequate arrangements for the notification, recording, investigation and reporting of incidents occurring on the site. The stated reason for this requirement is so that the regulator can be confident that incidents are reported to the regulator, that causes are identified, and that lessons are learned.[8] The system in place exceeds the licence requirements for the site.

In addition, the UK nuclear regulatory regime includes an arrangement whereby a specific government inspector spends a significant proportion of his/her time at sites checking documentation and field practices to ensure that licence requirements are being met and that safety is being managed appropriately. This means that many of the operational experience meetings described above are attended by a government inspector. It requires a mature safety understanding on both sides for this to be a

---

8   See the standard nuclear licence conditions at www.hse.gov.uk/nuclear/silicon.pdf.

positive experience — one that allows the organisation to air its problems in front of the regulator in the interest of finding solutions.

Broader organisational learning

As illustrated by the above examples, various technical groups at the nuclear power station make a concerted attempt to learn from their operational experience as recorded in the incident reporting system. The data could also be used in a similar way to learn and feed back management experiences that impact safety (or loss) performance. This organisation is less successful at using the data in this more challenging way. It is unclear why this is the case. While a piece of new equipment was being designed by the projects department, some safety issues had been raised by the operations department relating to the design pressure and pressure relief capacity. The equipment needed to be able to operate in a variety of modes and the design apparently did not take all of these into account. These concerns had been fed back to the projects department as part of the normal project review process, but they were ignored, and the equipment was built and installed without any changes being made to the original plans. The anticipated problems were indeed experienced: in some operating modes, a high pressure alarm was activated continuously and the throughput had to be reduced to ensure that the new equipment operated within appropriate safety margins. As far as the projects department was concerned, the project was complete, but the operations department had been left with a piece of equipment that did not function as required.[9] No one was actively working on fixing the problem.

This failure had been flagged by a report and was seen to merit an investigation. The person who undertook the investigation attempted to address not only the specifics of getting the equipment working as had originally been intended, but also the broader organisational issues raised by this experience. In the operational experience meeting at which he presented the findings of his investigation, he attempted to initiate a discussion about the reporting lines of the projects department and the level of authority that this large and expanding group seemed to be developing. The chair of the meeting did not take up this discussion.

It is difficult to know why this was the case, but the lack of understanding of the link between small incidents and organisational structures, policies and procedures was widespread in the senior management team. This potentially rich source of information about organisational effectiveness in managing safety remained untapped.

---

9 In the author's experience, this is not a particularly unusual situation. It is addressed in most large organisations of this type by a formal handover procedure between projects and operations whereby the work of the projects people is not complete until operations formally accepts the installed equipment as complete. Such a system was not in operation at the nuclear power station.

Conclusion

Incident reporting systems can provide organisations with a comprehensive method for ensuring that problems are fixed quickly, and a rich source of information about overall organisational safety. Process plant systems are usually based on the safety triangle and hence focused towards action tracking. High reliability organisation ideas such as the Swiss cheese model provide a basis for trend analysis and wider learning from incident reports.

As described above, the reporting rate at the nuclear power station was impressive, with over 2,000 reports raised per year. Incident reporting was encouraged and supported by senior and middle management, and most staff and contractors at the site were clearly seeing the system as a positive initiative. It is interesting to consider why this might be the case, since the system was fundamentally based on theoretical thinking in line with the safety triangle. As discussed at the beginning of this chapter, this can encourage underreporting of incidents. The key point seems to be that the system was highly effective in getting small problems fixed quickly. It was generally understood that, at such a large and complex site, there would always be small errors and safety issues coming to the fore. Due to the high management attention on action items, the operational experience feedback system was an effective way of getting small problems attended to. This is perhaps epitomised by the number of reports that list "completed this form" as the first remedial action taken.

Both the general level of awareness of the system and the level of reporting achieved at the nuclear power station are impressive. There is a strong commitment to organisational learning in the form of operational experience feedback. Many groups had realised that the database was an excellent source of information about past technical problems that could make their working life more effective.

The organisation was less familiar with the concepts of the Swiss cheese model that would allow it to make improvements to management practices (based on its experience) in exactly the same way as it does for technical issues. While there are many lessons to be learned from the nuclear power station's system, incorporating this additional layer would make it the ultimate in operational experience feedback.

CHAPTER 7

OPERATIONAL DISCIPLINE

Richard J Angiullo

Introduction

Operational discipline is a characteristic of all organisations and groups of people organised to accomplish a task, whether they be a sports team, an army or a manufacturing organisation. The level of operational discipline of an organisation (or team) describes how well individuals in the organisation execute activities (especially when doing routine tasks) to achieve the goals of the organisation as a whole. While this characteristic is important for all teams and groups, it is critically important for manufacturing organisations — especially those involved in highly hazardous operations, such as the chemical, petrochemical and nuclear power industries.

The DuPont Company defines operational discipline as the "deeply rooted dedication and commitment by each member of the organization to carry out each task the right way, each time". Failures in operational discipline are regularly cited as the underlying cause of serious industrial incidents and accidents. An analysis of industrial accidents in DuPont has found that poor operational discipline was a factor in more than 50% of the cases. Failures in operational discipline are often described as "operator error", with the primary cause of an accident laid at the feet of frontline workers who, for example, didn't follow procedures or took a short cut instead of doing the job the right way, often with terrible consequences. We will see that operator error is seldom the primary or "root" cause of any serious accident.

Operational discipline is distinctly different from disciplining or punishing workers. Progressive discipline in the industrial environment, involving verbal and written warnings, suspensions and in some cases the discharge of workers, is an important management process. Although it will have an impact on the level of operational discipline achieved by an organisation, it is far from the only management process that impacts on the level of operational discipline — and, in my opinion, it is not the most important one.

During the course of my 35-year career in the chemical industry, I have had the opportunity to observe many different industrial manufacturing organisations (most were in the chemical industry). I have seen organisations which were characterised with both high and low (or poor) levels of operational discipline. More recently,

I have also had the opportunity to study a few organisations involved in nuclear power generation in the United States. In these organisations, I observed levels of operational discipline that I had not previously seen in the chemical or petrochemical industry. That is, the US nuclear power industry currently operates with the highest level of operational discipline that I have ever observed. Because of the industry's history and the level of risk involved, it carries operational discipline in many areas well beyond that seen in other industries.

Why is it that managers and supervisors in some organisations operate with outstanding safety performance, while many others do not? How can managers and supervisors develop and improve the level of operational discipline in their organisation? In this chapter, I will attempt to provide answers to these questions using a framework of organisational attributes and behaviour (identified by DuPont in the late 1990s) that illustrates the characteristics of organisations that have achieved some level of operating and safety excellence. I will also compare the level of operating excellence that I observed in the US nuclear power industry with that in other hazardous manufacturing industries (specifically, the chemical and petrochemical industries).

Before I describe the details of operational discipline and its characteristics in manufacturing organisations, let's think for a moment about what this type of discipline is at a fundamental level. All organisations or groups of people working together require some level of discipline in order to coordinate their activities. Sports teams require individual members to control their egos and desire for recognition, and to channel their energy and efforts into the success of the entire team. Military organisations demand that their members follow orders without question so as to reliably coordinate the activities of individuals and to operate as a unit. These are examples of operational discipline in a non-manufacturing setting. At its most fundamental level, operational discipline is the coordination achieved by an organisation or team when each member of the team follows a predetermined role and executes their tasks in an outstanding way, with strict adherence to established procedures.

Much of this chapter will discuss how to motivate workers and teams in order to obtain a high level of coordination among members of the team and to operate with as few errors and mishaps as possible. This is an especially important concern for organisations that are involved in hazardous operations (such as chemical manufacturing or nuclear power generation), where the consequences of operating errors can be catastrophic.

DuPont operates a large number of potentially hazardous manufacturing facilities involving toxic, flammable and explosive materials, and it has developed a well-deserved reputation for doing this in a very safe way. The company has developed many different programs and processes to ensure the safe operation of its facilities and manufacturing processes, for example, the process safety management (PSM) model. The essential features of the PSM model are illustrated in Figure 1. The model is called the "PSM wheel", with each of the 14 spokes describing an individual safety program or management process. "Management leadership and commitment" (which is shown at the centre or hub of the wheel) provides resources and is critical to the functioning of all of the programs. Management leadership provides the energy to make the wheel turn.

The PSM wheel is a representation of the various management programs and processes that must be executed to ensure the safety of the manufacturing-related processes at DuPont, but they are only effective when (and if) they are executed well. How effectively these programs are implemented is directly determined by the level of operational discipline in the organisation. Therefore, operational discipline is an essential part of the PSM system and is represented as the rim of the PSM wheel. It connects with all of the elements and programs, and it translates these management processes into real results, that is, the prevention of injuries and incidents.

Characteristics of operational discipline

In addition to the PSM wheel and its various management safety programs, DuPont has developed the following list of 11 characteristics (or criteria) to define

Chapter

7

FIGURE 1: DuPont's process safety management model

Copyright © 2006 DuPont. All rights reserved.

and describe operational discipline and the level of operational discipline in an organisation:

1. leadership by example;
2. common shared values;
3. pride in the organisation;
4. sufficient and capable resources;
5. strong teamwork;
6. employee involvement;
7. active lines of communication;
8. up-to-date documentation;
9. practice consistent with procedure;
10. absence of short cuts; and
11. excellent housekeeping.

The extent to which these characteristics describe an organisation is entirely a matter of judgment, based on the observations of individual assessors. However, it is interesting to note that, when team members are anonymously surveyed about these characteristics, the findings are usually in agreement with the perceptions of outside observers.

For the purposes of this discussion, the preceding 11 characteristics can be conveniently grouped into three categories: leadership characteristics; well-defined and followed management processes; and maintenance of high standards.

Leadership characteristics: leadership by example, common shared values, pride in the organisation, strong teamwork

In my experience, the most important determinant of the level of performance of any organisation (including safety performance) is strong leadership. By strong leadership, I mean the leadership skills and capabilities of managers and supervisors throughout the entire organisation, from the CEO to the local shift supervisor on the manufacturing floor. There is a distinct difference between managing and leading an organisation. Both are important when determining organisational performance and developing a high level of operational discipline. Leadership inspires and motivates, as well as directs. Management provides resources and controls the activities of the organisation.

When strong leadership is integrated into other business parameters, it becomes outwardly visible. It is important for managers to take every opportunity to demonstrate their leadership abilities and to effectively communicate their personal values regarding safety, health and environmental issues. In this respect, direct communication and action are more effective and have much more impact than the written word.

Perhaps the most important role of management leadership is deciding what the priorities, values and boundaries will be for an organisation and its employees. Establishing the primacy of safety and operational discipline among competing priorities is absolutely essential for manufacturing managers in hazardous industries. Although managers and supervisors often verbally express a priority for safety, it is their actions that will be studied by their staff, and that determine the priority that safety will be given by the organisation. "Leadership by example" is the most powerful way that management can establish a value for safety and operational discipline. Clearly communicating standards and expectations, and consistently demonstrating a commitment to outstanding performance and discipline through actions, are hallmarks of effective leadership by example.

Although often established and promoted by management, values and beliefs need to be broadly held by the organisation if they are to have an impact on performance. All employees need to understand and be aware of management's commitment to safety and the goal of zero injuries and incidents. The belief that all injuries and incidents can be prevented needs to be espoused and acted on by management in order to be shared by everyone in the organisation. I found that the extent of this belief among employees inversely correlated with the number of injuries and incidents in an organisation. The more broadly this belief is held, the lower the number of injuries and incidents.

The US nuclear power industry is a good example of management establishing and acting on a priority for operational discipline and safe operation. In this industry, management clearly recognises the potentially disastrous consequences of errors and failures in the operation of its facilities, and has established and demonstrated the highest priority for operational discipline. The industry uses the term "human performance" to describe many of the attributes that I have called operational discipline. While not an exact match to operational discipline, human performance focuses on the situations and attitudes that lead to errors, injuries and incidents, and in many ways parallels and extends what I have described as the characteristics of operational discipline.

By "human performance", the US nuclear power industry means the avoidance of errors by anyone in the organisation (both active and latent human errors during the execution of any task). The following is an excerpt from a pamphlet published by the Institute of Nuclear Power Operations:

> "Striving for excellence in human performance is an ongoing industry
> effort to significantly reduce plant events caused by human error.
> Human error is caused by a variety of conditions related to individual

Chapter 7

behavior, management and leadership practices, and organisational processes and values. Behaviors at all levels need alignment to improve individual performance, reduce errors, and prevent events."

Organisations in this industry train employees (including managers and supervisors) on the nature of, and contributing causes for, errors. The reporting, investigation and analysis of every plant event is strictly enforced. Events are defined in the US nuclear power industry as "an undesirable consequence (or situation) to the plant, generally in terms of reduced safety margin". Investigations of events identify, in addition to the initiating or root cause, underlying situations that contributed to the error, especially organisational weaknesses. Organisational weaknesses that contributed to an incident are defined as deficiencies in the management control processes or values that allowed the workplace conditions that provoked the event. Examples of error events that are tracked and analysed are plant "upsets", personal injuries and near misses where an injury almost occurred, plant "trips" or operating shutdowns, spills or environmental releases, and any human error that negatively impacts on the operation of the plant or unit and thereby reduces the safety factor for plant operation.

The nuclear power industry supports a Human Performance Centre which researches and promotes mechanisms for avoiding errors and subsequent incidents in nuclear power generation sites.

One of the ways in which organisations involved in nuclear power generation can build value for excellence in human performance is by measuring the elapsed time between error events on a running clock, called the "human performance clock". This digital clock is situated so that it is visible to the whole organisation. Each time there is an unwanted event, the clock is reset to zero. The elapsed time since the last clock reset for the entire plant (or an individual unit) is a metric on which management puts a great deal of emphasis, as milestones and achievements in the length of time between events are acknowledged. The human performance clock gives the entire organisation a visible indication of performance, and it gives management the opportunity to emphasise the importance and value that it places on excellence in human performance (or operational discipline).

Management ensures that employees in the nuclear power industry know how well they are doing in human performance compared with others in and out of the industry. Employees take great pride in their performance and the fact that they are recognised for achievements. It is relatively easy for a visitor or observer to sense that pride by simply talking to employees and noting the level of awareness of their unit's performance. Pride is nurtured and encouraged through management's recognition of organisational performance compared with various benchmarks (for example, average injury or event frequency rates for the industry) and internal indicators (such as the previously-mentioned elapsed time since last incident measured on the performance clock).

One of the challenges with this type of program is how to ensure that all injuries and events are reported — given the negative consequences to the organisation that may follow their occurrence. This is a problem in both the nuclear power industry and the chemical industry, and I would guess that minor errors involving single individuals acting alone do not get reported in either industry. In DuPont, management makes it clear that the consequences to an employee of not reporting an incident are much more serious than the consequences associated with the investigation of an incident. This was also the case in nuclear power stations that I observed, where management worked hard to demonstrate that the purpose of investigating events was to learn rather than to punish. Either way, there is no doubt that any event that involves or is witnessed by more than one person will be reported and investigated.

To my knowledge, there are no programs in the chemical or petrochemical industry that enhance operational discipline as well or as extensively as the performance clock. However, this does not mean that operational discipline is not recognised and aggressively managed in these industries. In my experience at DuPont, managers and supervisors are routinely judged, rewarded and coached based on the performance level of the organisation and the level of operational discipline that they create.

Well-defined and followed management processes: sufficient and capable resources, up-to-date documentation, active lines of communication, employee involvement

It is useful to think about manufacturing activities as a series of *management processes* that parallel the actual manufacturing processes. By management processes, I mean the overall activities undertaken by people in different roles, with each person passing pertinent information from one to another to accomplish a task. A simple example of a management process is scheduling the amount of product to manufacture to meet an estimated customer demand. Sales personnel will estimate the amount of sales in an upcoming time period based on their interactions and discussions with customers. They then communicate this estimate to operating planners or schedulers who develop a production plan and order raw materials for an upcoming time period. The schedulers then communicate to the operating supervisors and managers a proposed production schedule for that time period.

A well-defined management process clearly identifies the actions and activities to be completed at each step, and specifies who has the accountability for that step in the overall scheme or process. As noted above, the level of operational discipline can be defined by how well people adhere to the defined and established processes and procedures. It is clear that, in order to achieve strict adherence, established procedures need to be well-defined and broadly understood, and they need, to some extent, to anticipate what can go wrong and how to deal with problems.

We might initially think about this in terms of frontline workers following written procedures in the course of their job. While this is certainly fundamental to achieving a high level of operational discipline, how well managers and supervisors execute the processes by which they control their operations is equally important to operational discipline. For example, how closely followed and well executed are procedures for conducting injury and incident investigations? Are all required preventative maintenance procedures and equipment inspections conducted and documented within established timelines? Does management use a standardised approach for prioritising repairs and upgrades, especially those involving safety issues? These questions provide examples of common management processes used in all manufacturing industries, and answers to these questions provide insight into the level of discipline that managers and supervisors exhibit on a routine basis. These processes are analogous to the operating and maintenance procedures that frontline workers are expected to follow when doing their job. The point I want to emphasise is that frontline workers cannot be expected to strictly follow defined procedures if management doesn't follow similar procedures.

Two extremely important management processes that are necessary to ensure safe operation warrant special mention: (1) assessing and providing "capable" resources to the organisation; and (2) maintaining up-to-date operating documentation.

Managers and supervisors are constantly under pressure to improve productivity and reduce costs, and they cannot afford to waste any valuable resources (financial or human). Assigning people and making time and money available to ensure the safety of the workforce and operations are essentially a matter of balancing these short-term costs with the immense potential costs in the event of a major safety incident. Deciding on the priority that should be given to identified issues must be based on a judgment of the risk involved in the particular issue. The best-performing organisations (that is, organisations with high levels of operational discipline) have developed formalised processes for making these kinds of decisions — usually involving a cross-section of individuals in the organisation. In addition to making better-informed decisions, this kind of involvement results in improved morale and motivation among frontline workers.

One area that requires the commitment of resources (and is all too often neglected) is maintaining the documentation for process and operating technology and procedures. While the importance of clearly-defined and up-to-date procedures is widely recognised in the chemical industry, there have been too many examples of this not being the case in practice (often due to the lack of adequate resources being assigned to the task), and poorly written and unclear or inadequate procedures have contributed to many incidents. Maintaining accurate and up-to-date operating documents is one of the major challenges to achieving a high level of operational discipline in most organisations.

Closely related to maintaining up-to-date documentation is the management process for regulating change. It should be noted that managing change appears on DuPont's PSM wheel in three different locations (technology, subtle facility change, and management of personnel change). Good records and documentation are essential to managing both technology and facility changes. Regularly assessing and updating operating technology, and translating that technology into sound operating procedures and techniques, must be priorities for managers and supervisors — especially in potentially hazardous industries. Managers need to ensure that adequate and capable resources are assigned to this task, as it is critical to maintaining safe operations and fundamental to a high level of operational discipline.

Managing change is an area where I observed significant differences between the chemical and nuclear power industries in the US. Any proposed change to the manufacturing technology in the nuclear power industry — whether to equipment or to procedures — is challenged and scrutinised by engineers and managers prior to implementation. The proposed change is subjected to rigorous evaluation, using standardised approaches to investigate whether there are any safety implications. A good example of the cautious approach to change by the nuclear power industry is in the area of computerisation and process control.

The electronic revolution of the past 20 to 30 years has had a dramatic impact on the instrumentation and process control technology used in the chemical, petrochemical and power generation industries. New coal or gas-fired power plants, as well as chemical and petrochemical operations, have evolved from pneumatic control instruments to the widespread use of programmable logic controllers and computers for monitoring and controlling operations. Visiting the control room of a US nuclear power station, on the other hand, is like travelling back to a control room in the chemical industry in the 1960s. Although controllers and instrumentation had been modernised since original construction of the plant, changes had been made very slowly and carefully. The industry has approached computer-based monitoring, and especially process control, with great caution. Contrast this with the situation in the chemical and petrochemical industries where many plant upgrading and expansion projects included the modernisation of instrumentation and control technology. Undoubtedly, there is a difference in philosophy between the nuclear power industry and the chemical industry. The nuclear power industry is under strict regulations, with a good deal of political scrutiny. Managing change in the chemical industry, although recognised as critical to operational safety, has, in general, not been executed with nearly the same degree of rigor as in the nuclear power industry.

An important management process that will strongly impact on the level of operational discipline is communication between managers, supervisors and frontline workers. Clear and regular communication, both up and down the organisational structure, is essential to motivation, morale and operational discipline. Frequent open communication fosters a spirit of teamwork, encourages employee involvement in the organisation, and demonstrates acceptance of the organisation's goals and values. In some manufacturing organisations, frontline workers (individually and in teams) are actively involved in analysing and writing procedures, designing safety programs, investigating incidents and accidents, and prioritising capital improvements and other significant expenditures. This is a key characteristic of organisations with high levels of operational discipline.

Maintenance of high standards: practice consistent with procedure, absence of short cuts, excellent housekeeping

A "standard" in the context of operational discipline means the acceptable level of performance of an organisation, especially in regular or routine activities. Standards exist for most aspects of routine activities, from the neatness and orderliness of the workplace to the adherence by employees to workplace rules and regulations. The level of performance in the activity demonstrates employees' adherence to established practices. This adherence to a standard is what many would think about in terms of "a disciplined organisation". Standards are determined by managers and supervisors as the lowest level of performance that they will accept from themselves and their subordinates. Standards exist in all areas of operations, including how processes are executed by management and how routine activities are executed by frontline workers (such as the use of personal protective equipment). The standards in a manufacturing organisation are usually quite obvious — even to a first-time visitor who will be able to observe how things vary from one part of the organisation to another.

Establishing and maintaining high standards in safety and operational discipline are, for high-performing organisations, particularly important in the following areas: (1) the alignment of practice with established procedures; (2) the absence of short cuts taken by workers; and (3) excellent housekeeping, that is, the old cliché "a place for everything and everything in its place" is pertinent in these organisations.

Aligning activities on the shop floor with written and established procedures is important to both the quality and safety of operations. While important in the chemical and petrochemical industries, it is an especially high priority in the nuclear power industry. Managers demand and regularly remind operators and frontline workers to challenge any procedure that cannot be followed exactly as written.

Workers are constantly reminded in meetings and by numerous posters and signs in the work area to identify aspects of the procedure that they find ambiguous or where they don't completely understand what is written. Managers and supervisors regularly conduct scheduled audits of jobs in the field, comparing observed activities with written procedures in order to ensure consistency between the two. This priority undoubtedly requires management and technical resources be made available to operating personnel so that issues with procedures identified by frontline workers can be addressed. Procedures need to be corrected and adjusted, and the proposed change needs to be reviewed and analysed according to the management of change procedures (this involves a review by a number of experts who have different roles and skills). While some of these practices exist in the chemical industry, they are not executed with the same level of energy and discipline as they are in the nuclear power industry.

The nuclear power stations that I have visited categorised procedures according to the level of detail in the written procedure, and the potential consequences of an error when executing the procedure, and therefore the strictness of adherence required. The most detailed procedures were identified as category one, and they were associated with the most "safety-critical" operations and tasks. Category one procedures are written in an extremely detailed way, and critical steps in the procedure require two operators (one to execute the step and another to observe and check that the step was executed correctly). Both operators are required to sign a check sheet indicating that the step was completed, and to record the date and time accurately. Less critical operations, designated as category two, are not written in quite as much detail, and do not require sign-off by a second operator on completion. The least critical operations, category three, are written in the most general way, relying on operators to fill in the necessary details.

The following instructions are examples of the three categories of written operating procedures:

1. "establish fluid circulation in the re-boiler" — a category three procedure;
2. "open valve 123 and then start pump 321 to establish fluid circulation in the re-boiler line" — a category two procedure; and
3. "open valve 123 and then start pump 321. Note the date and time on the check sheet and have the operation of the pump and establishment of flow verified by another operator and so note on the check sheet" — a category one procedure.

Writing and categorising procedures according to how critical they are to operational safety is an example of a management process used in the nuclear power industry to ensure safe operations. The degree of effectiveness of this management process is determined by the level of operational discipline of the entire organisation when executing the process. Operational discipline is required from: engineers and managers in their process of analysis when deciding which are the safety-critical operations; supervisors and operators who must write the procedures clearly; and frontline workers who actually follow and execute the procedures. This is a good example of how operational discipline must be present at all levels of the organisation. To be effective, it is not simply a matter of how frontline workers execute their duties. In high-performing organisations, managers and supervisors demonstrate and lead by example when executing their responsibilities.

Closely related to the adherence to established procedures is the absence of short cuts taken by all employees. It is almost a cliché to say that many injuries have occurred when operators have bypassed a step in the procedure or failed to take a precaution, either because they forgot, they wanted to save time, or the particular step was inconvenient at that moment. This is a classic example of a failure of operational discipline in an organisation. It is insightful, I think, to point out that the human performance model of the nuclear power industry is built on the premise that most people do not intentionally make mistakes or commit errors. The teaching here is that errors are distinctly different from violations. An error is an action that unintentionally departs from an expected behaviour according to some standard. Conversely, a violation involves a deliberate deviation from an expected behaviour. Error involves problems with the mental processing of task- or work-related information. Violation involves motivational factors that are characteristic of the individual or organisation. Both errors and violations need to be eliminated by management to ensure safe operation. Errors are more prevalent than violations, and they require much more of management's attention. This observation is consistent with my experience in the chemical industry.

The last characteristic of operational discipline is good housekeeping. Good housekeeping in the context of safety and operational discipline is a cultural concept that recognises how little things often lead to bigger things. Good housekeeping is, in essence, an employee involvement and quality program. Maintaining tools and parts in carefully planned storage that is readily accessible is essential to safety and efficiency. No significant difference between the petrochemical and nuclear power industries was evident here, although there were large differences between one organisation and another (even on the same site), thus demonstrating the importance of local supervision when establishing standards — not only for housekeeping, but for all aspects of operational discipline.

Conclusion

Operational discipline describes an organisation's level of commitment to doing each and every task the right way each and every time. It is an essential element for safe operation in potentially hazardous manufacturing facilities, such as those in the chemical, petrochemical and nuclear power industries. Any well-designed safety program or system is only as effective as the day-to-day ability of everyone in the organisation to rigorously follow procedures correctly and safely every time.

I have found that the highest levels of operational discipline exist in the US nuclear power industry. This industry has identified human errors as a serious source of incidents and has researched ways to improve organisational performance through its study of human performance. It has provided various programs to educate managers, supervisors and employees on how to improve organisational and individual performance on the job. The chemical and petrochemical industries in general can learn a great deal by studying the nuclear power industry in the US.

Chapter

7

CHAPTER 8

OPERATIONAL DECISION-MAKING

Jan Hayes

Introduction

This chapter describes research on decision-making by operations supervisory personnel in three different high-hazard industries. A large body of research on industrial decision-making already exists, but the focus is almost invariably control room operators, field staff and other frontline personnel. Another large body of research on managerial decision-making covers strategic issues. The focus of the research presented in this chapter is quite different — those who supervise frontline personnel and essentially provide the organisational link between senior management and the minute-by-minute operations of the organisation.

For all technical and managerial personnel in high-hazard organisations, decisions that potentially impact on safety are a routine part of day-to-day business. Many operational decisions are typically made for field personnel in advance by requiring them to follow specific and detailed procedures for routine tasks. At their best, such procedures minimise the potential for human error by incorporating appropriate technical and human factors considerations, but the research shows that senior managers overestimate the extent to which operational decisions are proceduralised. When discussing safety decision-making, senior managers and organisational systems focus on analysis, codification and rules. The role of experience and expertise tends to be hidden and hence undervalued, but research shows that these professional qualities play a significant role in operational safety decision-making.

This chapter describes common approaches to safety decision-making that are espoused by high-hazard organisations, and details the results of research into how decisions are actually made by operations personnel in three high-hazard organisations — a chemical plant, a nuclear power station, and Airservices Australia.

Decision-making in the field

The particular focus of the present research is operational decision-making by operations supervisory staff that requires a trade-off (in some form) between safety and cost. Data were collected by interview, workplace/meeting observations, and documentation review. Interviewees were senior shift personnel who have the responsibility of deciding whether production should be allowed to continue, or those personnel who support decision-makers at that level. They were asked to recount specific instances when they had made decisions that required a trade-off between safety goals and production goals. Most had no difficulty in recalling several such cases and describing how each situation unfolded. This research is a "normal operations" study — in other words, focusing on how safety is managed in typical situations, rather than looking at errors made in situations that have led to an accident or serious incident.

Operations personnel in three organisations participated in the research — a chemical plant, a nuclear power station, and Airservices Australia (Australia's air navigation service provider). Fieldwork at the three research sites was undertaken during 2006 and 2007. The chemical plant is a well-established industrial site in the suburbs of Melbourne (operating since the 1970s). It is licensed under the Victorian major hazard facilities regulations. The nuclear power station is located in the United Kingdom and has been operating since the 1970s under a safety case-style licensing regime. Airservices is also a well-established organisation, operating under a risk-based safety case-style regulatory framework.[1]

The nature of the technology and the political circumstances under which the nuclear power industry has been operating for several decades in Europe and the United States has resulted in a strong focus on safety management in that industry. With a small number of well-known exceptions, the industry record is good, and nuclear safety practices and regulatory approaches have tended to be used as a model for other high-hazard industries. Similarly, the organisation that owns and runs the chemical plant also operates complex and potentially hazardous technologies in an environment where good safety performance is a sociopolitical necessity. The activities are also subject to significant commercial pressure. On the other hand, the nature of air traffic control (ATC) is somewhat different (that is, the provision of a service to a broad sector involving customers and stakeholders ranging from commercial airlines to sports aviators). Airservices' mission is to provide safe and environmentally sound air navigation services to approximately 11% of the world's airspace on behalf of the Australian Government. Airservices is a government business enterprise operating under its own Act, which essentially puts it on a similar commercial basis to large private sector corporations.[2] All three organisations could therefore be characterised as high reliability organisations (HROs) and might be expected to use similar strategies for managing safety in such challenging circumstances.

1　Airservices has been operating in its current corporate form since it was established under its own Act in 1995. Prior to that time, the functions now undertaken by Airservices were part of the Civil Aviation Authority.

2　Airservices is established under the *Airservices Act 1995*. It is an Australian Government-owned corporation. The board of directors reports to the Minister for Infrastructure, Transport, Regional Development and Local Government.

The following discussion about the research results uses the term "production" in the broadest sense (meaning the commercial activities of each organisation). It is acknowledged that, although the chemical plant manufactures a polymer and the nuclear power station produces electricity, Airservices could more accurately be described as a service provider. Despite this, what I have termed the production side of the safety/production balance is essentially the same in nature. In all three organisations, trade-offs are required between safety and economics in the form of either cost or income.

All three organisations operate with multiple levels of safety devices and procedures to prevent accidents. Despite the highly hazardous nature of the technologies involved, no single error or poor decision can, on its own, result in serious safety consequences (such as a release of radiation, an aircraft collision or a serious fire) if the rest of the system is operating correctly. On the rare occasions when accidents occur, they are caused by a chain of faults and failures, many of which have typically gone undetected for an extended period. Most decisions, therefore, even if they are wrong, result in a decrease in safety margins, rather than a serious accident.

This chapter is structured as follows. First, the field research in each organisation is described. Next, the key aspects of decision-making practices are developed. Finally, the broader implications for safety decision-making are described, followed by some conclusions.

Research results

At the nuclear power station: "we put a line in the sand"

There are two nuclear reactors at the nuclear power station, and it has a total generation capacity of 980 MW. Approximately 650 people are employed at the site. The operational arrangement includes three eight-hour shifts each day, with 23 people per shift.[3] Each shift includes 20 operators, two team leaders, and a shift charge engineer (the person with final responsibility for operating decisions on each shift). Research interviews focused on shift charge engineers and those with whom they consulted when making operational decisions.

The minute-by-minute operation of the plant is the responsibility of the plant operators. Many of the systems are fully automated, while others require manual intervention to ensure that they are functioning appropriately. The work of the operators is therefore a combination of monitoring and intervention or operation of plant and equipment. The shift charge engineer has very limited involvement in the operation of the plant when things are running smoothly. His attention to

Chapter

8

---

3   As is typical for this type of staffing, there are five shift teams in total to fill the roster.

the details increases when something out of the ordinary is planned (for example, a startup or shutdown) or when a significant operating anomaly develops.

Complex plant such as the nuclear power station operates in a quasi-steady state where minor equipment faults and small deviations in the process conditions occur constantly. The status of major equipment items (pumps, compressors, major valves, etc) is shown by lights on the control room panel, and a change in status causes an alarm (both audible and visual). If, for example, a pump stops automatically due to a problem detected by its control instrumentation, an alarm sounds in the control room and the status lights move from on to off. Similarly, many process parameters (pressure, temperature, flow, etc) are measured and displayed on control room panels (in the form of paper strip charts or computer screens). Deviations from the expected value cause alarms at pre-defined levels.

In general, it is the job of the operators to analyse the causes of process deviations and minor equipment problems, and to initiate changes to plant operation as required. The types of process deviations that the shift charge engineers become involved with are those cases that are significantly out of the ordinary.

In this operating environment, the operational decision-making in the face of a developing operating anomaly follows a clear two-stage process.

Stage one: compliance with station operating instructions

First, when an abnormal operational situation with potential safety implications is initially discovered, the shift charge engineer makes a decision about the need for immediate action to bring the system to a safe state. This usually (but not always) means deciding that a reactor shutdown is necessary, with the attendant interruption to power generation. This step is often dictated by the application of formal rules in the form of station operating instructions.

A decision to take a reactor offline then becomes one of compliance with the relevant station operating instruction. Shift charge engineers are well aware that a compliance breach (that is, not shutting down a reactor when such a shutdown was required according to the formal rules) is considered to be a major disciplinary breach, with potentially serious career consequences. The station operating instructions derive their authority directly from the statutory operating licence of the facility.

The operators also make decisions about whether a particular situation complies with the station operating instructions and may act without consulting the shift charge engineer, depending on the available time for decision-making and the nature of the potential breach of the overall operating envelope. However, if more time is available to make the decision (that is, if there is no immediate clear breach of a station operating instruction), and there are broader (plant-wide) implications for the action (for example, shutting down a reactor, rather than one section of plant), then the final decision will be made by the shift charge engineer. This is partly due to the production interruption involved, but also because there are hazards associated with an unplanned shutdown of the system.

The decision to shut down a reactor is certainly not taken lightly. Nuclear reactors produce enormous amounts of energy and this must be removed from the reactor in a safe manner, even if the energy is no longer to be used for power generation. The physical shutdown of a nuclear reactor (either planned or unplanned) is the job of a licensed control room operator. The required sequence of activities is complex and much of the sequence is manually (not automatically) initiated based on the operator's judgment that it is safe to proceed to the next step. These sequences are practised in the plant simulator and the demonstrated ability to manage such events is a key part of an operator's licence testing.[4] The supervisory staff have no direct operational role once the decision has been made that the shutdown is necessary — unless they are required to manage broader aspects of the incident that resulted in the decision to shut down in the first place.

There are other reactive cases where the supervisor decides that a situation is so abnormal that an immediate shutdown is required, even if there is not a strict breach of a formal rule. As one power station supervisor described it:

> "… if there are enough pieces of the puzzle missing and I can't say
> hand on my heart that I know we are safe at the moment, then I need
> to go to some arrangement, status, condition where I do know that we
> are safe. It may well mean shutting the plant down." (interviewee 2)

Within the operating envelope represented by the formal rules, supervisors rely on their own experience, and that of their colleagues, to make these types of operational decisions. The result may be a decision to shut down part or all of the system, even though the plant is within its formally defined operating envelope.

Stage two: the line in the sand
The second stage in the decision-making process comes about if the supervisor decides that no immediate shutdown is required. In this case, operations can continue, but with the situation being closely monitored due to a reduced safety margin. While the safety margin is reduced from the normal and desired level, it has not yet reached a situation that the shift charge engineer sees as unsafe. This might be due to an equipment breakdown with some associated downtime required for repairs, or an unusual operating condition that needs further investigation.

---

4   This site has a full control room simulator facility located on site, but it is completely independent of the operating plant. It is used for training and licence testing purposes.

Again, this emphasises that, just because no published operating limit was in danger of being breached, it was not assumed that the situation was necessarily safe:

> "Had we met any specific criteria for taking this reactor off in our technical specifications? No we hadn't. We hadn't got anything definitive. So it's now building up this gut feeling. This ain't right." (interviewee 2)

Personnel at the nuclear power station developed and imposed limits on operation under these types of conditions. The relevant limit is often, but not always, time. As interviewee 4 said: "We put a line in the sand. If it's not fixed in the second week, we're coming off."

These limits are articulated explicitly to control room staff and many cases were recounted by interviewees where the limit was reached and shutdown initiated (as well as many cases where the problem was fixed within the self-allocated window).

All three participating organisations operate some form of maintenance works approval system where specific authorisation is required from the operations supervisor for equipment to be taken offline for maintenance. If the equipment involved has a safety function, these types of decisions also require a trade-off between safety and production or cost. Unlike the operating situations described above, these decisions are made proactively in that the supervisor can choose the time at which the work is done. At the nuclear power station, the station operating instructions described above include a list of minimum equipment that must be available at all times for systems with a safety function. This is used as a conservative guide for determining whether equipment can be taken out of service for maintenance or inspection purposes.

In summary, operating outside (or even within, but close to the boundary of) the defined operating envelope was seen by all shift charge engineers as unsafe. Deliberately putting or allowing the plant to be in such a condition was almost unimaginable to the shift charge engineers and their operating crews. However, operations within the defined boundary were not always seen as necessarily safe. The shift charge engineers accepted that, as a normal part of their job, they would come across unusual operating combinations that were not considered in the definition of the operating envelope. In such cases, it was up to them to decide whether production could continue safely and to seek whatever specialist advice they felt they needed to make that decision.

At the chemical plant: "if it's not safe, we don't do it"

The chemical plant uses feedstock and creates products that are both highly flammable and toxic. The product is manufactured in several reactor vessels called autoclaves. The chemical reaction that converts the feedstock to product also produces energy, and would accelerate if not controlled by the removal of heat. The reaction section of the plant operates by converting batches of feedstock into product, that is, this part of the plant cycles through a series of steps that must be carefully controlled to ensure that an appropriate product yield and quality are produced safely.

The site is staffed on a 24-hour, seven days a week basis by five shifts. Over 100 people are employed at the site. Each shift includes five operators and a shift manager. The role of the shift manager and the relationship between the operators' duties and the responsibilities of the shift manager are similar to the nuclear power station case described above.

While smaller and less complex than the nuclear power station, operations at the chemical plant are similar in many ways. The flow of various chemicals is monitored electronically and the current status of a wide range of operating parameters (pressure, temperature, flow, etc) is shown on plant instrumentation. The details are always changing, partly because of the quasi-steady state nature of such complex facilities and partly because, in this case, the heart of the plant operates on a batch basis, that is, the product is produced in batches (like baking cakes) rather than in a continuous process.

An immediate decision to stop production

At the chemical plant, some developing operational situations result in an immediate decision by the shift manager to shut part or all of the plant. All shift managers interviewed saw such decisions as being based on their judgment and experience and not on the application of formal rules or procedures, as the following interview extract shows (this refers to the decision to continue running the plant with one or more process control instruments out of service):

> Interviewee 7: "As far as making a judgment with an instrument [about] how critical it is as far as the plant's concerned, that's where my training comes into it as far as decision-making is concerned."
>
> Interviewer: "So you don't look it up in a register to see how it's classified or something like that?"
>
> Interviewee 7: "No."
>
> Interviewer: "It's based on your knowledge of the plant and your experience?"
>
> Interviewee 7: "Yes, absolutely."

Some interviewees took exception to the way the research questions were framed and claimed that there was no conflict between safety and production as safety is always number one. The following are typical statements from interview:

> "Safety, health and environment issues, the plant comes off. Depending on the severity of the issue, the plant comes off. It's straightforward." (shift manager interviewee 1)

> "If it's going to cause anybody harm or potentially cause anybody harm, we won't run it. We won't do it." (shift manager interviewee 3)

> "Safety or production, production loses out." (shift manager interviewee 5)

No interviewee was able to articulate any analytical process regarding how he came to a conclusion about whether a particular situation or course of action was safe or otherwise. Most interviewees said that it was based on their experience and judgment, and several then told stories as to how they developed their sense of what is safe. As one interviewee explained:

> "I guess like any decision you use your frame of reference in terms of what happened in the past and what I've seen in the past and what I have seen other people from other industries or other chemical plants or ... mining plants [do]. You take all that into account." (shift manager interviewee 6)

These stories were often very personal accounts of past experiences, focusing not on the technical sequence of events, but on thoughts and feelings about what had happened. Although they were not directly asked about the incident, most interviewees recounted in various ways the story of the most serious incident to have occurred at this site (approximately seven years earlier). For many interviewees, this incident taught them about the potential for serious safety consequences at the plant. The incident resulted in a significant release of flammable (and toxic) material, but it did not ignite and no one was injured — although there was a full call-out of external emergency services. The material was released from the process in an unexpected and complex way that took some time to diagnose and bring under control. Shift manager interviewee 7's summary is typical of how the incident was described:

> "I was involved here maybe five years ago now, where we had an incident which was potentially quite hazardous ... That was quite interesting and is certainly something I will never forget. It was quite, in a lot of ways, it was quite traumatic from a personal perspective, from my own personal perspective anyway ... I think at the time your training kicks in and you just think about making the plant safe. Afterwards, you just think what could have happened ... and

you think what happened at Longford.[5] Those are the sort of things that go through your mind, particularly afterwards when the dust has settled."

While interviewee 7 was present during this incident (which occurred on night shift), the sense of shock at "what might have been" extended to others who worked at the site at the time. One worker (interviewee 9) described how concerned he was to arrive at the site for the day shift to find a large number of fire trucks already there.

Dealing with unusual operating conditions

For the cases in which no immediate shutdown was deemed to be required, supervisors responded in a similar way to those at the nuclear power station. The equivalent parameters (such as estimated time to repair) were taken into account when deciding how to proceed — although there were some key differences. The operating environment at the chemical plant is different in that the physical plant and equipment have a much lower degree of redundancy (that is, duplication of critical components) than at the nuclear power station. Also, the chemical plant personnel have had no specific training in a process that encourages them to use their experience to set limits, articulate them and stick to them. Despite there being no company system in place, the approach of creating a situation-specific limit or rule was a practice that some people had informally adopted for themselves.

Reviewing the range of stories told, the shift managers were less disciplined in sticking with their self-imposed limits than their counterparts at the nuclear power station. I heard several stories where the shift manager decided to continue operation on the basis that repairs would be put in place by a certain time, only for that time to be exceeded for other operational reasons. In two of the stories recounted in interview, this resulted in an adverse outcome and the interviewees realised in hindsight that they perhaps should have stuck to their initial judgment.

Chapter

8

Another key factor was the number of safety barriers in place. If a safety system were offline (for example, for maintenance), then available alternatives would be put in place.

In summary, the shift managers take a strong professional pride in their judgment and experience — in particular, their ability to produce product safely. Their judgment about safety relies not only on their technical knowledge of the plant, but also on their real appreciation of the dangers associated with hazardous chemicals and industrial activities. In their view, there is no conflict between production and safety, because safety always wins out.

---

5   The fire and explosion at the Longford gas plant in Gippsland, Victoria, in September 1998.

At Airservices: "when you kick a ball you don't know where it's going to land"

Research into operational decision-making at Airservices was carried out in the Melbourne ATC centre and the Sydney operations room. Staff in the Melbourne centre are responsible for providing ATC services to all aviation traffic from an east-west line just south of Brisbane as far south as Antarctica. Their coverage also extends from the middle of the Indian Ocean in the west, and half-way to New Zealand in the east. The number of air traffic controllers required varies according to the time of day (and hence traffic level), but is typically around 50. Each controller sits at a console with radar displays and communications equipment to locate aircraft and talk to pilots. The controllers are divided into six rows and each group of two rows has an aisle supervisor. When the fieldwork was being conducted, the most senior operations personnel in the operations room were the system supervisor and the operations director.

The arrangement in Sydney is similar but on a smaller scale. Staff in the operations room are responsible for aviation traffic within 45 nautical miles of Sydney airport. A traffic manager supervises approximately five to 10 air traffic controllers (depending on the time of day).

For both the chemical plant and the nuclear power station, if a significant operating safety issue arises, the appropriate response is to shut the system down. While in both cases there are hazards associated with the shutdown process itself, this is still the safest response to most serious safety issues. At Airservices, the situation is different. Perhaps the most serious safety issue that can arise is an unexpected loss of a major part of the operating system. The physical system (equipment and software) that allows the controllers to locate, monitor and talk to pilots is highly integrated and includes multiple levels of redundancy. Air traffic controllers are trained in how to respond in the event of unexpected loss of communications or radar capability. There are well-established contingency plans and hierarchies to ensure that air traffic in any airspace immediately impacted by an equipment failure is managed to the ground (the safest place) in an orderly manner. This transition is relatively hazardous, so there are no cases in which supervisors would choose, for safety reasons, to immediately shut down the system for which they are responsible due to the potential breach of some kind of operating limit.[6] Having the system running, even in a degraded state, is always a safer option.

Repair work following less serious failures also involves safety and cost trade-offs. Time limits are proceduralised in the form of service restoration times (SRTs). When

---

6   There may be circumstances in which this decision may be made for security reasons. These types of contingencies were not discussed and are not part of the research described here.

equipment items fail, the urgency with which they must be repaired is specified by the SRT. Service restoration times have been developed based on the cost to repair the item balanced against the increased risk to aircraft and passengers due to the item being out of service. They form part of the overall reliability specification of the system (along with the acceptable failure rate, etc). The cost to repair is a function of the restoration time due to the overtime costs of bringing specialist staff in at night and on weekends. For some items that are in remote locations, a short SRT might also mean a special trip (even chartering a plane), whereas a long SRT might mean fixing a fault on the next scheduled visit at a much reduced cost. These requirements are proceduralised by published SRTs agreed between operations and maintenance, but operational supervisors can request a variation to the published times if they believe that particular circumstances warrant it.

On the other hand, there are cases when some redundancy in the system is removed to allow for planned maintenance activities. The decision to release equipment for inspection, testing and maintenance lies with the supervisor. An example of this is the decision about the best time of day to allow testing of the backup power supply to be carried out on an in-service operational system with a clear safety function (as aircraft traffic levels change over the course of the day). There are no rules to cover this or similar situations, which can be a direct trade-off of maintenance (overtime) costs versus safety.

Weather issues are another instigator of safety and traffic trade-offs. A set of fixed operating limits cover many potentially hazardous situations (for example, the maximum allowable cross wind on a runway), but these rules apply at the local or individual aircraft level. It is the job of the air traffic controllers, rather than the supervisors, to deal with these issues. In the event that a service interruption occurs in a specific location, supervisors generally get involved in the knock-on effects, making decisions about operating modes in other parts of the country due to, for example, significant weather delays at a major airport. These types of situations generally take some time to develop (and the longer the duration of the interruption, the more widespread the impact becomes).

Chapter

8

The supervisors work hard to make sure that they can manage such service interruptions proactively, rather than allowing small issues to compound into a major problem. Traffic manager 4 (session 5) described this as "manoeuvring to keep the ship on course". There are often direct trade-offs between safety and potential airline schedule interruptions as a result of rules being applied by the air traffic controllers, but the supervisors try to prevent operations from getting to the situation where application of the rules is necessary. An example of this is that aircraft are not permitted to land if the cross-runway component of the wind is greater than 20 knots. This rule is enforced by the tower air traffic controllers, but the traffic managers select the duty runway. When making that selection, they take the weather forecast into account so that the tower air traffic controllers should not be in a situation where this rule needs to be invoked.

Traffic manager 2 (session 3) described his job as acting as a buffer for the air traffic controllers to ensure that there were enough staff, that there were no distractions from phones or visitors, that equipment was working, and that they were in the right operating mode for the prevailing conditions.

Traffic manager 4 (session 6) said that he believed that a key feature of experience is managing one's workload as an air traffic controller so as not to become overloaded. He felt that inexperienced air traffic controllers have a tendency to take on too much and get themselves into strife. Part of the role of the traffic managers is to make sure that environmental factors do not encourage this. This would appear to be similar to traffic manager 2's buffer concept. Melbourne operations supervisor 1 (session 14) made a similar comment: "It's like a frog in a pot of hot water. The problems can sneak up on you [when you are an air traffic controller]. My job is to keep an eye on traffic levels and make sure this doesn't happen."

Similar decisions are required in cases regarding air traffic controller workload. If staffing levels are suddenly found to be short (for example, due to someone calling in sick), the supervisor may be faced with a situation that requires a trade-off between cost (overtime), safety (increased workload for the remaining air traffic controllers), and customer service (formally deciding that some services will be withdrawn). There are detailed procedures for how each option would be put into practice and some firm constraints on the options available, but the decision regarding which operating mode is appropriate lies with the supervisor.

In all of these cases, conservatism was seen as the key. Traffic manager 6 (session 7) said: "The key to safety in this job is to be conservative. It is better to overreact in that situation on the off-chance that things might go bad, than to assume everything will be OK and get caught out." He has been in the job for 30 years.

Undoubtedly, there are many rules for air traffic controllers to follow. Traffic manager 1 (session 1) said that "it's a very structured environment" but, while many detailed aspects of the air traffic controllers' work are completely specified, any real operating situation is a set of complex interactions between one or more aircraft (and hence pilots) and a wide range of environmental factors. As these combinations of circumstances are not — and cannot be — completely defined, integrated responses cannot be determined in advance and specified in procedures. One supervisor described his thoughts about the rules regarding ATC. He said that, despite the enormous number of rules and procedures under which the air traffic controllers and pilots operate, it is a myth that the outcomes are clearly determined by these rules. The metaphor he used was "when you kick a ball you don't know where it's going to land". The point he is making is that he is acting in the present to ensure that the outcome in the future is as desired. No matter how accurately we control action in the present, it is impossible to ensure that the future outcome is always pre-determined. This is because some things that impact on the outcome are either not predictable or are outside our control (or both).

In the face of dynamic complexity, anticipation, conservatism and buffering are key strategies adopted in decision-making by operations directors, system supervisors and traffic managers. At their level, operational decisions are mainly based on experience and judgment rather than rules.

Common themes

The organisational expectations are that safety decisions are made in accordance with rules. The perception of senior management is that this generalisation applies to operational managers as much as frontline staff. Prior to conducting the fieldwork, senior management at two of the sites indicated that they did not think there was much to study in this research project other than procedural compliance, as all operational decisions relating to safety were completely defined in specific rules. At the third site, it was emphasised that decisions were based on identification and analysis of options (essentially, a description of the classical decision-making process). The research data suggest that, to a greater or lesser extent, rules *are* used as part of safety decision-making by the operational managers in all three organisations.

While rule compliance plays an important role in safety decision-making, the research data indicate that this is far from the full story for operational managers. There were many examples given in interview where managers relied on experience-based judgment — rather than the recollection of a published rule — when deciding whether a significant production interruption was necessary. Such examples included:

- deviating from the expected value of more than one parameter, but all within the stipulated operating envelope;
- responding to an unplanned equipment failure or outage; and
- the situation-specific knock-on effects of complying with a safety rule.

In some cases, the operational managers created a new, situation-specific rule for themselves as a way of formalising their judgment-based decision. Creating a "line in the sand" seems to be an effective way of preventing such decisions from drifting when repairs and responses take longer than originally expected.

The other factor in decision-making is a set of common elements associated with the experience and judgment of the operational managers. Their stories and descriptions show a desire to act conservatively and responsibly — showing a high degree of dedication to professional tasks (generating power safely, making product safely, and managing the safe, orderly and expeditious movement of aircraft). In contrast to the compliance behaviour of the operational managers — rooted in their identity as organisational employees — these other characteristics come from the operational managers' sense of professionalism. These dual occupational identities (as employees and as professionals) and the associated implications for safety decision-making are explored in the rest of this chapter.

Decision-making and identity

Many people and many organisations believe that good decisions are made on the basis of rational choice, that is, where the decision-maker, faced with a problem, identifies the available options, analyses them, and choses the best one based on rational, generalised criteria. Much research has shown that operational decisions, especially those made by experienced people who are under significant time pressure, are not made like this, nor necessarily should they be. Researchers from the field known as "naturalistic decision-making" (or NDM) have studied how firefighters, intensive care nurses and other highly skilled specialists make time-pressured high-stakes decisions (Klein 1998). The generalised models that they have produced show that decisions like these are made based on (often unconscious) pattern recognition.

Weick (who is well known for his work on HROs) takes this further with his work on sensemaking (Weick 2001). In his view, decisions are not really decisions, but simply the actions required by the understanding or the sense that an individual has of an unfolding situation.

Snook makes this point when he uses sensemaking as one frame for his analysis of the accidental shoot down of US Blackhawks over northern Iraq (which resulted in 26 "friendly fire" fatalities):

> "I could have asked, 'Why did they *decide* to shoot?' However, such
> a framing puts us squarely on a path that leads straight back to the
> individual decision-maker, away from potentially powerful contextual
> features and right back into the jaws of the fundamental attribution
> error. 'Why did they decide to shoot?' quickly becomes 'Why did they
> make the *wrong* decision?' Hence, the attribution falls squarely onto
> the shoulders of the decision-maker and away from potent situational
> factors that influence action. Framing the individual-level puzzle as
> a question of meaning rather than deciding shifts the emphasis away
> from individual decision-makers toward a point somewhere 'out there'
> where context and individual action overlap. Individual responsibility

is not ignored. However, by viewing the fateful actions of TIGERS 01 and 02 as the behaviours of actors struggling to make sense, rather than rational attempts to decide, we level the analytical playing field toward a more complete and balanced accounting of all relevant factors, not just individual judgment." (Snook 2000, pp 206-207)

This leads to the idea that decision-making is not a rational process occurring in isolation of context. Instead, decision-making is seen as a richly context-dependent process. For all of the participating operational managers, the context in which they work has two key characteristics: they are all very long-term members of their employer organisation, and they are all very experienced in their given professions. This gives them two strong occupational identities — on the one hand as an employee, and on the other hand as a member of a professional peer group. These senses of self or parts of their identity play a key dual role in their safety decision-making.

Looking first at organisational identity, it is clear that the operational managers have stable employment histories. Many of them have only ever worked for one employer, or at one facility.[7] The average level of experience is approximately 25 years. For most interviewees, this is their entire working life — indicating a long and stable relationship between employer and employee. Also, the operational managers are all in upper middle management, holding positions that are two to four levels below the CEO of their respective organisations. While this gives them significant organisational authority, they are still required to follow policies and procedures for many aspects of their role, including operational decision-making. In this context, authority lies with their organisational superiors, and the operational managers are expected to adopt organisational goals about safety and production as their own, and to follow decision-making procedures laid down for them.

The implications of organisational identity on decision-making were most obvious at the nuclear power station and at Airservices. At the nuclear power station, the organisational requirements for safety decision-making were clearly documented and the level of compliance from the operational managers was high. At Airservices, operational changes were occurring when the fieldwork was being conducted, and the operational managers were acutely aware of the preferences of their superiors when it came to operational decision-making. So, in one sense, all operational managers take their priorities and direction from their organisational superiors, but in another important sense, senior operational staff are in charge. In all three organisations, documented procedures clearly state that operational staff are responsible for all major and minor operating decisions, including whether or not

Chapter

8

---

7   In the case of two of the participating sites, ownership of the site has changed several times during the working life of the operational managers.

the facilities stay on line. This is normal for such facilities, where delays in decisions to stop operations have contributed to accidents. This was a lesson well learned after the Piper Alpha disaster in the 1980s. In that incident, 167 people lost their lives when an offshore oil and gas platform in the North Sea was destroyed by a series of large fires. The platform was a hub for a series of collection pipelines from other platforms in the area. One factor in limiting the inventory of fuel available to burn was the time taken by the managers of adjacent facilities (who could see the fire) to stop the production of oil and gas. In at least one case, shutdown was delayed until the facility manager received permission to stop production from more senior management in the onshore office.

At Airservices, this concept is known as "operational command authority" and is respected in practice to the point that, if the person holding that authority has to leave the operations room (even if only for a few minutes), he hands over that authority to someone else before departing. It was also very clear at the nuclear power station that the operating crew is in control of operating decisions. The operations manual says: "If management representatives are present during operations, there should be no doubt who is responsible for decision-making." The writer is trying to say that senior management is actually not in charge when they are in the control room. Similarly, at the chemical plant, the operational managers know that they have full authority to interrupt production (if they believe it is necessary) without reference to more senior management. Final operational authority lies with the professional operating crew in all cases, even when their organisational superiors are present.

When exercising this authority (which operates parallel to, but outside, organisational lines of authority), operational managers are acting from their professional identity, rather than their organisational identity. By fostering this system of authority, organisations are implicitly acknowledging the professional identity of operational managers, even though this is rarely stated explicitly. This identity has other significant implications for safety decision-making that generally remain unacknowledged. The stories and conversations about decision-making show a number of ways in which operational managers think and behave as professionals, rather than employees. This includes:

- using their judgment, rather than rules, to make decisions;
- showing dedication to professional goals, standards and ethics;
- consulting with peers to make decisions;
- learning by sharing stories with peers; and
- being trustworthy and responsible towards colleagues and the public.

This chapter now explores in some detail the safety implications of decision-making based on both organisational and professional identities.

Rules and procedures for decision-making

Rules and procedures are an important way for organisations to communicate to staff in advance what it is that they are required to do in a range of situations. The types of rules used by the operational managers take two quite different forms. Some rules fix the limits of operations (boundary rules). While operational activities are left to the discretion of the decision-maker, a rule fixes limits or boundaries to operations that must not be breached. The station operating instructions at the nuclear power station are boundary rules. The other form that safety decision-making rules take is that of process-based rules. This type of rule lays down a process that the operational managers must follow in order to decide on the best course of action. Rules of this type are used in all three organisations studied.

Goal-based (boundary) rules

Of the organisations that participated in this research, the nuclear power station had the strongest focus on rules at the operational manager level (and probably overall, but this was not investigated systematically). As described above, the facility had a very well-defined operating envelope in the form of station operating instructions. It was unconscionable for any operational manager to allow the plant to continue to operate if there was a chance that one of the published limits might be breached.

The engineering department is responsible for writing the station operating instructions, which are largely based on technical evaluations of hazards and risks. Some station operating instructions are about permitted combinations of equipment that must be available at all times to ensure that the reactor can always be controlled. These rules limit the number of equipment items that, for example, might be released for maintenance work at the same time. The rules are determined based on fault tree analysis. "Always" (as used earlier in this paragraph) actually means with a calculated failure frequency that is less than a predetermined limit. Other station operating instructions limit plant operating parameters, such as pressure, temperature or concentrations of contaminants. These values have also been determined by engineers based on calculations of the consequences of going beyond the defined point and the frequency of undesired outcomes. This is the main way in which risk assessment influences safety decision-making by operational managers. The managers themselves rarely consider specific situations in risk terms, as will be described further below.

Definitions of a firm operating envelope are also becoming increasingly common in the chemical industry (CCPS 2007), although such limits were not in operation at the chemical plant that participated in this research. In the ATC environment, many operating limits apply to the work of air traffic controllers (for example, the specified minimum separation distances between aircraft). However, few similar parameters apply at a system level and hence few operating limits are relevant to the work of the operational managers.

The station operating instructions at the nuclear power station are an example of goal-based rules. They specify a goal (that various parameters must not be breached) without prescribing the actions to take to prevent the limit from being breached. In a sense, they act as a supervisory rule, working in parallel with the operating procedures that detail how various tasks and activities are to be done by the operating crew. Another type of rule is relevant to decision-making by operational managers. These are process-based rules (described below).

Process-based rules

The idea behind using process-based rules for safety assurance is that, if the series of steps that a skilled individual is required to perform is specified, when performing those steps the individual will come to the best decision. Examples of process-based rules commonly used in manufacturing and process industries are permit to work systems and job safety analysis requirements. When going through these processes, it is expected that experienced workers will identify potential problems and fix them before they occur.

Two of the participating organisations had process-based rules that were designed to apply to decision-making by operational managers. At the chemical plant, operational managers (along with other technical staff, including engineers) had received training in a decision-making system known as the revolution model. This model basically follows the five steps known as classical decision-making: define the problem; identify the possible solutions; evaluate the solutions; implement the chosen solution; and check whether the problem is solved. Decision-making tools based on these generic steps will be familiar to anyone who has done any management training in this area. The operational managers completely ignored this procedure to the point where, in approximately 15 hours of interviews, none of them mentioned its existence.

A process-based procedure for decision-making by operational managers was also in place at the nuclear power station. This was for situations within the defined operating envelope, but where the situation was still abnormal in a way that was giving the operational manager some safety concerns. In these cases, the operational manager was required to review the situation and fix a limit — a situation-specific point at which troubleshooting would stop and the plant or equipment involved would be shut down. Often, but not always, this line in the sand takes the form of a time limit. The field data from the nuclear power station include many examples of setting a line in the sand and sticking to it. In some cases, the problem was fixed within the self-imposed limit and, in other cases, the plant was shut down.

Several of the stories told by the operational managers at the chemical plant followed a similar pattern. In one case, the manager said: "I knew I had about 30 minutes to fix it." This was not based on a procedure or anything specific that would occur after 30 minutes, but rather his view about how long it was safe to run in a set of abnormal circumstances. In another case, the operational manager was involved in temporary repairs to a leaking cooling water system. Since the plant was still operating, he had set the control room operator the task of monitoring a plant parameter, with instructions to shut equipment down if a specific limit was reached. The difference at the chemical plant was that there were also several stories told where the limit set in the first instance was then ignored as repairs were delayed for a range of practical reasons. In some of these cases, the situation deteriorated and an emergency trip (rather than a controlled shutdown) resulted. The stories show our human tendency to say, "well, it's been OK so far", just like the frog in the pot of hot water mentioned by the Airservices' operational manager cited above. In some instances, we revise our original view that the activity or operation was undesirable. This leads to an acceptance of continuing operation with decreased safety margins.

In her study on the *Challenger* space shuttle disaster, Vaughan found that, over a period of years, National Aeronautical and Space Administration technical staff came to accept observed damage to solid rocket booster seals as normal, even though it was initially seen as a problem (Vaughan 1996). Eventually, the seals were so damaged on one launch that they failed and the shuttle was lost. She calls this shift in what is normal or accepted practice as "the normalisation of deviance". The present research on operational managers indicates that such normalisation can occur very quickly in cases where the self-imposed limit is not strongly articulated and/or recorded.

The operational managers at Airservices were also observed creating situation-specific rules to limit operations. For example, one day in Sydney when a revised weather forecast was received predicting significant deterioration during the afternoon, the traffic manager immediately reworked the schedule of flight arrivals and departures for Sydney airport using a reduced cap on the maximum number of movements per hour. He chose the cap based on his experience of past similar situations — what it would be possible for the air traffic controllers to manage in the weather conditions and other environmental factors likely to exist later in the day. The new arrangements for the afternoon were distributed to the airlines and the air traffic controllers, so there was no question that the new situation-specific limit could be ignored. It simply became the new planning basis for the day.

Both goal-based and process-based rules are used by operational managers when making decisions. There is generally significant respect for the rules that have been set by an organisation, although, given the opportunity, operational managers will

Chapter

8

ignore rules if they do not believe they are useful. In all three organisations, the operational managers were observed making their own situation-specific rules. When generating and applying such rules, the operational managers rely on their professional experience and are acting from their professional, rather than organisational, identity. This is the subject of the next part of this chapter.

Professionals at work

In all three organisations, the operational managers' highest priority is to do what they believe is a good job. They see themselves as professionals, taking great pride in the standard of their work. We all have a sense of what it means to be professional, but there is no universal definition. The various aspects of professionalism can be distilled into the following list:

- "technical and theoretical expertise and the authority and status flowing from such expert and highly valued knowledge, understanding and skill;
- the establishment and the exercise of trust as a basis for professional relationships (with clients and between professionals);
- adherence to particular standards and professional ethics often, but not always, represented by the granting of a licence;
- independence, autonomy and discretion; and
- specific attitudes towards work, clients and peers involving dedication, reliability, flexibility and creativity in relation to the 'unknown'." (Middlehurst & Kennie 1997)

Many of these features are seen in the attitudes and behaviours of the operational managers.

Expertise and judgment

Undoubtedly, individuals at the operational manager level have a great deal of technical knowledge about how their systems operate. This is partly abstract or theoretical, but heavily based on many years of practical experience.

In these days of organisational "churn", employees in these types of jobs provide an island of stability and a source of corporate history. Clearly, operational managers rely on their extensive understanding of the technical aspects of the operation of the facilities and systems for which they are responsible when making decisions. This was not specifically addressed in this research, but many stories included references to factual knowledge held by the operational managers simply due to the length of their involvement and the richness of their experience. One operational manager at the chemical plant said that he knew immediately how to fix a problem that was giving the operating crew trouble:

"I had the advantage of seeing the plant grow from the ground and there are things that you see that other people, they are there for them to see but, because of what else is happening around them, they don't necessarily see them in the way that you see them."

Apart from understanding the technical implications of any given situation, the other aspect of decision-making is whether a situation is safe or unsafe. When asked to describe or generalise about this issue, interviewees rarely talked in theoretical terms, but often recounted stories about their past experiences. This was especially common in the interviews held with the operational managers at the chemical plant (as described above).

Several people talked of occasions that had brought home to them the reality of the danger associated with the technologies with which they work. Sometimes these were stories of disaster averted where the events that had occurred were well known to all at the site. On other occasions, the stories were far more personal. One interviewee at each site described the technological system within which they work as "the beast". Looking at the quotes in context, the qualities of the beast are common to all three interviewees. In each case, the beast is:

- complex;
- unknown and, to some extent, unknowable and unpredictable;
- difficult to control;
- powerful; and
- dangerous and somewhat malevolent.

These themes were also reflected in other stories that did not use this specific metaphor, for example:

- the story of the first time that the plant did not behave as the young plant operator (now an operational manager) had expected and the shock he experienced as a result;
- the personal cost of having to tell relatives that someone had been injured at work; and
- stories of what the system "likes" and "hates".

The common theme to all of these stories of events large and small is the inherent danger and unpredictable nature of the systems for which the operational managers have responsibility — in other words, the vigilance required to keep "the beast" under control.

The research data give some insight into how the judgment was made that the developing situation was unsafe. In the specific decision-making scenarios described in interview, individuals focused on context-specific loss of defences or deviation from the normal level of control, rather than on a judgment about the likely outcome. Also, very few references were made to any theoretical considerations of what constitutes safe or unsafe operation. Risk and risk assessment were not commonly articulated terms, and while the erosion of system defences was clearly being considered in a context-specific manner, terms such as "defence in depth" or "Swiss cheese" or any other generalised references to the role of defences were not used.

Trust

Organisations generally show a high degree of trust in operational managers. They have significant authority and, certainly at the nuclear power station and at the chemical plant, the most senior company managers went to significant lengths to show the operational managers that they were trusted. Several operational managers cited support from senior managers as the most important thing in helping them to make good decisions. The attitude of senior management at the nuclear power station towards decisions made by the operational managers is described below. The attitude of senior management at the chemical plant was not quite so supportive, but the operational managers' judgment was never questioned and they knew that their judgment would be accepted. If the operational managers chose to interrupt production for safety reasons, then senior management would seek to find out why such action was necessary so that the underlying problem could be fixed and further production interruptions avoided. The decision to interrupt production was never directly challenged. Both senior management and operational managers understood the importance of absolute trust on this issue.

The importance of trust was most obvious at Airservices, where industrial circumstances meant that trust was somewhat strained. When the fieldwork was being conducted, major operational restructures were underway and many existing operating practices were being challenged by the organisation. Senior management was asking operational managers to make changes to some long-established practices that management felt were overly conservative and unnecessarily costly, although, at least with regard to operational decision-making, it was emphasised that the final decision (and responsibility) was always with the operational managers. The responses of the operational managers varied. Some felt that their professionalism was being challenged; they stuck with past practices and responded with hostility to the requirement to justify what they had decided. Others moved to the new way of operating and, when asked why they were happy to change when some others were not, they said that it was clear what the organisation wanted them to do, so as employees they felt it was their duty to do what was required of them. This was the clearest case in the research data where professional and organisational identities seemed to be promoting different behaviour.

The complicating factor in this particular case is that many of the controversial issues related to staffing arrangements, so it was easy for senior management to see the resistance to change as being at least partly driven by self-interest. I am in no position to judge the technical pros and cons of the disputed practices and, to a large extent, that is irrelevant to the issue at hand. All I can say is that the safety of the system as a whole relies on the professionalism of the operational managers and, at the time that the fieldwork was done, they felt that their professional judgment was under attack.

Relationships with peers

A third important aspect of the professional identity of the operational managers was their relationship with their peers. Due to the nature of their working arrangements, it is extremely rare for the operational managers to meet together as a group (since they must cover 24-hour continuous shifts between them). Nevertheless, relationships with peers were universally important to reinforce professional judgment. All decision-makers viewed consultation with other experienced people as important. Sometimes specialist technical advice is needed, but on many occasions the reason for telephoning colleagues for advice is different. As someone at the nuclear power station who is regularly called by shift charge engineers put it: "Out of hours you are lonely on shift and you've got the SOIs [station operating instructions], but usually these kind of events don't fit in with procedures ... I've done it myself when I was shift charge. You get all sorts of funny things and you ring [other experienced people] up at two and three in the morning. You just want to test your argument with someone else ... what they want is a sounding board, just to test their arguments I think." The sensemaking view of decision-making emphasises the social nature of the processes involved: "How can I know what I think until I hear what I say?" Consulting professional peers was equally valued by operational managers in the other two organisations.

In addition to consulting each other regarding specific decisions in the heat of the moment, the operational managers universally valued the opportunity to share "war" stories of the types described above. Each of the three organisations has a comprehensive system in place for reporting, investigating, acting on, and looking for trends in incidents and accidents. While not the specific focus of this research, the systems appear to play an important role in resolving specific safety issues in a timely manner, and in identifying longer-term trends. Reporting rates at all sites are high. While the operational managers use all aspects of these systems on a daily basis, the incidents that are of interest to them in increasing their system understanding are usually not reported or reportable in the site or organisation-wide system. This is because the nature of the incidents reported relates to loss or potential loss (in the case of the chemical plant and nuclear power station) and error (in the case of Airservices). However, incidents that are of interest to operational managers relate to unusual and unexpected system interactions and events. While some incidents fall into both categories, many do not. In all three organisations, the operational managers had developed informal systems (based on stories) outside the main incident reporting arrangements for sharing their experiences with their peers. None of the organisations specifically supported the use of these types of occurrences in training or simulations.

Good and bad decisions

If our objective is to support operational managers in making better decisions, it is useful to consider what that means before we turn to the implications of their dual identities as employees and professionals.

At first thought, it might seem that it should be obvious (at least in hindsight if not in advance) whether a given safety-related decision was a good one or not. In practice, this is often far from clear if we focus entirely on the outcome. Of course, there are cases where someone makes a poor choice and things go badly. In these cases, the decision-maker and others can hopefully learn from that experience and not make the same mistake again.

Simplistically, a good decision might be seen as disaster averted, but this introduces some major problems if it is used to determine the effectiveness of real decisions in context. There are some cases in the research data where a decision was made to interrupt production, and further analysis showed that there was indeed a significant problem in the system that might have resulted in a serious incident if no intervention had been made. In these cases, it is clear that a real problem was averted, but there are also many cases that do not conform to this pattern and yet the decisions can still be classified as good ones. In some cases, the fact that the intervention occurred makes it impossible to know what would have happened otherwise. For example, if an aircraft had not been grounded as bad weather developed at its destination, what would have happened? Whether any individual judgment was correct in context or overly conservative remains a matter of opinion, even after the event. In other cases, further analysis shows that, however appropriate the judgment to intervene seemed at the time, there was, in fact, no serious threat to safety and the interruption to production was unnecessary if judged only by the situation-specific outcome.

At the nuclear power station, a routine inspection of one of the reactors found some unexpected cracking. The operational manager on duty at the time asked the inspection engineers whether they could guarantee that the same fault was not present in the other reactor (which was still on line) and further, if similar cracks were present, that it was safe to continue to operate. The inspection engineers were unable to provide such assurances, so the operational manager decided to take the second reactor offline. A week later, further engineering work showed that there was no issue with the reactor integrity and the reactor was restarted. The plant manager praised the conservative thinking on the part of the operational manager, even though he had cost the organisation one week's production for something that turned out not to be a problem.

This is surely very impressive on the part of senior management at the nuclear power station, and is in significant contrast to some of the stories told at one of the other sites where operational managers felt under pressure to allow work to be done on live systems on the basis that it had been done before at other locations without any problems. Senior management at these two organisations seem to have different views about what constitutes a good decision. In one case, a good decision is one based on the identification of a potential problem. Evidence has been interpreted in the most conservative way and the worst possible outcome is assumed to be possible until proven otherwise. In the other case, evidence is interpreted in the most optimistic way: "We didn't have a problem last time, so it will be OK to do the same activity again."

Decisions, risks and barriers

Some readers may be surprised that this chapter is not about risk assessment. After all, most high-hazard organisations have a strong emphasis on risk management and many say that they use risk-based decision-making.

This research has shown that risk is important in operational decision-making, but only indirectly. As described above, many of the operational limits that impact on safety decision-making are formulated as a result of risk assessments. This applies not only to the station operating instructions at the nuclear power station, but also to limits used at the other organisations, such as the fatigue management scores used by operational managers at Airservices to make rostering decisions.

On the other hand, the operational managers rarely used terms such as risk, probability or chance when describing their own judgment-based decisions for cases where prewritten rules do not apply. Instead, consideration of the appropriate action centred on the barriers in place to prevent an undesirable outcome.

The operational managers believed that, in its normal operating state, the system is safe. As described above, this does not mean that the operational managers are unaware of the dangers inherent in the activities that they perform, but, in all three participating organisations, the general belief is that sufficient barriers are in place so that the normal situation is safe. When departures from that situation occur, the operational managers become uneasy. They seek to repair, replace or substitute the missing, failed or ineffective barriers. At their best, they anticipate a problem with a barrier and provide an alternative in advance. Examples include:

- providing alternative hand-held gas detection while the automatic gas detection system is being repaired;
- calling in additional staff in anticipation of further problems when redundancy has been lost in communications systems (due to an extreme weather event); and
- planning equipment maintenance to ensure that relevant safety systems are always available.

Situations are understood by the operational managers to be unsafe once barriers are compromised in situations in which they may be required. This can lead to an immediate decision to shut down or lead to a "line in the sand" being invoked (formally or informally), depending on the operational manager's judgment about how important the missing or compromised barrier is in the given situation.

Of course, this situation can be described in risk terms. Risk is higher with one or more barriers compromised and the line in the sand limits the time at risk. The operational managers do not see such situations in probabilistic terms, that is, they make no conscious assessment of the chances of something further going wrong. This could be because, fundamentally, an assessment of the chance of something going wrong is of no use to them in the heat of the moment. They are faced with a dichotomous choice — to (plan to) interrupt operations or continue to operate. The present research suggests that they make this decision based on the state of barriers, not consideration of risk.

Conclusion

This research has shown that senior managers often have a relatively poor understanding of what drives the decision-making by operational managers. The reliance on rules, while a significant factor in decision-making at all sites, is not as all-encompassing as many organisations believe. In many ways, it must be obvious that the professionalism of the operational managers as a group (including such aspects as their judgment, skills and experience, and commitment to the job) plays an important part in good decision-making. This raises the question as to whether it matters that these factors are not openly acknowledged.

The fact that operational managers act as professionals as well as employees *should* matter to organisations which seek to improve safety performance. If judgment-based processes are acknowledged and valued, then those judgments can be refined and improved — to the benefit of all.

There are a number of ways in which organisations can assist operational managers to make better safety decisions.

Clarifying the boundary of the system operating envelope

Consistent decision-making is supported by a shared understanding of what constitutes "unsafe" in the sense of the operating envelope of the system. The range of parameters that need to have limits assigned will vary from facility to facility, but will typically include:

- physical parameters such as pressure, temperature, composition, etc in the case of the process plants, and traffic levels in the case of Airservices;
- other internal parameters such as the minimum number of people with certain skills;
- external environmental parameters such as maximum or minimum weather conditions;
- limits on the availability of safety systems or other equipment items; and
- limits on the acceptable combinations of simultaneous activities.

Sometimes limits can be independently defined, but often it is the combination of various factors that forms the necessary limit. While operational managers and others in the operating crew have important insight into the operating limits of the system, some limits are inherent in the design. These are generally engineering issues that may not be at all obvious without reference to the original design calculations. Such information must be communicated to the operational crew, and fixing operational boundaries is one simple way to achieve this.

As this research has shown, while operating outside the design envelope is unsafe, the operational managers also identified many cases where they believe that operations not specifically proscribed are still potentially unsafe. In my view, such cases are not an indication that the operating envelope has been incorrectly defined, but simply a sign that not every operating mode of a dynamic and complex system can be predicted in advance. In order for rules regarding operating limits to be accepted by operational managers, it is important to emphasise that they are designed to support operational decision-making rather than to completely define it, and that judgment remains an important aspect in decision-making.

Formalising judgment-based decision processes: the line in the sand

All of this points to the importance of process-based rules for decision-making. The decision-making process defined at the chemical plant was not accepted by the operational managers because it makes no allowance for the role of experience and judgment. Senior management's focus on classical decision-making processes did not sit well with the cognitive processes already in use. However, the concepts of conservative decision-making as defined at the nuclear power station were universally accepted by the operational managers precisely because they provide a formal framework for their experience. Once an unusual operating condition has been detected, the steps in this process are:

- assess the current situation and decide if an immediate production interruption is required;
- if not, commence troubleshooting or repair, and also set a line in the sand that defines the point at which troubleshooting will end and production will be interrupted;
- record and communicate the line in the sand to all those involved;
- monitor the system for further changes to ensure that the line in the sand is still appropriate; and
- if the line in the sand is reached before the situation returns to normal, initiate whatever production interruption has previously been agreed on.

It is telling that operational managers at the chemical plant and at Airservices had adopted at least the first two steps of this process, including coming to a conclusion about how long they had to fix a problem. The steps in the process that were not always applied were recording, communicating and sticking to the self-imposed limit that the operational managers had determined when the operating anomaly first came to their attention. Instead, they had a tendency to allow the abnormal situation to continue, especially if there was no evidence that the situation was deteriorating. This provides strong evidence that what Vaughan calls "the normalisation of deviance" occurs readily in operating situations, and that a formal process to stick to self-imposed limits could limit the drift towards acceptance of unsafe conditions.

The present research suggests that operational safety would be enhanced if operational managers were trained to set a line in the sand and then stick to it for unusual operating situations. They should not be expected to continue operating simply because the system is within the defined operating envelope. This decision-making process seems to provide structure and support for professional judgment, rather than defining cognitive steps that do not come naturally to experienced decision-makers who are under time pressure.

Sharing professional knowledge

As described above, operational managers love to share stories about their experiences with their peers. This currently happens in all three participating organisations — but outside formal incident reporting systems and with no specific time allocation.

The scope of incident reporting systems is usually limited to loss or potential loss events. The types of stories of interest to operational managers about unusual system behaviour often do not fall into this category. They are stories about operating occurrences that may only have an indirect link to loss or loss prevention. None of the organisations studied systematically records such incidents so that lessons can be captured for the longer term and incorporated into formal training and/or simulation.

In modern organisations, all staff are under time pressure, and time for unacknowledged tasks is becoming more and more difficult to find. In days gone by, it was common to have regularly scheduled training days when operational staff could get together away from day-to-day demands to discuss matters of common professional interest. Such sessions have tended to suffer as a result of cost reduction pressures or have been taken over by organisations as time to promote the latest management programs, rather than professional development time for operational staff.

Acknowledging the role of professional judgment in decision-making might make it easier to justify the costs associated with professional development time and prevent such time from being taken over by other organisational communication requirements.

Consultation

In a similar vein, the operational managers at all three organisations were happy to assist their colleagues by receiving out-of-hours phone calls and requests for assistance. This was largely unacknowledged by the wider organisation.

All three organisations also have emergency call-out arrangements that are designed to be triggered in the event of a serious emergency at the site. People who are included on the emergency roster have allocated emergency roles and have been trained to fill them. At the nuclear power station, this system had been adapted gradually and informally to include consultation in non-emergency situations. This has created some anomalies regarding training for inclusion on the roster and remuneration for duties.

The research data suggest that consultation should be encouraged. If organisations agree that this is appropriate behaviour, it should be resourced and appropriate rewards provided. This is not to say that consultation between professional colleagues needs to be authorised or controlled by senior management. It is simply that modern business practices, such as business process definition and re-engineering, give no value to activities that are not identified and seen as being in accordance with organisational business needs.

Clarifying goals and how to achieve them

The operational managers in all three organisations were well aware of the financial environment within which their organisations operate, and the importance of meeting production targets and keeping costs down. However, they take their safety responsibilities seriously and are prepared to make "sacrifice decisions" whereby these longer-term goals must sometimes be traded off against short-term safety concerns.

One of the most strongly articulated issues about safety decision-making was the attitude of senior management—specifically, the response to particular decisions that were made. It is important for senior managers to foster a common understanding with operational managers of overall safety and production goals, and to develop and demonstrate their trust in the ability of the operational managers to achieve those goals. Senior managers frequently say that safety is their number one priority without understanding what this might mean on a day-to-day basis. If safety is truly to be top priority, then complexity and uncertainty will mean that there are sometimes legitimate production interruptions in cases where hindsight will show that the interruption was unnecessary.

The operational managers in all three organisations were sensitive to senior management responses in these situations.

Emphasis on barriers, rather than risk

As discussed above, risk assessment (the consideration of hazards, consequences and frequency) plays an important role in establishing the operating envelope of the system. On the other hand, the concept of risk appears to have little impact in day-to-day operational decision-making. This is not a recommendation for more training or focus on risk assessment techniques for operational staff; rather, it is an observation about the limits of the concept of risk in practical situations.

Formal risk management processes are ultimately aimed at ensuring that there are sufficient controls in place to ensure that risk is as low as reasonably practicable. With this in mind, many operational risk management regimes are moving their focus from risk per se to risk controls or barriers. This is more consistent with the way in which operational personnel think about safety, and perhaps explains the popularity of risk management tools such as bow ties (which focus on barriers) with operational personnel. If overall risk management processes focus on ensuring that the right risk barriers are in place for normal operations, then the decision-making strategy of looking at deviations from that set of barriers seen in this research data will be a successful risk management approach.

Operational managers are stable long-term employees who show a high degree of skill and respect for organisational goals when making operational decisions. They also have a rich professional life that is largely ignored by formal organisational processes. This research has provided some insight into the importance of their identity as professionals, as well as employees, in safety decision-making. It has also highlighted some ways in which organisations might support operational managers in making better safety decisions.

CHAPTER 9

THE "NO-BLAME" APPROACH: INVESTIGATING BLAME IN SYSTEMIC ACCIDENT ANALYSES

Kate Branford

Introduction

The International Civil Aviation Organization (ICAO) states that: "The sole objective of the investigation of an accident or incident shall be the prevention of accidents and incidents. It is not the purpose of this activity to apportion blame or liability" (ICAO 2001, p 3-1). This approach is essential for improving safety. Accident investigations must be prevention-focused, so that inadequacies can be addressed to prevent future occurrences. They must also refrain from allocating blame, so that the individuals involved can provide information without fear of "becoming a target" (Prichard 2003), and so that investigators can focus on identifying what happened without having to consider issues of culpability.

Reason's systemic approach to accident analysis is widely advocated for this purpose. It focuses on prevention by identifying the organisational and systemic problems that contribute to organisational accidents, and promotes a "no-blame" approach (House of Representatives 2002, p 2) by focusing not on "who blundered", but on "how and why the defences failed" (Reason 2000, p 768). However, given the strong tendency that people have to blame after serious accidents, the question arises as to whether analyses based on this approach succeed in deflecting blame. This chapter draws on an example of an accident analysis to provide insight into this question.

Reason's approach

Reason argues that complex technological systems are designed with a series of barriers, safeguards and defences in place to protect the systems, assets and potential victims from hazards (Reason 1997, 2000). Ideally, each defensive layer prevents accidents from being possible. In reality, however, there are always weaknesses and gaps in a system's defences. Reason notes that weaknesses in any one defensive layer do not usually cause accidents, but that accidents can occur "when the holes in many layers momentarily line up to permit a trajectory of accident opportunity — bringing hazards into damaging contact with victims" (Reason 2000, p 769).

Such weaknesses, Reason claims, are caused by active failures and latent conditions. Active failures are unsafe acts performed by people at the front line of the system, such as pilots and control room operators. Reason argues that accident analysis must go beyond identifying these errors to examine how and why they occurred. Latent conditions are, he says, like "resident pathogens" in a system, producing ongoing weaknesses in its defences and generating active failures by creating circumstances that promote human error (Reason 2000, p 769). These include local workplace factors, such as poor design and impractical procedures, and the organisational factors (relating to budgeting, resource allocation and communication, for instance) that generate these problems (Reason 1997).

Reason therefore sees organisational accidents as occurring when system deficiencies combine with local events and human errors to penetrate the system's defences. In such accidents, he views human errors not as the *causes* of accidents, but as the *consequences* of systemic problems, claiming that the contribution of operators to accidents is "usually that of adding the final garnish to a lethal brew whose ingredients have already been long in the cooking" (Reason 1990, p 173). He consequently argues that it is essential in accident analysis to consider the *context* within which errors occur, because only then can the individual's behaviour be understood and the underlying causes uncovered.

Reason notes that there are occasions when workers can justifiably be blamed for their errors, namely, when their behaviour is "unreasonably reckless, negligent or ... malevolent" (Reason 1997, p 205). However, if other workers with similar experience and qualifications to the individual in question would have made the same mistake, it is likely to be a "blameless system-induced error", and blaming the individual will only mask the systemic deficiencies involved (Reason 1997, pp 208-210). Reason suggests that the vast majority of unsafe acts are of this type. Thus, Reason's approach is intended to be "blame-free", not in the sense that it provides blanket protection against blame, but in the sense that it refrains from blaming individuals for mistakes that others would have made in the same circumstances (Reason 1997). However, accident analyses making use of this model are intended to be blame-free, viewing accidents as "a failure of the system and not simply as the failure of a person, or people" (Maurino, quoted in MOT 2002a, p 103). Issues relating to blame and liability are intended to be addressed through a separate process, so as not to interfere with the analysis (House of Representatives 2002).

The inclination to blame

It is essential to recognise that achieving blame-free accident analyses may be difficult. Typically, people's behaviour is not viewed as determined or overly constrained by external circumstances. Rather, people tend to be viewed as "free agents", with choice and control over their behaviour. When someone makes a mistake, we tend to focus on dispositional factors (such as their carelessness or incompetence), rather than the circumstances that may have promoted their error (Moghaddam 1998; Reason 1997). We tend to assume that they could have acted differently, and we therefore hold them responsible. This is frequently what happens after a major accident.

Where there is no one in particular to blame, attention often shifts to the companies involved (Hunt 1996, p 4). Wells claims that the "pressure for vengeance is ubiquitous" and that, in cases where no individuals were at fault, accident survivors and victims' relatives have a "manifest desire" to hold companies themselves responsible for their errors (Wells 1995, p 177). Thus, while improvements in safety depend on accident investigations being blame-free, it is clear that identifying the causes of major accidents in a way that prevents the attribution of blame may, in practice, be difficult.

The Singapore Airlines crash

This chapter illustrates how blame can be read into systemic analyses based on Reason's approach by examining an actual aviation accident. The chosen example involves the investigation into the crash of Singapore Airlines flight SQ006. This Los Angeles-bound aircraft was scheduled to depart from Chiang Kai-Shek Airport, Taiwan, on the evening of 31 October 2000. A typhoon was approaching at the time and a situation of low visibility, heavy rain and strong winds prevailed. The Singapore Airlines pilots had been cleared to take off from runway 05 left (05L), but mistakenly lined up on the parallel runway 05 right (05R) — a "partially closed" runway which was intended to be used for taxiing purposes only (ASC 2002, p i). About half-way down runway 05R and out of the sight of the pilots at its entrance, a portion had been closed for construction work. The pilots were aware of the construction work on runway 05R but believed they were on runway 05L and so commenced take-off. The partially airborne aircraft collided with the construction equipment and ignited, killing 83 and seriously injuring 39 of the 179 people on board (ASC 2002; MOT 2002a).

Causes of the accident

The causes of the crash remain in dispute. On the one hand, the accident can be viewed as the result of pilot error, as the pilots "failed the basic test of navigation — to ensure that the aircraft ended up on the correct runway" (surviving passenger, quoted in Air Safety Week 3 June 2002, para 4). The pilots, who had a navigation chart of the airport, entered runway 05R instead of taking the next turn into runway 05L. There were several indications that they were on the incorrect runway. For instance, the instrument landing system (primarily used to locate the runway for landing) and the paravisual display (used to identify the runway centreline in low-visibility conditions) would both have indicated that the aircraft was not aligned with the runway 05L centreline. Runway 05R also had green taxiway centreline lights rather than white runway lights, and was 15 m narrower than the intended runway. There were also runway and taxiway signs and markings on the airport surface to inform the flight crew of their location (ASC 2002; MOT 2002a). It is evident, then, that the pilots had made an error by commencing take-off from the incorrect runway.

On the other hand, the accident can be understood as the result of airport deficiencies. A range of markings, signage and equipment at the airport did not meet ICAO requirements and recommendations. For instance, in accordance with ICAO requirements, the centreline markings on the taxiway should have branched into two paths (one to the right towards runway 05R and the other leading ahead towards runway 05L) to clearly show that there were two alternative taxi routes. However, at the time of the accident, the centreline markings led only towards the closed runway and did not continue ahead towards runway 05L (MOT 2002a). In accordance with ICAO recommendations, there should also have been 16 taxiway lights (no less than 7.5 m apart) leading from the taxiway towards the runway 05L holding position. There were, however, only four taxiway lights in the direction of the correct runway and only two were working properly, so that the first fully functional taxiway light was 116 m away from the point where the taxiway curved towards the closed runway (MOT 2002a). Thus, in the limited visibility of the evening, the only visible path led towards the closed runway 05R (MOT 2002a). It can therefore be argued that the airport lighting and markings did not provide "clear guidance" to runway 05L and instead provided a "compelling visual pathway" towards runway 05R (MOT 2002a, pp 17, 83).

In low-visibility conditions, ICAO standards also require flashing guard lights to be installed on either side of runway holding positions and stop bar lights to be placed at the holding line (MOT 2002a, p 9). Had these lights been present, they would have been directly in front of the aircraft before it turned onto runway 05R, indicating that runway 05L was still ahead (MOT 2002a).

International Civil Aviation Organization standards also require runway designation signs (for example, saying "05R") on either side of the holding positions of runways. However, at the time of the accident, there was only one sign for each runway and these signs were not in the required locations. Correct signage might have provided additional visual cues of the presence of runway 05L further along the taxiway (MOT 2002a, p 8).

There were also deficiencies in the measures taken to ensure that the closed runway did not appear to be operational. International Civil Aviation Organization annex 14 requires that, when a runway is closed, the threshold markings (or "piano keys") and designation signs should be removed and a runway closure marker added. However, at the time of the accident, runway 05R (which was to be permanently redesignated as a taxiway) still had all runway markings intact. Thus, it can be argued that, on entry to the closed runway 05R, the pilots "were presented with a picture of an operational runway" and were therefore not alerted to their mistake (MOT 2002a, pp iv, 30).

In accordance with international practice, there should also have been physical barriers across the threshold of the closed runway. Had these barriers been in place, the pilots would probably have realised that the runway was closed and, more significantly, the aircraft would have been physically prevented from entering the wrong runway and commencing take-off (MOT 2002a). Thus, the accident can be alternatively explained in terms of airport deficiencies since, had these safety precautions been in place, the accident would not have occurred.

Analysis of the accident

Unusually, two separate investigation reports were produced for this accident. The first, which was not a Reason-style analysis, concluded that the crash was primarily caused by pilot error. The second, a systemic analysis adopting Reason's approach, included airport deficiencies as causes of the crash. These reports, and the circumstances surrounding their production, provide valuable insight into the issue of blame in accident analysis.

The Taiwanese Aviation Safety Council's analysis

After a major aviation accident, the ICAO requires the state of occurrence to conduct an investigation. The body responsible for civil aviation accident investigation in Taiwan is the Aviation Safety Council. This Council conducted the accident analysis. Taiwan is not a contracting state of the ICAO, but nevertheless chose to investigate the crash in accordance with ICAO requirements (MOT 2002a).

According to ICAO annex 13, accredited representatives from relevant states other than the state of occurrence are permitted to "participate in all aspects" of the investigation, such as examining the evidence, visiting the accident scene, and participating in meetings regarding the analysis and causes of the accident (ICAO 2001, p 5-4). However, the annex comes with a note that it "is recognized that the form of participation would be subject to the procedures of the State in which the investigation, or part thereof, is being conducted" (ICAO 2001, p 5-5). The Taiwanese Council interpreted this note as meaning that it had "the full right to decide the extent of participation of the accredited representatives" (ASC 2002, p iii). On this basis, it decided that it would allow other parties (such as the Singapore Ministry of Transport, representing the state of operator, and the

United States National Transportation Safety Board, representing the state of manufacture) "to participate in all aspects of the investigation ... with the exception of item (h)" (ASC 2002, p iii). Item (h) concerns participation in "investigation process meetings including deliberations related to analysis, findings, causes and safety recommendations" (ASC 2002, p ii). The reason given for excluding other parties from participating in this phase of the analysis was that this allowed the Taiwanese Council "to maintain its independence" (ASC 2002, p iii).

The format that the Taiwanese Council used to list the causes of the accident was unusual. The ICAO recommends that the conclusions of an accident report should "list the findings and causes established in the investigation", including "both the immediate and the deeper systemic causes" of the accident (ICAO 2001, app 2). The ICAO recommends the use of Reason's approach in such situations (MOT 2002a). However, the Taiwanese Council chose not to categorise the conclusions into findings, immediate causes and systemic causes, but instead to categorise all of the conclusions as "findings". In what was described as "a few minor modifications" to annex 13, the findings and causes were grouped into three categories, defined as follows:

> "The **findings related to probable causes** identify elements that have been shown to have operated in the accident. These findings are associated with unsafe acts, unsafe conditions, or safety deficiencies associated with safety significant events that played a major role in the circumstances leading to the accident.
>
> The **findings related to risk** identify elements of risk that have the potential to degrade aviation safety. Some of the findings in this category identify unsafe acts, unsafe conditions, and safety deficiencies, including organizational and systemic risks, that made this accident more likely; however, they cannot be clearly shown to have operated in the accident alone. Further, some of the findings in this category identify risks that are unrelated to this accident, but nonetheless were safety deficiencies that may warrant future safety actions.
>
> **Other findings** identify elements that have the potential to enhance aviation safety, resolve an issue of controversy, or clarify an issue of unresolved ambiguity." (ASC 2002, pp iv, v)

The Taiwanese report identified eight "findings related to probable causes" for this accident. One of these was poor weather. The remaining seven related to the flight crew, including that they entered the wrong runway, inadequately verified the taxi route, and overlooked numerous indications of their error. These were the only findings that the Taiwanese Council concluded were "shown to have operated in the accident" (ASC 2002, pp iv-vi).

There were 36 "findings related to risk" listed in the Taiwanese report, that is, findings that may have made the accident more likely but "cannot be clearly shown to have operated in the accident alone", or may have been "unrelated to this accident" (ASC 2002, p v). These included the deficiencies at the Taiwanese airport, including the list of items of airport infrastructure that did not meet ICAO requirements or "internationally accepted standards and recommended practices" (ASC 2002, p vii). The report suggested that the airport deficiencies were not causes, stating that:

> "Appropriate attention given to these items could have enhanced the situational awareness of the flight crew … however, the absence of these enhancements was not deemed sufficient to have caused the loss of situational awareness of the flight crew." (ASC 2002, p vii)

Thus, the Taiwanese report concluded that pilot error and poor weather, but not the airport deficiencies, were the causes of the accident.

Responses to the Taiwanese report: the Taiwanese report received a negative response from many parties, particularly Singapore Airlines and the Singapore Ministry of Transport. Singapore Airlines argued that the findings section of the report did not give "due weight" to the airport deficiencies that "misled the pilots into taking off from the wrong runway" (Channel NewsAsia 26 April 2002b, para 4). Similarly, the Singapore Ministry argued that the report presented an inadequate account, as it "downplays significant systemic factors which contributed to the accident", namely, the airport's shortcomings and failure to conform to ICAO standards (Channel NewsAsia 26 April 2002c, para 2). The International Federation of Air Line Pilots' Associations reported being "dismayed" that the effects of "obvious critical airport deficiencies" were not considered (Channel NewsAsia 26 April 2002a, paras 1, 2).

The Singapore Ministry also criticised the report for failing to take a systemic approach. It argued that, in placing the primary focus on the flight crew, the Taiwanese report did not "consider the accident as a systemic failure" and consequently failed to account for the numerous factors contributing to this crash (MOT 2002c, p 31). The Singapore Ministry suggested that a systemic approach would have included causes such as the absence of warnings and barriers to prevent aircraft from entering and taking off from runway 05R (MOT 2002b).

In addition, the report was heavily criticised for its non-standard format. The Singapore Ministry claimed that, by listing only "findings" rather than the "immediate" and "systemic" causes of the accident, the report failed to conform to ICAO requirements (MOT 2002c, p 39). It insisted that the major airport deficiencies should have been categorised as "probable causes" of the accident rather than "findings related to risk" because, had the correct safety measures been in place, the accident would not have occurred (MOT 2002a, pp v, 101, 102). The Singapore Ministry criticised Taiwan's Council for classifying the factors and causes of this accident in an "arbitrary" manner, with the result that attention was directed "disproportionately towards particular factors" (MOT 2002c, p 39).

Interestingly, identifying the pilots as causing this crash was inevitable, given the format adopted by the Taiwanese Council. The definitions of the three categories of findings meant that human errors that contributed to the accident could only be listed in the "probable causes" section. However, systemic and organisational risks were, by the definitions provided, part of the findings related to risk category and so could not be classed as causes because the definition specified that such failures "cannot be clearly shown to have operated in the accident alone" (ASC 2002, p v). In light of the definitions used, the Singapore Ministry criticised the Taiwanese team for placing the causes of the accident with the weather and flight crew before the analysis had even begun (MOT 2002c, p 39).

Attribution of blame in the Taiwanese report: although the Taiwanese report began by stating that its intention was to be blame-free (ASC 2002), it was widely perceived to apportion blame. By concluding that seven of the eight causes of this accident related to the flight crew (and the other one to poor weather), the Taiwanese report indicated that the pilots should have acted differently and that no other factors were directly causal to the outcome. The managing director of Taiwan's Aviation Safety Council reinforced this conclusion, stating that: "There are many resources for the flight crew to use but they did not ... and if any one of them had been used or if the flight crew had used them properly ... it would have prevented the accident from happening" (Ming 2002, para 8). The Singapore Ministry claimed that, since the findings related to probable causes related only to the pilots and bad weather and not to the airport deficiencies, the outcome, whether intended or not, was that the pilots were "effectively 'blamed' for the accident" (MOT 2002c, p 39).

The causal analysis was also interpreted as an attribution of blame by numerous journalists who were reporting on the findings. For instance, CNN, Channel NewsAsia and the *Taipei Times* reported that the Taiwanese report blamed the pilots, or pilot error and bad weather, for the crash (CNN 26 April 2002; Dobson 2002; Ming 2002). Similarly, a number of *Straits Times* reports indicated that the Taiwanese report laid or "pinned" the blame for the accident mainly on the pilots (Get for me Singapore 2002). A spokesperson from the International Federation of Air Line Pilots' Associations noted that, while "responsible investigation authorities" no longer apportion blame in accident investigations, the causal statements in the Taiwanese report were "very clearly an assignment of blame" (Channel NewsAsia 29 April 2002, para 10).

The Singapore Ministry of Transport's analysis

The Singapore Ministry of Transport was dissatisfied with Taiwan's analysis, claiming that its inputs had not been considered adequately and that the report "presented an incomplete account" of the accident (MOT 2002a, p vii). The Singapore Ministry chose to conduct its own analysis of the accident, based on the "factual information" gathered by the Taiwanese Council (MOT 2002a, p vii). The Singapore Ministry stated that it hoped its alternative analysis "could lead to a better understanding of why the accident happened and how similar incidents could be prevented" (Channel NewsAsia, 26 April 2002c, para 9).

The Singapore team conducted a Reason-style analysis of the investigation, acknowledging that the pilots commenced take-off from the wrong runway, but seeking to understand how they made this error and why it resulted in the accident (MOT 2002a). In addition to considering the flight crew's actions and performance, it aimed to identify the organisational factors that contributed to the accident (in line with Reason's approach and ICAO requirements).

The Singapore team's report concluded that the accident was the result of "a failure of the aviation system" (MOT 2002a, p v). It listed 86 findings and contributing factors, and stated that the accident resulted from many factors at both the individual and organisational levels, all of which must be taken into account to prevent similar occurrences in the future (MOT 2002a, p 82).

In addition to pilot error, the Singaporean report included the deficiencies at the Taiwanese airport as contributing factors, arguing that the accident would have been prevented had barriers and visual warnings been present, "in accordance with ICAO standards and recommended practices, and with prudent safety practice" (MOT 2002a, p 101). The report highlighted the absence of guidance to lead the pilots towards the correct runway, barriers to prevent them from entering the incorrect runway, and cues to alert them of their mistake among the accident findings and contributing factors (MOT 2002a, p 101).

The Singaporean report also noted that two other pilots had almost made the same error as the Singapore Airlines flight crew within two weeks before the accident. Both pilots had recalled that there were no barriers to stop them from accidentally entering runway 05R and one had commented that, without "local knowledge" of the airport, it would have been easy to line up on runway 05R accidentally (MOT 2002a, pp iv, 28). From these occurrences, the Singaporean report concluded that "airport safety measures are critical in preventing crews from mistaking a closed runway for an operational runway" (MOT 2002a, p 58).

Responses to the Singaporean report: like the Taiwanese report, the Singaporean report was criticised on a number of points. It was referred to as an "over-the-top response" designed to "deflect blame" from the Singapore authorities (Singh nd, para 2). Singapore's Ministry was criticised for disputing almost every point made by the Taiwanese Council, resulting in "legalistic quibbling" (Hannon 2002, para 17). The report was also criticised for "downplaying" the critical role and responsibility of the pilots (Singh nd, para 2).

Attribution of blame in the Singaporean report: there were some suggestions in the media that the Singaporean report apportioned blame, with *BBC News* and *New York Times* articles summarising the report as blaming inadequacies at the airport for the crash (BBC 26 April 2002; Bradsher 2002, para 5). However, the Singaporean investigation was not widely criticised for apportioning blame.

Discussion

The circumstances surrounding the analysis of this accident raise an interesting question. Why did the Taiwanese Council avoid a standard systemic analysis in its investigation into this accident? The answer can be found if we examine its approach to the investigation.

The Taiwanese Council's approach was unusual in three significant respects. First, against the requirements of ICAO annex 13, the Council did not allow the other accredited representatives to participate in establishing the causes of the accident. Second, it developed a new format which was inconsistent with ICAO regulations and the format used by other major accident investigation bodies. Third, this new format did not permit organisational or systemic risks to be classified as "causes".

The Taiwanese Council was apparently familiar with Reason's approach to accident analysis, as is evident in the statement that it would use a "systemic approach" to the accident "in accordance with the general guidelines in ICAO annex 13 ... and the work of Reason" (ASC 2002, p 167). It is therefore reasonable to assume that the Council knew that a standard Reason-style investigation would have identified systemic and organisational failures among the causes of the accident. As is evident by its list of findings related to risk, the Taiwanese Council was also aware that the systemic and organisational failures included the major deficiencies at the Taiwanese airport and a lack of oversight and monitoring on the part of the Civil Aeronautics Administration of Taiwan (ASC 2002, pp vi-x). It can, therefore, be inferred that the Council knew that a systemic Reason-style analysis of the accident would identify deficiencies in Taiwan's aviation system among the causes of the crash.

Apparently, the Taiwanese Council felt that the blame for this accident would be attributed to the parties identified as responsible for its causes, as is clear from the statement that the report had not used the term "specific causes" because the issues of blame and liability were for the courts to decide (BBC 26 April 2002, paras 4, 5). The Council's notable departure from normal procedures can therefore be understood as an effort to ensure that the causes identified in the report would not lie with the Taiwanese authorities so that they could not be blamed for the accident. The Singapore transport minister made a similar point, suggesting that, when compiling the analysis, the Taiwanese authorities were trying to protect their own reputations rather than trying to search for the truth and prevent future accidents (Popatlal 2002).

Blame in systemic accident analysis

The Singapore Airlines example can be used to provide insight into the issue of blame in relation to systemic accident analyses using Reason's approach. Although such analyses are clearly intended to be blame-free, the effort on the part of Taiwan's Council to avoid such an analysis, as well as the suggestion that the Singaporean analysis blamed airport inadequacies for the accident, indicate that blame can nevertheless be inferred from these analyses.

It is important to recognise that the identification of causes and the acknowledgment of errors in these types of analysis do not logically imply blame. Rather, it seems that the strong tendency that people have, after accidents, to blame those responsible for the causes means that the identification of the causes in accident analyses can be *perceived* as an attribution of blame.

In systemic analyses based on Reason's model, the broader context within which an accident occurred — rather than the errors made by frontline individuals — is the focus of the analysis. However, such an approach does not necessarily eliminate blame from accident analyses, as blame can still be perceived as lying with those responsible for the cause(s) identified. Thus, rather than removing blame from accident analyses, such analyses may simply shift the blame from the frontline operators to those responsible for the systemic deficiencies identified. This conclusion can explain why those affiliated with the parties responsible for the systemic deficiencies may prefer to conduct a non-systemic analysis that identifies the causes elsewhere.

Clearly, such a situation is not conducive to uncovering the causes so that these can be rectified to prevent future accidents. If investigation reports are perceived to apportion blame to those responsible for the systemic deficiencies uncovered, investigators may not feel free to focus solely on gaining a comprehensive understanding of what went wrong for accident prevention purposes. Rather, a situation may occur in which efforts are directed towards blame-avoidance.

Managing blame in systemic accident analysis

Having concluded that systemic analyses can be perceived as attributing blame and that this situation may impede the capacity to learn from accidents, it is useful to consider how this problem might be resolved. The problem relates to the attribution of blame at the point where the causal analysis stops. If the analysis goes no further than identifying human errors as the cause of an accident, the result is that individuals are effectively blamed for the accident, as was arguably the case in the Taiwanese investigation. However, if the analysis goes beyond this point to consider *why* errors were made and *why* they resulted in the accident (in line with Reason's logic), the blame is shifted away from those individuals. In the Singapore Airlines crash, for instance, had the appropriate lighting, markings and barriers been in place, the pilots would have been less likely to turn into the incorrect runway and would not have been able to take off from it. If the analysis stops at this point, the blame for the accident shifts to airport management because, had it ensured that these defences and changes were implemented, the accident could not have occurred. In addition, had Taiwan had a system in place to ensure that airport management upheld international safety standards, runway 05R would probably have been properly closed and the accident would have been prevented. Concluding the analysis at this organisational level, as was done in the Singaporean report, means that blame is essentially shifted from the pilots and rests with the airport management and Taiwanese authorities. Reason-style analyses typically stop at this level — not because it is impossible to proceed further, but for practical reasons. Specifically, it is suggested that analyses should continue until the factors that can be corrected to improve the system's safety have been identified. The people who are "most concerned and best equipped to do this", it is argued, "are those within the organization(s) involved, so it makes practical sense to stop the analysis at these organizational boundaries" (Maurino et al 1995, p 4; Reason 1997, p 15).

However, if we go on to consider *why* these organisational failures and deficiencies occurred, the blame will be shifted to the next level. This process could be continued until a point is reached where blame is shifted to a level where it no longer impedes the analysis process. This can occur once the causes identified are sufficiently remote from the event under investigation so that the people responsible for them cannot reasonably be blamed for the accident. Alternatively, it can occur if blame is simply shifted beyond the level at which conflicts of interest arise. It may be the case, for instance, that blame rests with political or societal trends with which investigators need not be concerned.

Reason notes that the extension of accident analyses to such levels is certainly possible, but rejects this move because the focus should be on controllable factors. Such extensions, he points out, reveal causes that are beyond the control of system managers and are essentially "given and immutable" (Reason 1997, p 16). However, the given and immutable nature of such factors can alternatively be seen as the reason why it is useful to conclude analyses at this point. It is easy to associate blame with factors that could and should, in hindsight, have been different. When this is not the case, the association between cause and blame becomes less intuitive.

There are obvious difficulties with extending accident analyses to these higher levels. Identifying remote causes requires considerable research into why the organisational failures occurred. The answers are likely to relate to political or social issues which may be complex, difficult to establish as direct causes, unrelated to the accident under investigation, and beyond the area of expertise of accident investigators. However, numerous analysts have shown that it is possible to continue analyses in this way, extending their analyses beyond the organisation(s) involved to include causes at the broader regulatory and government levels (Rasmussen & Svedung 2000; Woo & Vicente 2003). Others have shown that the causes of organisational accidents can, in fact, be traced back to broader societal factors such as market forces, outsourcing, political events, privatisation, and public pressures (Hopkins 2000a, 2005; RAAF 2001; Snook 2000). If analyses are extended in this way, the context within which the organisational deficiencies occurred is understood, and blame for the accident is shifted beyond both the immediate individuals involved and the organisation(s) and regulatory bodies. Thus, investigators can direct their efforts towards identifying the causes of accidents and preventing recurrence, rather than deflecting blame. Such an approach would not necessarily eliminate blame, since blame may simply be shifted to these higher levels. Several rail accidents, for instance, have been "blamed on privatisation" (ABC 16 March 2004; BBC 21 September 1999). However, shifting blame to this level means that it no longer interferes with the causal analysis. The adoption of such an approach may, therefore, be useful in cases where blame avoidance is thought to interfere with the analysis process.

This type of solution can be illustrated by continuing the causal sequence described in the Singapore Airlines crash and considering *why* the Taiwanese Civil Aeronautics Administration may not have ensured that international safety standards were upheld by airport management. If the analysis extends to this point, reasons behind this failure can also be explored. While the reason was not addressed as a "cause" of the crash in either analysis, the Taiwanese report referred to it in its findings:

> "Being a non-contracting state, the [Taiwanese Civil Aeronautics Administration] … does not have the opportunity to participate in ICAO activities in developing its airport safety enhancement programs to correspond to international safety standards and recommended practices." (ASC 2002, p viii)

Chapter

9

For the purposes of this example, it could be argued that, if Taiwan had been a contracting state of the ICAO, the Taiwanese Civil Aeronautics Administration would probably have ensured that international aviation standards were upheld and the airport would therefore probably have had the required safety precautions in place. The analysis can be continued. Taiwan is not a contracting state of the ICAO because the ICAO is a suborganisation of the United Nations, of which

Taiwan is not a member. Taiwan's exclusion from the UN, in turn, relates to the one-China policy in which Taiwan is considered to be a province of China rather than a sovereign state, and thus ineligible to join the UN as a separate state.

The purpose of extending the analysis in this way is simply that it shifts the blame away from the Taiwanese authorities to a point where it no longer interferes with the accident analysis process. Obviously, those responsible for the circumstances which exclude Taiwan from the UN in this example cannot meaningfully be blamed for the accident. Although it may be possible to trace the causes of the accident back to them, their actions are so unrelated to, and distant from, the events leading up to the crash that they cannot be blamed.

Conclusion

Drawing on an example of the analysis of an aviation accident, this chapter has shown that, while systemic analyses incorporating the Reason model are theoretically blame-free, such analyses can nevertheless be perceived as apportioning blame. As a result, the identification of relevant causes may be impeded by the desire to avoid blame. It was suggested, however, that such analyses could potentially be extended so that the allocation of blame no longer interferes with the analysis process. While such modifications raise a number of practical issues, they could allow the full benefits of this form of analysis in improving system safety to be realised.

CHAPTER 10

GUIDELINES FOR ACCIMAP ANALYSIS

Kate Branford, Neelam Naikar and Andrew Hopkins

Introduction

This chapter focuses on a systems-based technique for accident analysis, referred to as the AcciMap approach.[1] The technique involves the construction of a multilayered diagram in which the various causes of an accident are arranged according to their causal remoteness from the outcome. It is particularly useful for establishing how factors in all parts of a sociotechnical system contributed to an organisational accident,[2] and for arranging the causes into a coherent diagram that reveals how they interacted to produce that outcome. By identifying these causal factors and the interrelationships between them in this way, it is possible to identify problem areas that should be addressed to improve the safety of the system and prevent similar occurrences in the future.

AcciMaps have been used to analyse accidents involving the contamination of drinking water (Vicente & Christoffersen 2006; Woo & Vicente 2003), the Toronto severe acute respiratory syndrome outbreak (Piché & Vicente 2005), the Esso Longford gas plant explosion (Hopkins 2000a), the Glenbrook train crash (Hopkins 2005), and several Australian Defence Force aircraft accidents (Naikar, Saunders & Hopkins 2002; RAAF 2001), among others. However, a lack of consistency in how the technique has been applied and the absence of documentation regarding how to conduct such analyses have prevented the approach from being readily accessible to new users. The aim of this chapter is to present a standardised AcciMap format (based on elements of the existing AcciMap varieties) and guidelines for applying the technique. The first part of this chapter discusses the development of the standardised AcciMap approach. The second part presents guidelines for conducting AcciMap analyses.

---

1   Pronounced *axi-map*, for the *map* of an *accident*.
2   *Organisational* accidents (the type of event that AcciMaps are designed to analyse) are those accidents that take place in complex sociotechnical systems (such as nuclear power stations, chemical process facilities, and aviation, marine and rail transport systems), have "multiple causes involving many people operating at different levels of their respective companies", and can result in damage to people, assets or the environment (Reason 1997, p 1).

Part A: Standardising the AcciMap approach

The AcciMap approach

The AcciMap was developed by Rasmussen (1997) as part of a process for generating proactive risk management strategies for complex sociotechnical systems. Rasmussen views organisational accidents as the result of the loss of control over potentially harmful physical processes, and therefore sees safety as requiring "control of work processes so as to avoid accidental side effects causing harm to people, environment, or investment" (1997, p 184). The AcciMap was developed as a means of analysing the series of events and decision-making processes that interacted to result in this loss of control. For Rasmussen, the AcciMap was one part of a broader process for generalising from a series of accidents to define the conditions for safe operation in a particular type of system, so that risk management strategies could be devised (Rasmussen & Svedung 2000).

However, the AcciMap approach has also been used independently of this broader process to analyse the causes of single accidents. Woo and Vicente (2003), for instance, have used the approach to analyse separate accidents in an effort to determine the types of risk factor that might be common to different systems. Other analysts (Hopkins 2000a, 2005; Naikar, Saunders & Hopkins 2002; RAAF 2001) have used it solely to analyse accidents and assist in safety recommendation development.

The AcciMap approach involves the construction of a causal diagram depicting the events and conditions that interacted to result in an accident. The AcciMap itself is a tree-shaped diagram, with the accident located near the bottom and the causes of that event branching upward (with the more immediate causes in the lower sections of the diagram and the more remote causes towards the top). The causal factors are arranged into a series of levels representing the different parts of the sociotechnical system in which the event took place. The lower levels show the immediate precursors to the accident, while the higher levels incorporate organisational, governmental, regulatory and, in some cases, societal factors that played a role in the occurrence. Each of the causal factors in the diagram is linked to its effects in a way that illustrates how that factor influenced other factors and contributed to the outcome. An AcciMap is therefore a graphical representation of the events and conditions that came together to produce an organisational accident.

There are a number of advantages to this approach. First, it enables analysts to compile large amounts of information — regarding the numerous causes of an organisational accident, the area of the sociotechnical system in which each factor arose, and precisely how the factors came together to produce the accident — within a single, coherent diagram. Such an approach is useful, not only for conveying this information to others in a succinct and logical form, but also for assisting the analyst in building and maintaining an understanding of the complex combination of factors that resulted in the outcome.

Second, the approach promotes a systemic view of accident causation. The AcciMap diagram extends well beyond the immediate causes of an accident to uncover the range of factors throughout the system that promoted the conditions in which an accident occurred, or which failed to prevent the negative outcome. The diagram identifies the factors that led directly to the accident and then progressively identifies the causes of each of these factors, so that the decisions, events and conditions that created the circumstances in which the accident took place are identified. The diagram therefore provides the necessary context for gaining a comprehensive understanding of how and why an accident happened. It also prevents excessive attention from being directed towards the immediate causes of accidents (such as human errors) because the diagram shows that these are the result of higher-level factors, rather than the sole causes. The approach therefore promotes Reason's (1997, 2000) *systems approach* to accident analysis, which is recommended by major accident investigation bodies. The systems approach acknowledges the influences and constraints on the behaviour of individuals working in a system and aims not to blame them for honest errors, but to uncover the systemic deficiencies that provoked those errors and/or failed to prevent them from resulting in an accident. Such an approach focuses on repairing systemic deficiencies to prevent future accidents, rather than reprimanding the individuals involved and leaving the deficiencies that promoted their actions unaddressed.

A third major advantage of the AcciMap approach is that it assists in safety recommendation development. The way the causal factors and their flow-on effects are illustrated in an AcciMap means that analysts can work systematically through the diagram to pinpoint the factors that, if corrected, could prevent a range of potentially hazardous situations from arising. The grouping of the factors into the levels of the sociotechnical system assists in this respect by separating the factors for which corrective actions are useful (namely, those at the organisational level and above) from the *consequences* of those factors (which should not be addressed directly in accordance with a systems approach to accident analysis). The capacity of AcciMaps to incorporate contributing factors beyond the organisational level (for example, factors relating to legislation, regulations, certification, auditing, and government decisions) is also beneficial because identifying these high-level causes enables equally high-level safety recommendations to be devised. This is a "particularly desirable feature" of AcciMaps "because the higher the level of the corrective action, the broader is the class of unwanted events which may be prevented" (Hopkins 2003, p 2). A safety recommendation directed towards a regulatory inadequacy, for instance, can help to improve safety in all organisations

Chapter

10

under the influence of that regulator, rather than just the single company affected by the accident in question. In addition, since high-level system problems generally have far-reaching negative effects, with the potential to contribute to a number of different types of accident (Reason 1997), addressing these problems can help to prevent a variety of negative outcomes, rather than just a recurrence of the same event.

A major disadvantage of the AcciMap approach, however, is its inaccessibility to new users. In the published examples of AcciMap analyses, the format, underlying logic, scope of analysis, and process taken have all varied, depending on the particular purpose and nature of the analysis. For this reason, a standard format and process for other analysts to follow has not been available. The purpose of this chapter is to present such a format, along with detailed guidelines for use.

The standardised AcciMap

The standardised AcciMap presented in this chapter was not developed by formalising any one of the existing varieties but, rather, by selecting and incorporating the factors common to these varieties and the factors judged most suitable for retrospective accident analysis purposes. The aim in bringing together the existing varieties in this way was to create a standardised approach that incorporates a strict causal logic for identifying causal factors and illustrates how they contributed to the outcome. In addition, the standardised AcciMap is intended to promote the development of safety recommendations and is not specific to a particular domain, so it can be used to analyse organisational accidents in any sociotechnical system. The standardised AcciMap format chosen for these purposes is shown in Figure 1, and the features of the format are described below.

The outcomes

The accident itself, that is, the final negative outcome to be analysed, is located in the lowest section of the diagram with the causes branching upward (as in AcciMaps by Hopkins). In some existing AcciMaps (Rasmussen 1997; Woo & Vicente 2003), the lowest level incorporates factors relating to equipment and physical surroundings, while the immediate accident sequence is located in the second-lowest level, ordered from left to right in temporal order. The placement of the outcome at the bottom of the diagram, in the standardised approach, enables all causes to be arranged strictly in terms of their causal remoteness from the outcome, rather than having causes located both above and below it. This means that all causal links in the diagram face downwards, making the causal chains easy to follow and giving the diagram a logical "tree" structure. Contrary to some versions, there is no suggestion here of a time line moving from left to right. The temporal order must be ascertained from the causal connections, as discussed below.

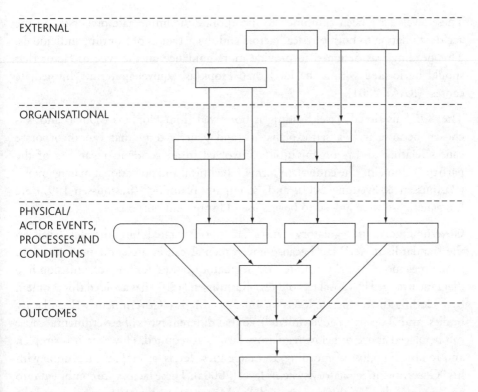

FIGURE 1: The standardised AcciMap format

AcciMap levels

The levels in the existing varieties of AcciMap vary, not only by the overall format adopted, but also by the system in which the accident occurred. However, all are generally modelled on the interacting levels in a complex sociotechnical system, ranging from government and regulatory levels down to the organisational and workplace levels (Rasmussen 1997). The criteria used to select the levels during the standardisation of the approach were that they should be unambiguous, that they should be non-domain-specific, and that they should preserve the causal remoteness in the diagram.

The "Outcomes" heading is adopted from one of Hopkins' AcciMaps (RAAF 2001). On occasions where one negative outcome leads to another (for example, a plane crash and a post-crash fire), more than one outcome can be located in this level.

The "Physical/actor events, processes and conditions" level combines the two lowest levels ("Physical processes and actor activities" and "Equipment and surroundings") of AcciMaps by Rasmussen (1997) and others (Vicente & Christoffersen 2006).

Chapter

10

These levels have been combined to incorporate the immediate precursors to the accident relating to both physical factors and the activities of frontline individuals. This heading was designed to provide more guidance on the type of factor that should be located within the level than Hopkins' equivalent term, "Immediate causes" (RAAF 2001).

The "Organisational" level heading is borrowed from Hopkins (2000a) and was chosen because it is a self-explanatory and generic term that can incorporate causes relating to any organisation(s) involved in an accident, regardless of the particular domain. The equivalent terms, "Technical and operational management" (Rasmussen & Svedung 2000) and "Company planning" (Rasmussen 1997) are less generic, so were judged to be less useful for present purposes.

Governmental and regulatory causes are not separated into distinct levels in the standardised AcciMap because governmental causes are sometimes less, and sometimes more, causally remote than regulatory causes, leading to confusion in a diagram arranged by causal remoteness. Rasmussen (1997) has avoided this problem by including three separate levels in some AcciMaps ("Government", "Regulatory bodies" and "Local area government"), so that different types of governmental cause can be placed above or below regulatory factors as required. However, it is simpler, and results in no loss of meaning, to merge these levels, as Hopkins has done with his "Government/regulatory system" level (2000a). These factors are combined into an "External" level in the standardised AcciMap, representing *all* factors beyond the control of the relevant organisation(s). This level includes all causes relating to the government and regulatory bodies and can also incorporate societal-level causes, as Hopkins has included in his AcciMaps (2000a).

Causal factors

The causes in the standardised AcciMap are factors that were *necessary* for the accident to occur, as in Hopkins' AcciMaps. This is because the diagram is designed to identify all of the factors that caused (or failed to prevent) a particular accident, so that an understanding can be gained of how it occurred and where corrective action could be taken to prevent similar occurrences in the future. However, to set useful boundaries on the causes identified, such causes are only included if they are of "practical significance" (that is, if something could conceivably be done about them) (Hopkins 2000a, p 22) or if they are *necessary for making sense of how and why the accident occurred* (that is, if the sequence of events does not make sense without them). The latter are included solely to ensure that the AcciMap contains sufficient information for readers to understand how the accident occurred. These factors are easily distinguished from the others because they are drawn in rectangles with curved edges (the symbol used by Svedung and Rasmussen (2002, p 407) to signify preconditions that are "evaluated no further").

To preserve the simplicity of the diagram, other symbols from the existing varieties of AcciMap are omitted in the standardised AcciMap. These include Rasmussen and Svedung's (2000, p 21) "Decision/action" boxes which show the decision and the "accidental side effect" of that decision in adjacent rectangles, and decision switches, phrased as "yes" or "no" questions (Woo & Vicente 2003). In the standardised approach, decisions which affected the outcome are displayed as rectangles, along with the other events and conditions that were necessary for the outcome. "AND gates", representing instances in which multiple factors were required in order for a consequence to occur, are also excluded from the standardised AcciMap. The same concept is represented simply by allowing several arrows to converge on a single outcome box.

The AcciMap guidelines (presented in Part B of this chapter) specify the process by which analysts can "extract" the necessary causes from the accident data.[3] The process involves the analyst identifying all factors for which he/she can say "had this been otherwise, the accident would probably not have occurred". The analyst is later required to ask *why* each factor took place, in order to identify all of the factors that caused or failed to prevent it. This process of asking "why?" is a common procedure for uncovering additional information in accident analyses and is used by Naikar, Saunders and Hopkins (2002), among others, to identify the systemic causes of accidents. A table providing examples of causes at each AcciMap level is provided in the guidelines to assist analysts in selecting the appropriate level for the causes uncovered. The guidelines suggest that analysts refer to this table during the analysis to check that they have not overlooked any relevant causes. The guidelines also encourage analysts to phrase these factors in a way that focuses the analysis on the systemic contributors, rather than the particular individuals involved.

Causal connections

For Rasmussen and Svedung, AcciMaps are not intended to be a "truthful representation of facts" but rather to identify "factors sensitive to improvement", that is, all of the decision-makers whose decisions could have influenced the events in the lower levels of the diagram. The arrows in their diagrams therefore refer to "influences", but do not necessarily imply causality (2000, pp 20-21). When using the AcciMap approach for the purpose of identifying the causes of accidents, as the standardised AcciMap approach is designed to do, it is useful to adopt more stringent criteria. The arrows in the standardised AcciMap therefore imply strict causation, in the way used by Hopkins (2000a) and Woo and Vicente (2003) in their AcciMaps. A factor is only linked to another if the first was necessary in order for the second to occur. The sequences of causal factors and arrows (or "causal

---

3 Note that the AcciMap guidelines are designed for analysing accidents using the data collected during the accident investigation, rather than during the initial data-gathering phase.

connections") in an AcciMap therefore illustrate the causes and effects that led to the outcome. In order to promote logical and coherent AcciMaps, the guidelines suggest that one cause should only be linked to another if the second was a *direct* cause of the first, that is, that no other factor needs to be inserted between them in order for a reader to understand how the first cause led to the second. The different ways in which causes can be arranged in the diagram are also specified in order to avoid repetition of causal factors and to ensure that broad problem areas are depicted appropriately.

Safety recommendations

The guidelines provide instructions on how to devise a list of safety recommendations from an AcciMap. Most AcciMap analysts have not extended their analyses to safety recommendation development. However, Hopkins (RAAF 2001) and Naikar, Saunders and Hopkins (2002) have continued their analyses to include safety recommendations since, if analyses identify the causes and do not go on to identify safety recommendations, the "hard won lessons will be to no avail" (RAAF 2001, p 1.4).

Safety recommendations are not generated automatically once an AcciMap is complete, and it is not the case that every cause identified should be addressed directly. Rather, safety recommendations "must stem from a consideration of where it is sensible to seek to make changes" (Naikar, Saunders & Hopkins 2002, p 4). The AcciMap guidelines therefore show how safety recommendation formulation should be approached but leave the analyst to judge how safety can best be improved. The guidelines specify the types of cause for which recommendations should be formulated, namely, all of those which could potentially be changed, controlled or compensated for to prevent a similar accident from occurring in the future. They also help the analyst to use the type of wording and level of specificity appropriate for a systems approach to accident analysis.

The guidelines for conducting an AcciMap analysis in the way described above are written in the following stand-alone section, and can be used by analysts who are unfamiliar with the AcciMap approach. They therefore begin with a background section and a sample AcciMap, followed by step-by-step instructions for performing the analysis. The AcciMap guidelines were developed on the basis of the published descriptions of AcciMap analyses (Hopkins 2000a; Rasmussen & Svedung 2000; Vicente & Christoffersen 2006; Woo & Vicente 2003), supplemented with the authors' experience in performing AcciMap analyses, and have been tested and revised in a series of pilot studies. This process was undertaken as part of a project for investigating the reliability and validity of AcciMap analyses (Branford 2007). The guidelines have subsequently been revised for the purposes of this chapter.

Part B: Guidelines for AcciMap analysis

Background to AcciMap analysis[4]

The AcciMap approach is a technique for analysing the causes of accidents. It involves arranging the various causes of an accident into a tree-shaped diagram, with the negative outcome(s) (the accident itself) at the bottom and the causes branching upward. The approach is useful for:

- identifying the broad range of factors that contributed to an accident;
- illustrating how those factors combined to result in the outcome; and
- indicating problem areas that should be addressed to prevent similar events from occurring in the future.

Sample AcciMap

Figure 2 is an example of an AcciMap analysis of a train accident that occurred near Waterfall, NSW, in 2003.[5] Details of the accident are as follows:

> "At approximately 0714 on 31 January 2003, State Rail Authority [SRA] passenger train service C311, a scheduled service from Sydney to Port Kembla, overturned at high speed and collided with stanchions and a rock cutting approximately 2 km south of Waterfall NSW. The train was carrying 47 passengers and two crew. As a result of the accident, the driver and six passengers were killed. The four-car Tangara train, identified as G7, was extensively damaged. The investigation found there was a high probability that the driver became incapacitated at the controls as a result of a pre-existing medical condition, shortly after departing Waterfall Station. The train then continued to accelerate, out of control, with maximum power applied. The deadman system and the guard were the designated risk controls against driver incapacitation. Both controls failed to intervene as intended and C311 overturned on a curve while travelling at approximately 117 km/h … The immediate cause of the accident was the train exceeding the overturning speed for the curve. The systemic causes of the accident were the simultaneous failures of risk controls in the areas of medical standards, deadman system and training." (Ministry of Transport 2003, p 5)

Chapter
10

4 This brief introduction is repetitive in the present context but it is included for readers who want to use Part B as a stand-alone document.
5 The AcciMap shown in Figure 2 is for illustrative purposes only and does not incorporate all information relevant to this occurrence. For additional details, see Ministry of Transport (2003). The AcciMap and safety recommendations are derived from information contained in this report.

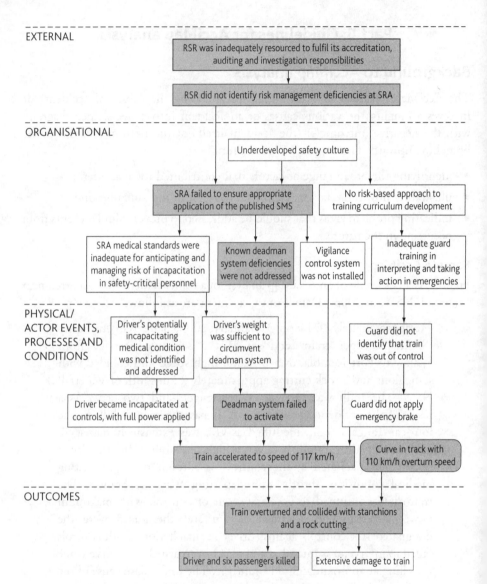

FIGURE 2: Sample AcciMap of Waterfall train accident

The sample AcciMap identifies the accident (in the lowest level of the diagram) and its causes (displayed as boxes and grouped according to their respective levels of causal remoteness). The arrows in the diagram signify causality, with an arrow from one factor to another indicating that the first *caused* the second. By examining the chains of causes in the AcciMap, it is possible to understand the sequence of events and the conditions that produced the accident, and to show that, had any one factor been otherwise, the accident would most likely have been avoided. By following the shaded chain of causes in Figure 2, it is evident that the train overturned and collided with stanchions and a rock cutting (resulting in multiple fatalities) because it accelerated to 117 km/h and exceeded the overturning speed for a curve in the track. One reason why the train accelerated to this speed was that the deadman system, designed to apply emergency breaking in the event of driver incapacitation, failed to activate. The reason for the lack of activation was that a known deficiency with the deadman system, namely, that it was ineffective as a defence against driver incapacitation for drivers weighing more than 110 kg, had not been addressed, and the incapacitated driver in this instance weighed in excess of 110 kg. Following the arrows upwards in the diagram, the reasons why this situation occurred, or was not prevented from occurring, become evident. Had the State Rail Authority (SRA) ensured that the published safety management system (SMS) was applied appropriately, the known risk with the deadman system would probably have been identified, assessed and controlled. The failure to ensure that the published SMS was applied appropriately therefore allowed this deficiency to remain unaddressed. The deficiency in the application of the SMS also remained unaddressed, in part because the rail safety regulator (RSR) did not identify the risk management deficiencies at the SRA and did not, therefore, take action to address them. Continuing to the top of the diagram, it is evident that the RSR did not identify these deficiencies because it did not have sufficient resources to fulfil all of its accreditation, auditing and investigation responsibilities effectively.

By following each of the causal chains up from the accident in this way, it is possible to develop an understanding of how each of the factors came about and how they combined to produce the final outcomes.

It should be noted that there is a potentially infinite number of causes for any event. As Reason (1997) points out, any causal chain could, in theory, be extended back to the big bang. However, for the purposes of accident investigation, only two types of cause are included:

1. causes of *practical significance*. These are causes that something could conceivably be done about (Hopkins 2000a). Note that the sample AcciMap does not show, for instance, that "had the train been scheduled to depart on a different day" or "had the passengers been travelling by bus" the accident would not have occurred. These causes are not of practical significance as no sensible actions can conceivably be taken to address them; and

2. causes that are not of practical significance, but that are necessary for making sense of why the accident occurred. These causes (depicted as ovals) are only included if the AcciMap *does not make sense without them*. The cause "Curve in

track with 110 km/h overturn speed" is included in the sample AcciMap for this reason. There is not much that can conceivably be done about it (since curves in rail tracks are not inherently dangerous and cannot always be avoided). However, it is necessary to include this cause in order for readers to understand why the train overturned. This category of cause includes factors that contributed to the negative outcome(s) but cannot conceivably be changed, either because it would not be sensible or would not be plausible or possible to do so. Causes relating to environmental conditions, physical surroundings, and ongoing social, political or economic conditions may fit into this category.

Safety recommendations

Once the AcciMap diagram has been completed, with the relevant causes identified at each level, a list of safety recommendations can be compiled. A list of recommendations from the sample AcciMap is shown in Figure 3. The recommendations are grouped in terms of the party responsible for carrying out the proposed action.

The types of recommendation made depend on the causes in the AcciMap:

- some causes can be *rectified directly*. For instance, the lack of a vigilance control system as an additional defence against driver incapacitation can be rectified directly by recommending that the operator considers installing such a system to its fleet of trains (recommendation 8);

- some causes cannot be rectified directly, but recommendations can be made to *prevent their occurrence*. For instance, the cause "Guard did not identify that train was out of control" cannot be dealt with directly, but recommendations can be made to improve the training provided to crews in interpreting and taking appropriate action in emergency situations so that this situation will be less likely to recur (recommendation 9); and

- other causes cannot be prevented (that is, those depicted as ovals), but efforts can be made to *compensate for their effects*, where appropriate. For instance, the cause "Curve in track with 110 km/h overturn speed" cannot reasonably be prevented. However, the overturn and collision that occurred, in part, as a result of this factor can be compensated for by strengthening the defences against excessive train speeds, such as those relating to driver health, deadman systems, vigilance control systems, and the guard (recommendations 6 to 9).

Note that there are no recommendations specific to the actual individuals involved in the incident. For example, there are no recommendations to punish or dismiss the guard for failing to apply the emergency brakes. This is because other guards in the same situation, with the same training and equipment, may easily have

---

Government

Recommendation 1: the RSR should be provided with sufficient resources to develop an effective rail safety regulatory regime and to fulfil its auditing and accreditation responsibilities.

Rail Safety Regulator

Recommendation 2: the RSR should review and improve its capacity to identify risk management deficiencies and effectively audit operator safety management systems.

State Rail Authority

Recommendation 3: the SRA should assess and take action to address safety culture deficiencies, particularly with regard to the application of the published safety management system.

Recommendation 4: the SRA should take steps to ensure that the published safety management system is understood and applied appropriately by all employees.

Recommendation 5: the SRA should adopt a risk-based approach to training curriculum development which ensures that hazards to be addressed through training are identified and incorporated into training.

Recommendation 6: the SRA should review and improve the medical standards applied to safety-critical personnel to ensure that risks relating to potentially incapacitating medical conditions are identified and addressed appropriately.

Recommendation 7: the SRA should address the deficiencies with the deadman system, particularly in relation to the risk of inadvertent circumvention for drivers with a body mass in excess of 110 kg.

Recommendation 8: the SRA should consider fitting vigilance control systems to its fleet of trains as an additional defence against driver incapacitation.

Recommendation 9: the SRA should ensure that all crews are trained adequately in interpreting and taking appropriate action in emergency situations.

FIGURE 3: Safety recommendations from sample AcciMap

made the same mistake.[6] Therefore, rather than aiming to change the behaviour of the particular individuals involved, safety recommendations should address the inadequacies that *allowed* this situation to occur at all, so that *any* individual in a similar situation will be prevented from making this type of mistake.

Instructions for AcciMap analysis

Chapter

10

AcciMaps can be constructed using a whiteboard or large sheet of paper and sticky notes (as described below) or electronically, depending on the analyst's preference.

---

6 See Ministry of Transport (2003) for full details of the factors contributing to the guard's behaviour.

Step 1. Create a blank AcciMap format on which to arrange the causes: separate the whiteboard or large sheet of paper into the four sections of the AcciMap, with the headings of the four levels on the left-hand side and horizontal lines separating each level (as in Figure 2).

Step 2. Identify the outcome(s): (1) from the accident data, identify the negative outcome(s) to be analysed; and (2) insert the outcome(s) into the "Outcomes" level of the AcciMap.

Step 3. Identify the causal factors: on a separate page, make a list of all causes in the accident data, that is, all factors for which you can say "had this been otherwise, the accident would (probably) not have occurred". If you are unsure as to whether or not a factor is a cause, include it in the list — it can always be eliminated at a later stage.

Step 4. Identify the appropriate AcciMap level for each cause: next to each cause, write down the name of the AcciMap level in which it belongs. Refer to Table 1 to determine the correct level. The first column in Table 1 defines the levels of an AcciMap and the second provides examples of the types of cause that may be found at each level.

TABLE 1: Level definitions and examples[7]

I. Level definitions	II. Categories of cause		
The EXTERNAL level includes causes that are beyond the control of the organisation(s). This level includes factors relating to →	GOVERNMENT, for example: • budgeting issues, government cost cutting • inadequate legislation • privatisation, outsourcing • inadequate provision of services	REGULATORY BODIES, for example, inadequate: • regulations, communication of regulations • certification, permits • safety standards • enforcement of regulations • auditing	SOCIETY, for example: • market forces • societal values, priorities (such as the public's requirement for quality, efficiency, comfort, affordability) • historical events • global politics

---

7 This list of examples incorporates causal factors identified by Hopkins (2000a), Kletz (1993), Naikar, Saunders & Hopkins (2002), Rasmussen & Svedung (2000), Reason (1997), RAAF (2001), Snook (2000), Vicente & Christoffersen (2006), and Woo & Vicente (2003).

I. Level definitions	II. Categories of cause	
The **ORGANISATIONAL** level incorporates causes relating to organisational processes. Factors are placed in this level if they are within the control of the organisation(s) involved, for example →	**FINANCIAL ISSUES**, for example: • organisational budgeting, cost cutting • resource allocation problems **EQUIPMENT AND DESIGN**, for example: • design problems (such as ergonomic issues, inaccessibility) • equipment problems (such as poor quality, defective, ageing, untidy, missing or poorly-maintained equipment or tools) • equipment not used as designed **DEFENCES**, for example, inadequate, insufficient or missing: • proactive system defences (such as alarms, warnings, barriers, personal protective equipment) • reactive system defences (such as hazard containment, protection, escape and rescue systems) **COMMUNICATION AND INFORMATION**, for example, inadequate: • information or knowledge • flow or organisation of information • communication of instructions, hazards, priorities, objectives, etc **AUDITING AND RULE ENFORCEMENT**, for example, inadequate: • implementation and enforcement of rules, regulations or procedures • internal auditing, inspection	**ORGANISATIONAL CULTURE**, for example: • incompatible goals (between safety and production or safety and budget, etc) • organisational acceptance or encouragement of short cuts, non-compliance, etc **RISK MANAGEMENT**, for example, inadequate: • hazard identification or risk assessment • hazard or defects reporting • processes for learning from past mistakes • awareness of risks • security (such as protection from unauthorised access) **MANUALS AND PROCEDURES**, for example: • inadequate, ambiguous, conflicting, outdated, absent or difficult to follow procedures, rules, regulations or manuals **HUMAN RESOURCES**, for example, inadequate or insufficient: • supervision, management, coordination, staff numbers • delegation, accountability • staff selection procedures or criteria **TRAINING**, for example, inadequate or insufficient: • training, training equipment, training exercises • training needs analysis

... continued

Chapter

10

I. Level definitions	II. Categories of cause	
PHYSICAL/ACTOR EVENTS, PROCESSES AND CONDITIONS are the immediate precursors to the outcome(s) and should include factors relating to →	**PHYSICAL EVENTS, PROCESSES AND CONDITIONS,** for example: • physical sequence of events (including technical failures) • environmental conditions and factors relating to physical surroundings which are necessary for making sense of the sequence of events	**ACTOR ACTIVITIES AND CONDITIONS,** for example: • human errors, mistakes, violations, actions, activities, etc • false perceptions, misinterpretations, misunderstandings, loss of situational awareness, etc • physical and mental status of actors (such as fatigue, ill health, inattention, unconsciousness, intoxication)

Step 5. Prepare the causes: write each identified cause on a sticky note (or equivalent), making sure that you:

- keep it brief;

- use wording that makes it clear how things might have been different, that is, don't just say "training" or "operator actions", say "inadequate training" or "operator failed to monitor temperature" so that what went wrong is clear; and

- use wording that suits the level that the cause is located in:
    - causes at the "Physical/actor events, processes and conditions" level should be phrased in terms of the actual errors, failures, conditions and events that led to the accident (for example, "life raft failed to inflate" or "pilot failed to adjust heading"); and
    - causes at the "Organisational" level and above should not focus on the particular individuals involved (for example, say "inadequate pilot training", *not* "Pete Smith had not been adequately trained").

Insert each sticky note (cause) into its appropriate level in the AcciMap.

If you have identified any causes which are not of practical significance but which need to be included so that the AcciMap makes sense, draw an oval around these factors to distinguish them from the other causes.

Step 6. Insert the causal links: rearrange the causes in the AcciMap so that the causes lie directly above their effects (whether the effects are in the same level or in the level(s) below).

Consider each cause in the diagram and insert a causal link between a cause and its effect if the following criteria are met:

- had A not occurred, B would (probably) not have occurred either; and
- B is a direct result of A; no other factor needs to be inserted between them.

If one cause does not obviously lead on to the next, leave a space where the missing information can be inserted later.

There is no limit to the number of causes to be included in any causal chain, and there may be multiple linked causes within the same level of the AcciMap:

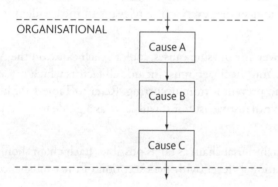

Causes do not have to be linked to effects in the same level or in the level immediately below — they may be linked to factors several levels below:

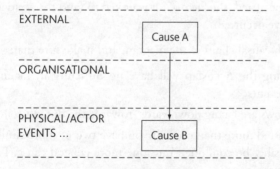

Some causes may be linked with more than one effect. Conversely, several causes may be linked to one common effect. This means that no cause ever needs to be listed more than once in an AcciMap:

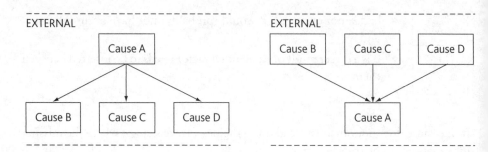

Step 7. Fill in the gaps: at this point, there may be gaps left in the causal chains where information is missing. These gaps must be filled so that the causal chains are unbroken from the earliest identified causes in each chain all the way down to the outcome(s), and so that every cause relevant to the accident is included in the AcciMap.

In order to uncover any missing causes, look at each cause on the AcciMap and ask why it occurred. Your AcciMap must include all factors which caused its occurrence or which failed to prevent it from occurring. Refer to Table 1 for help at this point. Table 1 is not an exhaustive list but it will serve as a guide to the types of factor that may be relevant.

Aim to follow each causal chain as far as possible. Each chain should extend at least to the "Organisational" level (with the exception of the oval-shaped causes).

Be sure to include as many (but only as many) factors as are necessary so that someone reading your AcciMap will be able to understand the sequence of events and conditions without difficulty.

Step 8. Check the causal logic: go through each cause in the diagram and make sure that, had it not occurred, the factor(s) it is linked to (and the accident itself) would probably not have occurred.

Go through each causal chain in the diagram and make sure that:

- anyone reading the AcciMap will have no difficulty in making sense of the sequence of events;
- all of the arrows are facing downwards, towards the outcome(s); and
- no cause is listed more than once. If you have two or more similar causes, see if they can sensibly be combined into one more general cause. For instance, the following causes:

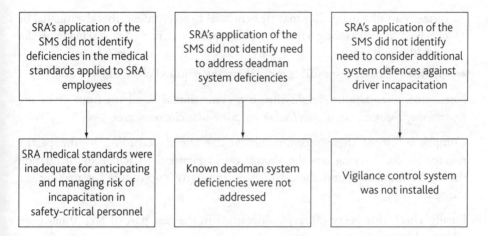

can be combined as follows (as they are in the sample AcciMap), to simplify the diagram and to highlight that the SRA's application of the published SMS was inadequate in a number of respects and is therefore a problem area that should be addressed.

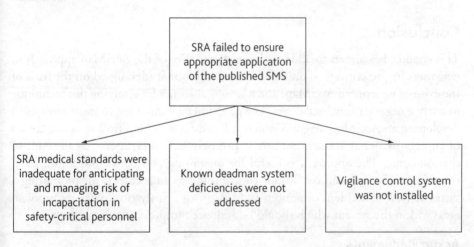

Step 9. Formulate safety recommendations: go through each of the causal factors in your AcciMap and identify those which could potentially be *changed*, *controlled* or *compensated for* so that a similar outcome could not occur again.

Bearing in mind that safety recommendations must be practical to implement:

- formulate safety recommendations that identify what *specifically* should be done to change, control or compensate for each cause;

- consider whether or not there is a more *general* problem area that should also be addressed (for example, if there are one or more problems relating to a

Chapter

10

certain part of a manual, it may be beneficial to recommend that the manual be reviewed, as well as the particular problem parts, to ensure that any inadequacies are addressed); and

- identify the party responsible for making the required changes.

Note: recommendations should aim to prevent similar accidents from occurring *regardless of the individuals involved or the particular circumstances.*

Compile a list of these recommendations, grouped according to the parties responsible for carrying out the actions (as in Figure 3). Each recommendation should be numbered and should identify the party responsible for making the change.

Finally, check that every cause you identified in the first part of Step 9 has been addressed by one or more recommendation, if appropriate.

Note: not all recommendations will necessarily be accepted by those responsible for implementing them. Issues of practicality, redundancy and cost-effectiveness may be relevant, and alternative solutions may be taken into consideration.

Conclusion

This chapter has aimed to address the inaccessibility of the AcciMap approach to new users by presenting a standardised AcciMap format (developed on the basis of the existing varieties of AcciMap) and a set of guidelines for applying this technique to analyse organisational accidents. The guidelines are intended to assist analysts in developing an AcciMap diagram which will illustrate the multiple systemic causes of an organisational accident and show precisely how they interacted to result in that outcome. The approach is useful for organising and conveying information regarding the events and conditions contributing to an accident, for promoting a systemic view of accident causation, and for assisting analysts to pinpoint problem areas within the system which should be addressed to prevent recurrences.

Acknowledgments

The authors would like to thank the Defence Science and Technology Organisation (DSTO) for granting the first author a PhD scholarship for conducting this research. They also appreciate the time and effort of those DSTO employees who participated in the pilot studies leading to the refinement of the AcciMap analysis guidelines.

CHAPTER 11

THE IMPORTANCE OF "COUNTERFACTUAL" THINKING: THE CASE OF THE 2003 CANBERRA BUSHFIRES

Madeleine Rowland and Andrew Hopkins

Introduction

In January 2003, massive bushfires swept into the suburbs of Canberra from the mountains to the west. Nearly 500 houses were destroyed and four lives were lost. The fires had been ignited 10 days earlier by lightning strikes, and they swept uncontrollably down from the mountains on the day of the disaster, driven by fierce winds. Weather conditions that day were extreme — arguably, unprecedented.

The coroner was highly critical of various emergency services personnel, arguing that their flawed decision-making contributed to the disaster. The individuals concerned took legal action in an attempt to prevent the coroner from making adverse findings about them, and this caused a long delay in the release of her report.

The coroner's criticisms are surprising, given that the stated purpose of her inquiry was "learning, not blaming" (Doogan 2006a, p 6). She saw her task as establishing the truth of what had happened so that lessons could be learnt. From this point of view, the output of the inquiry would be a set of recommendations to the authorities about how to reduce the risk of similar catastrophic fires in the future. Nevertheless, she said, blame was an inevitable by-product of this process: "Once the truth is established ... it is often impossible to learn from mistakes made without finding fault on the part of individuals." (Doogan 2006a, p 7)[1]

The coroner's view that the officials were at fault appears to have been based on two assumptions: first, that the decisions of these officials contributed significantly to the death and destruction on the day of the firestorm; and second, that those

---

1 There is a logical error in this statement. The coroner assumes that identifying mistakes amounts to finding fault. This is incorrect. A mistake, assuming that is what it is, can be demonstrated to be a mistake by some form of objective reasoning. Moreover, learning from a mistake means asking why that mistake was made, which again requires some form of objective reasoning. To attribute fault in these circumstances involves an additional step of making what is fundamentally a moral evaluation. It is to say that the mistake is blameworthy. There is no inevitability about this step.

decisions were inherently wrong. We address both of these assumptions in this chapter, but most of the discussion focuses on the first. Our main argument is that the coroner was wrong in suggesting that the decisions of these individuals contributed significantly to the death and destruction. The reason she made this mistake, we argue, is that she failed to carry out the kind of causal analysis described in earlier chapters in this book. This episode, then, provides a vivid illustration of the importance of such an analysis.

Counterfactual analysis

The causal analysis in question can be described as counterfactual analysis, in that it asks the question: what would have happened if certain things had been different (counter to the facts)?[2] For instance, if the houses that burnt down had been built of truly fireproof material, they would not have burnt down. That is a matter of logic. If they had been built merely of fire-resistant materials, the conclusion might be that they would *probably* not have burnt down. That is a matter of probability, rather than of logic. If we can say with some degree of confidence that, had a certain prior condition or occurrence been otherwise, the outcome would have been different, then it makes sense to talk about that prior condition or occurrence as a cause. In the above example, the fact that the houses were not built of fireproof or fire-resistant materials was a cause of their destruction.

This example demonstrates two points. The first is that, when talking about what would have happened had things been otherwise, we can seldom be certain. Our conclusions may only be "on the balance of probabilities", to use a well-known legal phrase. Second, a cause identified in this way is not the only cause. It is one of a potentially infinite set of factors which, had they been otherwise, might have forestalled the outcome. In the above example, had the fires not been ignited in the first place, the houses would not have burnt down; had the fires been extinguished after ignition, the houses would not have burnt down; and so on.

Lawyers are accustomed to describing this as "but-for" thinking, because it involves statements of the following kind: but for this occurrence or state of affairs, the outcome would not have occurred. For this reason, the causes of interest can be described as but-for causes. They can also be described as necessary conditions. They are conditions — more accurately, states or occurrences — that were necessary in order for the outcome to occur.[3]

---

2   There is a rich literature on this subject. See for instance, Ladkin & Stuphorn (2003), Snook (2000), and Griffin (1993).

3   That is not to say that they were *sufficient* to cause the outcome. On the question of sufficiency, see Fischer (nd).

The but-for test is important in law. If a court is trying to establish the liability of a defendant, generally speaking, but-for causation must be established.[4] It needs to be shown that, had the defendant behaved differently, the outcome would have been different. If the defendant's behaviour was actually irrelevant to the outcome under consideration, the defendant cannot be liable. In other words, but-for causation is a *pre-condition* for liability.

However, as lawyers are very quick to point out, the but-for test is not *sufficient* to establish liability. Someone's actions or inactions can be but-for causes, and yet it may not be sensible to hold that person liable. For example, the choice of Martin Bryant's mother to have children is a but-for cause of the Port Arthur massacre. (But for that choice, the massacre would not have occurred.) However, it would be absurd to hold her liable for the massacre (Stapleton 2001, p 147). Accordingly, the but-for test must be limited in some way, for example, with a "stop rule" (Rasmussen et al 1990), if it is to serve as the basis of legal liability. The prevailing legal view is that the but-for test must be qualified by "common sense" before it can serve as a basis for legal liability, that is, before it can be used to hold people responsible (Tobin 2008, p 25; Mendelson 2004, p 499; Lanham 2002, p 214; Lavery 1998, p 26; Travers 2002, pp 266-267; O'Meara 2005, pp 52-53).

The coroner appears to have taken a further step away from but-for causation and concluded that it is not a question of *qualifying* the but-for test with common sense, but *replacing* it with common sense. She does so primarily on the basis of her reading of the leading case in Australia on this matter, *March v Stramare (E & MH) Pty Ltd.*[5] We believe that the coroner incorrectly interprets this case, but we shall not develop the point here. The fact is that the coroner did indeed choose to rely on her own version of common sense, and she made little or no attempt in her analysis to apply the but-for test. We hope to show below that this was an error, with serious consequences.

The failure to attack the southern fire

There were two matters that the coroner paid particular attention to in her report and on the basis of which she found fault with various officials. The first of these was the failure to attack one of the fires with greater energy immediately after it had started, and the second was the failure to provide adequate warnings to the public. We deal with these in turn.

---

4   If X and Y fatally shoot A simultaneously, the but-for test gives the conclusion that neither shot is a cause. However, common sense tells us that both X and Y are responsible for A's death. In other words, the but-for test may fail to give sensible results where there are multiple simultaneous causes of an event (Hart & Honoré 1985, p 122ff).

5   (1991) 171 CLR 506.

Chapter

11

Four fires to the west of Canberra were started by lightning strikes 10 days before the firestorm struck the suburbs. Only two are relevant here: we call these the northern and the southern fires.[6] The northern fire was in New South Wales and therefore beyond the jurisdiction of Australian Capital Territory authorities. The southern fire was within the borders of the ACT. This is the one on which the coroner focused.

Firefighters got to the southern fire soon after it had started. However, the authorities decided on the first night to withdraw from the fire ground because the terrain was difficult and there was concern about the safety of firefighters working in the dark, especially as they were tired. By the time firefighters returned, the fire had expanded and they had lost the opportunity to black it out.

The decision to withdraw was made by an experienced operations officer. However, the coroner concluded that the decision was a mistake, the operations officer was incompetent, and the fire chief who appointed him had made a serious error. These judgments are questionable, and others took the view that the decisions were reasonable in the circumstances. It is only in the light of what happened, that is, with hindsight, that they can be construed as faulty decisions. The question of whether the decision to withdraw really was a mistake is something we shall take up later; what we want to explore here are the *consequences* of this decision. The question we address is: what difference would it have made if the firefighters had stayed and fought the fire?

The first question is: had the firefighters stayed on that night, would they have been able to extinguish the fire to the point where it was harmless? The evidence was that they might have "blacked out" the fire. Blacking out has been described as "extinguishing or removing burning material along or near the fire control line … trenching logs to prevent rolling and the like in order to make the fire safe" (Esplin, Gill & Enright 2003, p 20). Clearly, this does not mean entirely extinguishing the fire. The coroner effectively concedes this. She does not claim that the fire would have been extinguished; merely that "a significant degree of control would have been achieved" (Doogan 2006b, p 32). However, a fire that has been blacked out can continue to smolder for many days, and if extreme weather conditions subsequently develop, it can rapidly escape containment lines. In other words, even if firefighters had blacked out the fire at the time, it cannot be said with any confidence that this fire would not have redeveloped in the extreme conditions a week later. This in itself casts doubt on whether the failure to stay and fight the fire that night was a but-for cause of the disaster.[7]

---

6   They were, in fact, the McIntyres Hut fire and the Bendora fire.
7   An experienced firefighter who looked at an earlier draft of this chapter suggested that the southern fire was so small that firefighters could have extinguished it fully on the first night. Be that as it may, that was not the coroner's view, and had she recognised the implications of her view, as developed here, it would necessarily have changed her analysis.

Nevertheless, for the sake of argument, let us assume that firefighters had succeeded in extinguishing this southern fire totally. What difference would this have made? The answer is: relatively little. To understand why, we need to describe in more detail the behaviour of the northern and southern fires. These fires followed separate trajectories towards Canberra, but the coroner treats them as having contributed to a single firestorm that hit Canberra. The fact is, though, that these fires never combined to form a single fire front. It is true that they did merge many kilometres behind the fire fronts, back on the ACT border, but by then fire had already entered the suburbs of Canberra, and the merging of these two fires back on the border made no difference to what happened in Canberra's suburbs.

The northern fire was the real problem. It did not cross the border into the ACT until the day of the firestorm. It then travelled at great speed and quite uncontrollably to the outskirts of a part of Canberra known as Weston Creek. This fire was responsible for all four deaths in the ACT. Moreover, there were pine plantations along its way that fuelled its intensity. In fact, there was a pine plantation only 100 m away from the suburb where this fire struck first and with greatest intensity. Nearly all of the houses that were lost were destroyed by this northern fire.

As for the southern fire, on the day of the firestorm, it burnt rapidly towards the most southerly suburbs of Canberra. However, by good fortune, it did not enter those suburbs and not a single house was destroyed by flames from this fire! At this point, it is tempting to conclude that the alleged failure of the firefighters to stay and attack the southern fire on the first night had nothing to do with the destruction caused by the firestorm and was, from this point of view, quite inconsequential.

However, the situation is a little more complicated. A short time before the firestorm struck Canberra, a breakaway occurred from the southern edge of the northern fire (see Figure 1). This breakaway moved south for a short distance and then turned and travelled east in a corridor between the northern and southern fires. As it travelled, it remained separate from the main northern fire and, likewise, at no stage as it sped towards the suburbs did it merge with the southern fire.[8] This breakaway fire behaved quite remarkably. First, it travelled at much greater speed than either of the northern or southern fires. Second, it gave rise to a tornado that immediately preceded its leading edge. The tornado touched down at two quite specific locations within Canberra's suburbs where it did considerable damage, including removing the roofs of houses which enabled fire to take hold.[9] We estimate that, at most, 33 houses were lost to fire at these locations (Doogan 2006b, p 17). This is just under 7% of the 487 houses lost in Canberra as a result of the firestorm.

8   This is evident from plates 27-30 of Doogan 2006b, pp 15-16.
9   Lincoln Close, Chapman and Colquhoun Streets, and Sulwood Drive, Kambah (Doogan 2006a, p 350).

Chapter

11

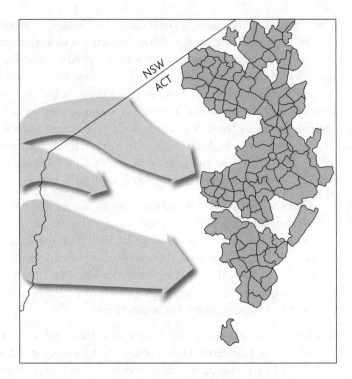

FIGURE 1: Fire trajectories

An explanation for the extraordinary behaviour of this breakaway from the northern fire was provided by an expert witness at the inquest and was accepted by the coroner. The witness believed that the strong updrafts created by the northern and southern fires had *in combination* produced the tornado (Doogan 2006a, p 350). In other words, it seems likely that, but for either fire and, in particular, but for the southern fire, there would have been no tornado. In that case, the 33 houses whose destruction by fire was facilitated by the tornado would probably not have been lost.

To summarise, the southern fire was not directly responsible for the loss of any houses. But because it contributed to the tornado, it indirectly contributed to up to 7% of the housing loss. And, to repeat, the southern fire was not responsible for any loss of life. Its contribution to the overall disaster that day was, relatively speaking, small.[10] In light of this analysis, the enormous focus placed by the coroner on the decision to withdraw from the southern fire on the first night is inappropriate. Had

---

10   We could reasonably take the argument a step further: had it not been for the northern fire, there would have been no tornado and the southern fire would have had no impact on Canberra at all.

she gone through the exercise of imagining what difference it would have made
if the firefighters had stayed, she would have realised that they would probably
not have been able to completely extinguish the fire, and that, even if they had,
this would have made no difference to the number of deaths and relatively little
difference to the extent of destruction. The most significant causes of the death and
destruction that occurred that day had nothing to do with the actions or inactions
of those responsible for fighting the southern fire. Had the coroner realised this, she
might have focused her inquiry elsewhere, and she would have been much more
careful to avoid creating the impression that the officials concerned were somehow
to blame for the firestorm.

The failure to warn the public

The second alleged failure, to which the coroner devoted 100 pages of her report,
was the failure of the authorities to adequately warn the citizens of Canberra of the
impending disaster, particularly in the preceding 24 hours. She argues that strong
warnings should have been given "at first light" (Doogan 2006b, p 158) on the day
of the firestorm, and even that a state of emergency should have been declared early
in the day (long before the fires began their run down from the hills) because of
the predicted extreme weather conditions. The question again, however, is: would
stronger warnings have made any difference?

Consider, first, the issue of fatalities. Of the four who died, two died actively
defending their houses with hoses, one died in her bathtub which she had filled with
water, apparently following instructions that had been broadcast on the radio, and
the fourth died because, although she was aware of the danger, she was apparently
awaiting a clear recommendation to leave (Doogan 2006b, p 189). The policy of
the fire authorities Australia-wide at the time was not that people should evacuate
areas threatened by fire, but that they should individually decide well ahead of time
whether they would stay and defend their houses or leave and go to a safer place,
and that they should prepare accordingly. That policy is now under review as a
result of the February 2009 Victorian bushfires, in which many people who stayed
to fight the fire lost their lives. However, it was the decide-in-advance policy that
was in place in Canberra in 2003.

So, what difference would it have made if, on the morning of the disaster, stronger or
clearer warnings had been given that the fire might attack the outskirts of Canberra
that afternoon? In particular, what difference would it have made if the warnings
had stressed that now is the time to decide either to stay and fight or to get out.
The coroner does not explicitly claim that better warnings would have made any
difference. Indeed, in the case of the woman who died in the bathtub, the coroner
explicitly states that she cannot conclude that this death was due to the inadequacy

of warnings. In the case of the two who stayed to fight, they were already responding to warnings, and the fourth individual was awaiting an instruction to leave, which was not a policy option at that time. It is hard to see how stronger warnings would have made a difference in any of these cases. Compulsory evacuation would certainly have saved their lives, but that is quite a different issue and nothing to do with the inadequacy of warnings. In short, the alleged inadequacy of warnings did not contribute to the deaths that occurred that day.

The next question to be asked is whether better warnings on the day in question would have resulted in more houses being saved. The coroner implies that the answer is: yes. She notes that the great majority of people who were at home on the day of the firestorm claimed that they knew how to prepare their houses for fire. The only problem was, she says, that they had not been given the opportunity to use their knowledge because they had not been given notice (Doogan 2006b, p 164). The fact is, however, that properly defending one's house against fire may take days, if not weeks. It requires gutters to be cleared, holes stopped up, vegetation cut down and removed, and so on. It may even require wooden fences to be replaced with steel ones. In other words, better warnings on the day in question could have made very little difference to the degree of preparedness.

Even if stronger warnings had been given much further in advance, it is not obvious that this would have made a significant difference. One particular street had been visited by the ACT bushfire service two months before the fires and was well prepared (Doogan 2006a, p 87). However, regardless of the high level of preparation, nearly every house in the street was burnt to the ground. This initiative by the authorities was to no avail in the extreme conditions that prevailed on the day of the firestorm.

Finally, it should be noted that, if more effective warnings had been given about the need to either prepare for fire or go, more people might have been encouraged to stay and fight and more people might have died. This is an obvious possibility in light of the 2009 Victorian fires, but it should have been obvious to the coroner following the 2003 fires in Canberra, since two of the four who died lost their lives as a result of a decision to stay and fight.

We can conclude, therefore, that the alleged inadequacy of the warnings on the day of the firestorm did not contribute in any obvious way to the number of houses lost.

Notwithstanding the previous discussion, there is one way in which stronger and clearer warnings on the day in question would have made a difference. Many people fled at the last minute, leaving behind personal possessions of great emotional value, such as photograph albums. If they had been urged a few hours earlier to implement their stay or go decision, they might have been able to rescue these personal possessions. It can be argued that the inadequacy of the warnings was a but-for cause of this loss.

The loss of personal possessions of this nature was not listed by the coroner as one of the matters necessitating the inquest (Doogan 2006a, p 3), but it became a significant issue during the inquiry. The fact that warnings had been insufficient to allow people to save some of their most treasured possessions generated great bitterness. It is hard to escape the conclusion that the coroner was influenced by these emotions and that her focus on the inadequacy of warnings was driven by losses of this nature, rather than the loss of life or property.

In summary, if the coroner had been thinking more clearly about but-for causation, she would have concluded that the loss of life and property had very little to do with the adequacy or otherwise of the warnings given to the public on the day in question.

Were the decisions inherently blameworthy?

The preceding analysis has demonstrated that the decisions in question did not contribute significantly to the death and destruction. Nevertheless, they might still be inherently blameworthy decisions. The best way to decide this issue is to resort again to counterfactual thinking.

Suppose the fires had been extinguished by rain some days prior to the firestorm. How would the decision to withdraw from the fire ground in the interest of firefighter safety then have been viewed? To begin with, the decision would not have been exposed to the glare of publicity. Any inquiry would have been much more low key and much less threatening to the individuals involved. Those who made the decision to withdraw would say that they had been engaged in a risk management process, balancing the risk to firefighters against the risk to the wider public. The critics might assert that firefighters must always give top priority to attacking small fires and that this is the time when resources must be mobilised to their full extent. It is hard to imagine an inquiry in these circumstances concluding that the decision to withdraw was a categorical mistake, let alone that those who had made the decision were at fault. The most likely outcome of such an inquiry would be that this was a matter on which opinions differed, that it was a question of expert judgment, and that no hard and fast policy could be developed to cover such situations.

The preceding conclusion is supported by the outcome of the inquiry by a NSW coroner into the northern fire. Fire crews had withdrawn from the northern fire on the first night, just as they had done at the southern fire. The NSW coroner stated that this was a reasonable decision, given what was known at the time (Milovanovich 2003, p 21).

Now consider a second counterfactual scenario in which, on the day that the fires were making their final run towards the suburbs of Canberra, the wind had changed and the fire was either stopped in its tracks or directed away from Canberra. As a result of the warnings actually given, numbers of people had begun preparing for the worst. Some of these people breathed a sigh of relief when the wind changed; others felt that the warnings had, in some respects, been unnecessary. In such circumstances, it is hard to imagine how anyone might subsequently have come to the view that the warnings actually given were inadequate.

These two counterfactual exercises reveal that there was nothing inherently blameworthy in the decisions that were made, and it is only with hindsight, that is, in light of what actually happened, that the coroner was able to find fault on the part of individual decision-makers in the way she did. Her criticism of these decisions depends entirely on their presumed contribution to the disaster. However, as we have shown, in neither case did the decisions contribute significantly to what happened. Had she carried out a but-for analysis, she would have made this discovery herself. She could then not have apportioned blame in the way she did, and the inquest would not have become bogged down in legal proceedings in which the individuals concerned sought to salvage their reputations.

Before moving on, there is one implication of the preceding analysis that we want to emphasise. Even if it had been possible to establish but-for causation, it would not follow automatically that the individuals concerned were blameworthy. We noted earlier that but-for causation must be qualified in some way before it can serve as a basis for legal liability. Similarly, in the case of the Canberra bushfires, there would need to be some additional fault before it would make sense to blame the decision-makers. Counterfactual analysis suggests that the decisions were reasonable, given what was known at the time. Hence, regardless of whether these decisions contributed to the outcome, they should not be seen as blameworthy.

Prevention

The first part of this chapter has shown how important but-for analysis is in any context where blame is being attributed. We consider now the relevance of but-for analysis for the development of disaster-prevention strategies. This is a complex matter that we cannot do justice to here. But there are a few observations that can be made on the basis of the present case.

A proper but-for analysis of the Canberra firestorm would have covered such matters as the proximity of pine forests, the inadequacy of controlled burning, the absence of any policy on compulsory evacuation, and the use of flammable building materials — in addition to the alleged inadequacy of early firefighting efforts and of the warnings provided on the final day. Some of these may have turned out to be but-for causes and others not.

Unfortunately, identifying but-for causes does not lead, *automatically*, to strategies for prevention. In some cases, there may indeed be a fairly straightforward policy implication. For example, if it had been established in the present case that the pine plantations were a but-for cause, a policy of keeping pine plantations well away from built-up areas would seem to be indicated. Generally speaking, however, policy-makers need to assemble a series of but-for analyses for a set of similar incidents and then identify any patterns that may emerge. These patterns may or may not reveal sensible prevention strategies. For instance, if a significant number of bushfires are found to have been started by arsonists, it may be sensible to develop policies for known arsonists that include intensive therapy and/or intensive surveillance at times of extreme fire danger. On the other hand, the fact that many bushfires are started by lightning strikes does not lead to any obvious preventive strategies. Moreover, while insisting that houses be built of fireproof materials would surely be effective in reducing the destruction wrought by bushfires, the cost may be such that policy-makers cannot impose this as a solution. So, to repeat, but-for analyses do not translate automatically into prevention strategies. They do, however, provide information that can be of use in developing such strategies.

Conclusion

Counterfactual thinking is an important aid to understanding the causes of incidents such as the 2003 Canberra firestorm. Had the coroner applied this style of thinking, it would have demonstrated two things: first, the actions and decisions of the officials that she criticised were not significantly related to the outcomes on the day of the firestorm; second, the decisions were in any case reasonable. If she had drawn these conclusions herself, she would not have been able to blame people in the way she did, and the inquiry would not have been disrupted by extraneous legal proceedings. Moreover, she would not have spent nearly so much time on matters that were of little causal relevance. As a result, the whole inquiry might have been better focused on identifying significant lessons — which, as she said, was its principal purpose.

Chapter

11

BIBLIOGRAPHY

ABC [Australian Broadcasting Corporation] 16 March 2004, "Rail accidents blamed on privatisation", *ABC News*, viewed 13 March 2009, www.abc.net.au/news/stories/2004/03/16/1066974.htm.

Air Safety Week 3 June 2002, "To blame or not to blame — that is the question", *Air Safety Week*, viewed 13 March 2009, http://findarticles.com/p/articles/mi_m0UBT/is_22_16/ai_86637461.

ASC [Aviation Safety Council] 2002, *Aircraft accident report: crashed on a partially closed runway during takeoff Singapore Airlines Flight 006 Boeing 747-400, 9V-SPK CKS Airport, Taoyuan, Taiwan October 31, 2000*, ASC, Taiwan.

ATSB [Australian Transport Safety Bureau] 1989, *Mid-air collision between Cessna 172-N VH-HIZ and Piper PA 38-112 VH-MHQ, near Tweed Heads, NSW, 20 May 1988*, ATSB, Canberra.

ATSB [Australian Transport Safety Bureau] 2004a, *Review of midair collisions involving general aviation aircraft in Australia between 1961 and 2003*, ATSB, Canberra.

ATSB [Australian Transport Safety Bureau] 2004b, *Bankstown midair collision, 5 May 2002*, ATSB, Canberra.

ATSB [Australian Transport Safety Bureau] 2004c, *Piper PA31T Cheyenne, VH-TNP, Benalla, Vic*, ATSB, Canberra.

ATSB [Australian Transport Safety Bureau] 2004d, *Limitations of the see-and-avoid principle*, ATSB, Canberra.

ATSB [Australian Transport Safety Bureau] 2008, *Analysis, causality and proof in safety investigations*, ATSB, Canberra.

Barach, P & Small, D 2000, "Reporting and preventing medical mishaps: lessons from non-medical near miss reporting systems", *British Medical Journal*, vol 320, pp 759-763.

BBC [British Broadcasting Corporation] 21 September 1999, "UK privatisation blamed for rail disaster", *BBC News*, viewed 13 March 2009, http://news.bbc.co.uk/1/hi/uk/453337.stm.

BBC [British Broadcasting Corporation] 26 April 2002, "Taiwan crash pilot ignored warnings", *BBC News*, viewed 13 March 2009, http://news.bbc.co.uk/1/hi/world/asia-pacific/1952406.stm.

Bendix, R 1966, *Max Weber: an intellectual portrait*, Methuan, London.

BFU [German Federal Bureau of Aircraft Accidents Investigation] 2004, *Investigation report Überlingen mid-air collision, AX001-1-2/02*.

Bird, FE 1975, *Management guide to loss control*, Loss Control Publications, Mt Waverley, Victoria.

Bird, FE & Germain, GL 1986, *Practical loss control leadership*, Institute Publishing, Loganville, Georgia.

Bourrier, M 1998, "Elements for designing a self-correcting organisation: examples from nuclear plants", in A Hale & M Baram (eds), *Safety management: the challenge of change*, Pergamon, Oxford, UK, pp 133-146.

Bradsher, K 2002, "Reports differ on causes of Taiwan runway crash that killed 83", *The New York Times*, 27 April, viewed 13 March 2009, http://query.nytimes.com/gst/fullpage.html?res=9F02E3DA103EF934A15757C0A9649C8B63.

Braithwaite, G 2001, *Attitude or latitude? Australian aviation safety*, Ashgate, Aldershot, UK.

Branford, K 2007, "An investigation into the validity and reliability of the AcciMap approach", PhD thesis, Australian National University, Canberra.

Brooker, P 2005, "Reducing mid-air collision risk in controlled airspace: lessons from hazardous incidents", *Safety Science*, vol 43, pp 715-738.

Buljan, A & Shapiro, Z 2005, "Attention to production schedule and safety as determinants of risk-taking in NASA's decision to launch the *Columbia* shuttle", in W Starbuck & M Farjoun (eds), *Organization at the limit: lessons from the* Columbia *disaster*, Blackwell, Oxford, UK, pp 140-156.

Cabinet Office 2002, *Risk: improving government's capability to handle risk and uncertainty*, Cabinet Office Strategy Unit, London.

CAIB [Columbia Accident Investigation Board] 2003, *The report*, vol 1, NASA, Washington.

CCPS [Centre for Chemical Process Safety] 2003, *Guidelines for investigating chemical process incidents*, Wiley Interscience, Hoboken, New Jersey.

CCPS [Center for Chemical Process Safety] 2007, *Guidelines for risk-based process safety*, Wiley Interscience, Hoboken, New Jersey.

Channel NewsAsia 26 April 2002a, "IFALPA press statement on the ASC's SQ006 report", MediaCorp Pty Ltd, viewed 13 March 2009, www.channelnewsasia.com/cna/sq006/ifalpa260402.htm.

Channel NewsAsia 26 April 2002b, "SIA's response to the ASC's SQ006 accident report", MediaCorp Pty Ltd, viewed 13 March 2009, www.channelnewsasia.com/cna/sq006/sia260402.htm.

Channel NewsAsia 26 April 2002c, "Singapore Ministry of Transportation's comments on the final report of the investigation into the SQ006 accident",

MediaCorp Pty Ltd, viewed 13 March 2009, www.channelnewsasia.com/cna/sq006/mot260402.htm.

Channel NewsAsia 29 April 2002, "The impact of the SQ006 reports on international aviation", MediaCorp Pty Ltd, viewed 13 March 2009, www.channelnewsasia.com/cna/sq006/rsi290402.htm.

CNN 26 April 2002, "Weather, pilot error blamed for Taiwan crash", Cable News Network, viewed 13 March 2009, http://archives.cnn.com/2002/WORLD/asiapcf/southeast/04/26/singapore.crash/index.html.

Cook, SDN & Brown, JS 1999, "Bridging epistemologies: the generative dance between organizational knowledge and organizational knowing", *Organization Science*, vol 10, no 4, pp 381-400.

COSO [Committee of Sponsoring Organizations of the Treadway Commission] 2004, *Enterprise risk management — integrated framework*, Altamonte Springs, FL.

Cullen, L 1990, *The public inquiry into the Piper Alpha disaster*, Her Majesty's Stationery Office, London.

Dekker, S 2007, *Just culture*, Ashgate, Aldershot, UK.

Dijkstra, A 2006, "Safety management in airlines", in E Hollnagel, D Woods & N Leveson (eds), *Resilience engineering: concepts and precepts*, Ashgate, Aldershot, UK, pp 183-204.

Dobson, R 2002, "Singapore cries foul over crash", *Taipei Times*, 27 April, viewed 13 March 2009, www.taipeitimes.com/News/front/archives/2002/04/27/133546.

Doogan, M 2006a, *The Canberra firestorm: inquests into four deaths and four fires between 8 and 18 January*, vol I, ACT Magistrates Court, Canberra.

Doogan, M 2006b, *The Canberra firestorm: inquests into four deaths and four fires between 8 and 18 January*, vol II, ACT Magistrates Court, Canberra.

Esplin, B, Gill, M & Enright, N 2003, *Report of the inquiry into the 2002-2003 Victorian bushfires*, State Government of Victoria, Melbourne.

Fischer, D nd, "Dependently sufficient causes in tort law — a reply to Professor Wright, University of Missouri-Columbia" (unpublished).

Get for me Singapore 2002, "Singapore Airlines' SQ006 crash at Chiang Kai Shek Airport", viewed 13 March 2009, www.getformesingapore.com/tragedy_sq006.htm.

Grabowski, M & Roberts, K 1996, "Human and organisational error in large scale systems", *IEEE Transactions on Systems, Man, and Cybernetics — Part A: Systems and Humans*, vol 26, no 1.

Grabowski, M & Roberts, K 1997, "Risk mitigation in large-scale systems: lessons from high reliability organisations", *California Management Review*, vol 39, no 4, pp 152ff.

Griffin, L 1993, "Narrative, event-structure analysis, and causal interpretation in historical sociology", *American Journal of Sociology*, vol 98, no 5, pp 1094-1133.

Hale, A 2001, "Conditions of occurrence of major and minor accidents", *Journal of the Institution of Occupational Health and Safety*, vol 5, no 1, pp 7-21.

Hale, A & Heijer, T 2006, "Defining resilience", in E Hollnagel, D Woods & N Leveson, *Resilience engineering: concepts and precepts*, Ashgate, Aldershot, UK, pp 35-40.

Hannon, B 2002, "Crash report on SQ006 not wrong", *Taipei Times*, 5 May, viewed 13 March 2009, www.taipeitimes.com/News/archives/2002/05/05/0000134701.

Hart, H & Honoré, T 1985, *Causation in law*, 2nd edn, Clarendon Press, Oxford, UK.

Helmrich, B 2006, "Red alert", *Flight Safety Australia*, September/October.

Hollnagel, E 2004, *Barriers and accident prevention: or how to improve safety by understanding the nature of accidents*, Ashgate, Aldershot, UK.

Hollnagel, E, Woods, D & Leveson, N (eds) 2006, *Resilience engineering: concepts and precepts*, Ashgate, Aldershot, UK.

Holmqvist, M 2003, "A dynamic model of intra- and interorganizational learning", *Organization Studies*, vol 24, no 1, pp 95-123.

Hopkins, A 1999, "The limits of normal accident theory", *Safety Science*, vol 32, pp 93-102.

Hopkins, A 2000a, *Lessons from Longford*, CCH Australia Limited, Sydney.

Hopkins, A 2000b, "A culture of denial: sociological similarities between the Moura and Gretley mine disasters", *Journal of Occupational Health and Safety — Australia and New Zealand*, vol 16, no 1, pp 29-36.

Hopkins, A 2001, "Was Three Mile Island a normal accident?", *Journal of Contingencies and Crisis Management*, vol 9, no 2, pp 65-72.

Hopkins, A 2003, *Fault trees, ICAM and AcciMaps: a methodological analysis*, Defence Science and Technology Organisation (internal publication), Melbourne.

Hopkins, A 2005, *Safety, culture and risk: the organisational causes of disasters*, CCH Australia Limited, Sydney.

Hopkins, A 2006a, "What are we to make of safe behaviour programs?", *Safety Science*, vol 44, pp 583-597.

Hopkins, A 2006b, "A corporate dilemma: to be a learning organisation or to minimise liability", *Journal of Occupational Health and Safety — Australia and New Zealand*, vol 22, no 3, pp 251-259.

Hopkins, A 2008, *Failure to learn: the BP Texas City refinery disaster*, CCH Australia Limited, Sydney.

House of Representatives 2002, *Transport Safety Investigation Bill 2002: second reading speech*, Parliament of Australia, Canberra.

Hunt, G 1996, "Corporate manslaughter, reforming the law, part 1: don't pay, won't listen", *The Whistle: Bulletin of Freedom to Care*, vol 10.

Hutter, B 2001, *Regulation and risk: occupational health and safety on the railways*, Oxford University Press, Oxford, UK.

Hutter, B 2005, "Ways of seeing: understandings of risk in organizational settings", in B Hutter & M Power (eds), *Organizational encounters with risk*, Cambridge University Press, Cambridge, UK.

Hutter, B & Lloyd-Bostock, S 1990, "The power of accidents: the social and psychological impact of accidents and the enforcement of safety regulations", *The British Journal of Criminology*, vol 30, no 4, pp 409-422.

ICAO [International Civil Aviation Organization] 2001, *Annex 13 to the Convention on International Civil Aviation: aircraft accident and incident investigation*, 9th edn, ICAO, Montreal.

ILGRA [Interdepartmental Liaison Group on Risk Assessment] 1996, *Use of risk assessment within government departments*, ILGRA and the Health and Safety Executive, London.

IRM [Institute of Risk Management] 2002, *A risk management standard*, IRM, National Forum for Risk Management in the Public Sector and Association of Insurance and Risk Managers, London.

Kiesler, S & Sproull, L 1982, "Managerial response to changing environments: perspectives on problem sensing from social cognition", *Administrative Science Quarterly*, vol 27, pp 548-570.

Kirwan, B 2007, "Safety informing design", *Safety Science*, vol 45, pp 155-197.

Kirwan, B & Perrin, E 2004, "Imagining safety in European air traffic management", paper presented to the 3rd International Conference on Occupational Risk Prevention, Santiago de Compostella, 2-4 June.

Kjellen, U 2000, *Prevention of accidents through experience feedback*, Taylor & Francis, London.

Klein, G 1998, *Sources of power: how people make decisions*, MIT Press, Cambridge, Massachusetts.

Klein, R, Bigley, G & Roberts, K 1995, "Organisational culture in high reliability organisations: an extension", *Human Relations*, vol 48, no 7, pp 771-793.

Kletz, T 1993, *Lessons from disaster: how organizations have no memory and accidents recur*, Gulf Publishing Company, Houston, Texas.

Ladkin, P & Stuphorn, J 2003, "Two causal analyses of the Black Hawk shootdown during Operation Provide Comfort", RVS Group, Bielefeld University, Germany, http://portal.acm.org/citation.cfm?id=1082052.

Lanham, D 2002, "Principles of causation in criminal law", in I Freckelton & D Mendelson (eds), *Causation in law and medicine*, Dartmouth and Ashgate, Aldershot, UK, pp 211-227.

La Porte, T 1996, "High reliability organisations: unlikely, demanding and at risk", *Journal of Contingencies and Crisis Management*, vol 4, no 2, pp 60-71.

La Porte, T & Consolini, P 1998, "Theoretical and operational challenges of high-reliability organisations: air-traffic control and aircraft carriers", *International Journal of Public Administration*, vol 21, no 6-8, pp 847-852.

Lavery, J 1998, "*Chappel v Hart*: The High Court's lost chance", *Australian Health Law Bulletin*, vol 7, no 3, pp 25-30.

Lawson, M 2001, "In praise of slack: time is of the essence", *The Academy of Management Executive*, vol 15, no 3, pp 125-135.

Logsdon, R 2001, "Why ask why?", *Rock Products*, vol 104, no 10, pp 52-53.

Macrae, C 2007, *Analysing near-miss events: risk management in incident reporting and investigation systems*, Discussion paper 47, London School of Economics and Political Science, Centre for Analysis of Risk and Regulation, London.

Mannarelli, T, Roberts, K & Bea, R 1996, "Learning how organisations mitigate risk", *Journal of Contingencies and Crisis Management*, vol 4, no 2, pp 83-92.

Marais, K, Dulac, N & Leveson, N 2004, *Beyond normal accidents and high reliability organisations: the need for an alternative approach to safety in complex systems*, paper presented to the Engineering Systems Division Symposium, Massachusetts Institute of Technology, Cambridge, Massachusetts, 29-31 March.

Matthews, S 2005, *The changing face of aviation safety*, paper presented to the Safety in Action Conference, Melbourne, 21-23 March.

Maurino, D, Reason, J, Johnson, N & Lee, R 1995, *Beyond aviation human factors: safety in high technology systems*, Ashgate, Aldershot, UK.

Mendelson, D 2004, "Australian tort law reform: statutory principles of causation and the common law", *Journal of Law and Medicine*, vol 11, no 4, pp 492-509.

Middlehurst, R & Kennie, T 1997, "Leading professionals: towards new concepts of professionalism", in J Broadbent, M Dietrich & J Roberts (eds), *The end of the professions? The restructuring of professional work*, Routledge, London.

Milovanovich, C 2003, *Inquiry into the fire at McIntyres Hut Brindabella Ranges, Kosciuszko National Park*, Coroner's Court, Queanbeyan, NSW.

Ming, Y 2002, "Taiwan says pilots, weather most likely to blame for SIA crash", *Channel NewsAsia*, 26 April, viewed 13 March 2009, www.clubs.mq.edu.au/SSA/ Newsletter/MayJune/pages/spore6.htm.

Ministry of Transport 2003, *Waterfall 31 January 2003 railway safety investigation final report*, Ministry of Transport, Sydney.

Moghaddam, F 1998, *Social psychology: exploring universals across cultures*, WH Freeman & Company, New York.

MOT [Ministry of Transport — Singapore] 2002a, *Analysis of the accident to Singapore Airlines Flight SQ006, Boeing 747-400, 9V-SPK at Chiang Kai-shek Airport, Taipei, Taiwan, on 31 October 2000*, Ministry of Transport, Singapore.

MOT [Ministry of Transport — Singapore] 2002b, "Comments from MCIT/ Singapore", in *Aircraft accident report: crashed on a partially closed runway during takeoff Singapore Airlines Flight 006 Boeing 747-400, 9V-SPK CKS Airport, Taoyuan, Taiwan October 31, 2000*, Aviation Safety Council, Taiwan, app 7, pp 22-25.

MOT [Ministry of Transport — Singapore] 2002c, "Comments from the Singapore Ministry of Transport Investigation Team on the ASC draft final report of the investigation into the accident to Singapore Airlines Boeing 747-400 at Taipei on 31 October 2000: executive summary", in *Aircraft accident report: crashed on a partially closed runway during takeoff Singapore Airlines Flight 006 Boeing 747-400, 9V-SPK CKS Airport, Taoyuan, Taiwan October 31, 2000*, Aviation Safety Council, Taiwan, app 7, pp 26-139.

Muermann, A & Oktem, U 2002, "The near-miss management of operational risk", *Journal of Risk Finance*, Fall, pp 25-36.

Naikar, N, Saunders, A & Hopkins, A 2002, *Profile of human error in the F-111 system*, DSTO Systems Sciences Laboratory, Edinburgh, South Australia.

O'Leary, M & Chappell, S 1996, "Confidential incident reporting systems create vital awareness of safety problems", *International Civil Aviation Organization Journal*, vol 51, pp 11-13.

O'Meara, M 2005, "Causation, remoteness and equitable compensation", *Australian Bar Review*, vol 26, no 1, pp 51-69.

Orr, J 1996, *Talking about machines: an ethnography of a modern job*, Cornell University Press, London.

Perrow, C 1982, "The President's Commission and the normal accident", in D Sils, C Wolf & V Shelanski (eds), *Accident at Three Mile Island: the human dimensions*, Westview Press, Boulder, Colorado.

Perrow, C 1994, "The limits of safety: the enhancement of a theory of accidents", *Journal of Contingencies and Crisis Management*, vol 2, no 4, pp 212-220.

Perrow, C 1999, *Normal accidents: living with high-risk technologies,* 2nd edn, Princeton University Press, Princeton, New Jersey.

Phimister, J, Oktem, U, Kleindorfer, P & Kunreuther, H 2003, "Near-miss incident management in the chemical process industry", *Risk Analysis*, vol 23, no 3, pp 445-459.

Piché, A & Vicente, K 2005, "A sociotechnical systems analysis of the Toronto SARS outbreak", *Proceedings of the Human Factors and Ergonomics Society 49th Annual Meeting*, Santa Monica, California, 26-30 September 2005, pp 507-511.

Pidgeon, N & O'Leary, M 1994, "Organizational safety culture: implications for aviation practice", in N Johnston, N McDonald & R Fuller (eds), *Aviation psychology in practice*, Ashgate, Aldershot, UK.

Pidgeon, N & O'Leary, M 2000, "Man-made disasters: why technology and organizations (sometimes) fail", *Safety Science*, vol 34, pp 15-30.

Pool, R 1999, *Beyond engineering: how society shapes technology*, Oxford University Press, Oxford, UK.

Popatlal, A 2002, "Transport minister says ASC report falls short in analysis", *Channel NewsAsia*, 27 April (no longer available online).

Power, M 2003, *The invention of operational risk*, Discussion paper 16, London School of Economics and Political Science, ESRC Centre for Analysis of Risk and Regulation, London.

Power, M 2007, *Organized uncertainty: designing a world of risk management*, Oxford University Press, Oxford, UK.

Prichard, R 2003, "On the trail of truth: conducting an accident investigation", *International Risk Management Institute Online*, April, viewed 13 March 2009, www.irmi.com/Expert/Articles/2003/Prichard04.aspx.

RAAF [Royal Australian Air Force] 2001, "Chemical exposure of Air Force maintenance workers", in *Report of the Board of Inquiry into F111 (fuel tank) Deseal/ Reseal and Spray Seal Programs*, Royal Australian Air Force, Canberra.

Rasmussen, J 1997, "Risk management in a dynamic society: a modelling problem", *Safety Science*, vol 27, no 2-3, pp 183-213.

Rasmussen, J, Nixon, P & Warner, F 1990, "Human error and the problem of causality in analysis of accidents", *Philosophical Transactions of the Royal Society of London*, vol 327, no 1241, pp 449-462.

Rasmussen, J & Svedung, I 2000, *Proactive risk management in a dynamic society*. Swedish Rescue Services Agency, Karlstad, Sweden.

Reason, J 1990, *Human error*, Cambridge University Press, Cambridge, UK.

Reason, J 1997, *Managing the risks of organizational accidents*, Ashgate, Aldershot, UK.

Reason, J 2000, "Human error: models and management", *British Medical Journal*, vol 320, pp 768-770.

Reason, J & Hobbs, A 2003, *Managing maintenance error: a practical guide*. Ashgate, Aldershot, UK.

Rees, J 1994, *Hostages of each other: the transformation of nuclear safety since Three Mile Island*, University of Chicago Press, Chicago, Illinois.

Roberts, K 1989, "New challenges in organisational research: high reliability organisations", *Industrial Crisis Quarterly*, vol 3, pp 111-125.

Roberts, K 1990, "Some characteristics of one type of high reliability organisation", *Organisation Science*, vol 1, no 2, pp 160-176.

Roberts, K 1992, "Structuring to facilitate migrating decisions in reliability enhancing organisations", in L Gomez-Mejia & M Lawless (eds), *Advances in global high technology management*, vol 2, JAI Press, Greenwich, UK.

Roberts, K 1993, "Cultural characteristics of reliability-enhancing organisations", *Journal of Managerial Issues*, vol 5, no 2, pp 165-181.

Roberts, K & Bea, R 2001a, "Must accidents happen?: lessons from high-reliability organisations", *The Academy of Management Executive*, vol 15, no 3, pp 70-78.

Roberts, K & Bea, R 2001b, "When systems fail", *Organisational Dynamics*, vol 29, no 3, pp 179-191.

Roberts, K & Gargano, G 1990, "Managing a high-reliability organisation: a case for interdependence", in M Von Glinow & S Mohrman (eds), *Managing complexity in high technology organisations*, Oxford University Press, New York.

Roberts, K & Rousseau, D 1989, "Research in nearly failure-free, high-reliability organisations: having the bubble", *IEEE Transactions of Engineering Management*, vol 36, no 2, pp 132-139.

Roberts, K, Rousseau, D & La Porte, T 1994, "The culture of high reliability: quantitative and qualitative assessment aboard nuclear-powered aircraft carriers", *Journal of High Technology Management Research*, vol 5, no 1, pp 141-161.

Roberts, K, Stout, S & Halern, J 1994, "Decision dynamics in two high reliability military organisations", *Management Science,* vol 40, no 5, pp 614-624.

Rochlin, G 1989, "Informal organizational networking as a crisis-avoidance strategy: US naval flight operations as a case study", *Industrial Crisis Quarterly*, vol 3, pp 159-176.

Rochlin, G 1993, "Defining 'high reliability' organisations in practice: a taxonomic prologue", in K Roberts (ed), *New challenges to understanding organisations*, Macmillan, New York.

Rochlin, G, La Porte, T & Roberts, K 1987, "Self-designing high-reliability organisation: aircraft carrier flight operations at sea", *Naval War College Review*, vol 40, no 4, pp 76-91.

Rosenthal, M & Sutcliffe, K (eds) 2002, *Medical error*, Jossey-Bass, San Francisco, California.

Sheaffer, Z, Richardson, B & Rosenblatt, Z 1998, "Early-warning-signals management: a lesson from the Barings crisis", *Journal of Contingencies and Crisis Management*, vol 6, no 1, pp 1-22.

Singh, P nd, "SQ006 — Clash of views or blame deflection?", viewed 13 March 2009, http://groups.yahoo.com/group/singaporeforum/message/25 (unpublished).

Smith, G 1988, "Towards a heuristic theory of problem structuring", *Management Science*, vol 34, no 12, pp 1489-1506.

Smithson, M 1989, *Ignorance and uncertainty: emerging paradigms*, Springer-Verlag, London.

Snook, SA 2000, *Friendly fire: the accidental shootdown of US Black Hawks over Northern Iraq*, Princeton University Press, Princeton, New Jersey.

Stapleton, J 2001, "Unpacking 'causation'", in P Cane & J Gardner, *Relating to responsibility: essays for Tony Honoré on his eightieth birthday*, Hart Publishing, Portland, Oregon, pp 145-185.

Sutcliffe, K & Vogus, T 2003, "Organizing for resilience", in K Cameron & J Dutton (eds), *Positive organizational scholarship: foundations of a new discipline*, Berrett-Koehler, London.

Svedung, I & Rasmussen, J 2002, "Graphic representation of accident scenarios: mapping system structure and the causation of accidents", *Safety Science*, vol 40, pp 397-417.

Svenson, O 1991, "The accident evolution and barrier function (AEB) model applied to incident analysis in the processing industries", *Risk Analysis*, vol 11, pp 499-507.

Tobin, P 2008, "Concurrent and sequential causes of delay", *Building and Construction Law Journal*, vol 24, no 1, pp 10-28.

Travers, R 2002, "Medical causation", *Australian Law Journal*, vol 76, no 4, pp 258-268.

Turner, B 1976, "The organizational and interorganizational development of disasters", *Administrative Science Quarterly*, vol 21, pp 378-397.

Turner, B 1978, *Man-made disasters*, Wykeham, London.

Turner, B 1994, "Causes of disaster: sloppy management", *British Journal of Management*, vol 5, pp 215-219.

Turner, B & Pidgeon, N 1997, *Man-made disasters*, 2nd edn, Butterworth-Heinemann, Oxford, UK.

Van der Schaaf, T, Lucas, D & Hale, A (eds) 1991, *Near miss reporting as a safety tool*, Butterworth-Heinemann, Oxford, UK.

Vaughan, D 1990, "Autonomy, interdependence, and social control: NASA and the space shuttle Challenger", *Administrative Science Quarterly*, vol 35, pp 225-257.

Vaughan, D 1996, *The Challenger launch decision: risky technology, culture and deviance at NASA*, Chicago University Press, London.

Vaughan, D 2005, "Organisational rituals of risk and error", in B Hutter & M Power (eds), *Organisational encounters with risk*, Cambridge University Press, Cambridge, UK, pp 33-66.

Vicente, K & Christoffersen, K 2006, "The Walkerton E. coli outbreak: a test of Rasmussen's framework for risk management in a dynamic society", *Theoretical Issues in Ergonomics Science*, vol 7, no 2, pp 93-112.

Visser, J 1998, Developments in HSE management in oil and gas exploration and production, in A Hale & M Baram (eds), *Safety management: the challenge of change*, Pergamon, Oxford, UK.

Wastnage, J 2005, "Airlines get new ice alert", *Flight International*, 25-31 October, p 12.

Weick, K 1987, "Organizational culture as a source of high reliability", *California Management Review*, vol 29, no 2, pp 112-127.

Weick, K 1990, "The vulnerable system: an analysis of the Tenerife air disaster", *Journal of Management*, vol 16, pp 571-593.

Weick, K 1995, *Sensemaking in organizations*, Sage, London.

Weick, K (ed) 2001, *Making sense of the organization*, Blackwell Business, Oxford, UK.

Weick, K & Roberts, K 1993, "Collective mind in organizations: heedful interrelating on flight decks", *Administrative Science Quarterly*, vol 38, pp 357-381.

Weick, K & Sutcliffe, K 2001, *Managing the unexpected: assuring high performance in an age of complexity*, Jossey Bass, San Francisco, California.

Weick, K & Sutcliffe, K 2007, *Managing the unexpected: resilient performance in an age of uncertainty*, Jossey-Bass, San Francisco, California.

Weick, K, Sutcliffe, K & Obstfeld, D 1999, "Organizing for high reliability: processes of collective mindfulness", *Organizational Behaviour*, vol 21, pp 81-123.

Wells, C 1995, *Negotiating tragedy: law and disasters*, Sweet & Maxwell, London.

Wildavsky, A 1988, *Searching for safety*, Transaction Publishers, Oxford, UK.

Wilpert, B & Fahlbruch, B (eds) 2002, *System safety: challenges and pitfalls of intervention*, Pergamon, London.

Wokutch, R & VanSandt, C 2000, "OHS management in the United States and Japan: the DuPont and Toyota models", in K Frick, P Jensen, M Quinlan & T Wilthagen (eds), *Systematic occupational health and safety management*, Pergamon, Amsterdam, pp 367-398.

Woo, D & Vicente, K 2003, "Sociotechnical systems, risk management, and public health: comparing the North Battleford and Walkerton outbreaks", *Reliability Engineering & System Safety*, vol 80, pp 253-269.

INDEX

Page

Accident analysis

AcciMap method . . . 92; 93; 193; 194; 201
  advantages and
    disadvantages. 195; 196
  analysis guidelines. 201
  constructing AcciMaps 205-212
  diagram. 197
  standardising the format 196
  Waterfall train accident. 201-205
airline industry. 92; 179
  inclination to blame 180; 181
  managing blame in systemic
    accident analysis 189-192
  "no-blame" approach . . . 179; 180; 192
  perceptions of apportionment
    of blame 186; 188; 189; 192
  Singapore Airlines crash:
    causes 181-183
  Singapore Ministry of Transport
    analysis 187; 188
  systemic and non-systemic
    approaches. 188; 189
  Taiwanese Aviation Safety
    Council analysis. 183-186
bushfire responsibility. 93; 213
  coroner's findings of fault 213
  counterfactual analysis, coroner's
    failure to apply 214; 215; 223
  counterfactual analysis in disaster
    prevention. 222; 223
  decisions perceived as
    contributing to disaster 215-222

AcciMaps 92; 93; 193; 194; 201
advantages and disadvantages . . . 195; 196
analysis guidelines 201
causal connections 199; 200
causal factors 198; 199
constructing AcciMaps. 205-212
diagram 197
levels 197; 198
position of outcome 196
safety recommendations 200

Page

standardising the format. 196
Waterfall train accident synopsis. 201
  AcciMap representation 202
  exposition of AcciMap
    representation 202-204
  formulating safety
    recommendations 204
  list of safety recommendations 205

Air traffic control (ATC)

functions of tower controllers and
  in-flight controllers. 23-25
incident reporting
  assessment of incident reports. . . .42-49
  ATC-attributable and non-ATC-
    attributable incidents. 28-31
  event reporting 34; 37; 38
  handling of incidents,
    examples 25; 26
  handling of overload event,
    example. 52-54
  incident reporting and
    attribution. 34-37
  monitoring effect of
    organisational change . . . 55; 56; 170
  monitoring safety performance. . .54; 55
  reporting culture. 38-40
  response to incident reports 50-54
  safety record 27; 28
operational decision-making
  compliance with procedures . . . 158; 159
  organisational assistance to
    decision-makers. 174-178
  professional judgment of
    operational managers. 168-172
  supervisor's judgment 159; 160
  types of rules. 165; 166; 167
risk management
  data collection. 78-83
  development of bow tie
    diagrams 64-76
  development of integrated
    Airservices Australia bow tie 77

Page

disadvantages of hazard
  registers 60-63; 76
implementation into safety
  management system. 84; 85
roles of personnel 23; 24; 158
United States Federal Aviation
Administration system as
HRO model 6

Airline industry

accident analysis 92; 93; 179
  inclination to blame 180; 181
  managing blame in systemic
    accident analysis 189-192
  "no-blame" approach . . . 179; 180; 192
  perceptions of apportionment
    of blame 186; 188; 189; 192
  Singapore Airlines crash:
    causes 181-183
  Singapore Ministry of Transport
    analysis 187; 188
  systemic and non-systemic
    approaches. 188; 189
  Taiwanese Aviation Safety
    Council analysis. 183-186
Australian legislative framework
  and watchdog bodies. 19
Australian safety record. 19; 20
impact on air traffic control risk
  management 78; 79
incident reporting 89; 95
  incident reporting and
    investigation systems 98-100
  role of risk managers 100-108
risk management approaches 97; 98
  analysis and learning from
    errors. 114-115
  participative network
    resolution 111-114
  risk resilience approach 107-111
threats to safety 47; 48

Airservices Australia

as high reliability organisation 3; 17;
          18; 23; 31; 39; 49; 55; 58; 85; 150
air traffic control function 23-31; 150

Page

goals of organisation
  potential for conflicting goals 22
  promotion of civil aviation 20; 21
  safety as primary
    goal 20; 21; 22; 77; 150
incident reporting 3; 33-58
  assessment. 42-49
  event reporting system 34; 37; 38
  immediately and routinely
    reportable matters 34; 35-37
  learning from incident reports. . . .50-55
  learning from incidents,
    examples 25; 26; 29
  learning from survey results. 40
  monitoring effect of
    organisational change . . . 55; 56; 170
  monitoring safety performance. . .54; 55
  reporting culture. 38; 39; 40
operational decision-making
  interplay between rules and
    supervisor judgment . . .158-160; 162
  organisational assistance to
    decision-makers. 174-178
  professional judgment of
    operational managers. 168-172
  types of rules. 165; 166; 167
risk management 3; 59
  bow tie risk management
    diagrams 60; 64-76
  development of integrated
    bow tie 77-85
  hazard registers 60-63; 76
  quantitative risk analysis
    modelling 75
roles of personnel 23; 24; 158
safety record 27; 28

Blame

contra-indications of
  counterfactual analysis 221-223
coroner's findings of fault 213
inclination to blame 180; 181
managing blame in systemic
  accident analysis 189-192
"no-blame" approach 179; 180; 192

Page

perceptions of apportionment
  of blame 186; 188; 189; 192
unwarranted blaming of
  operators. 135; 213

Blindness to risk 96; 97
normalisation of deviance. 167; 176

**Bow tie risk management
  diagrams** 59; 60; 64
advantages 65; 68-69
analysing controls and possible
  failure 70-73
development of Airservices
  Australia bow tie: data collection. . . . 77
  advantages. 79-81
  assurance to board and executives . . . 83
  delineation of direct and indirect
    risks. 78; 79
  opportunities to review
    controls 81-83
development of Airservices Australia
  bow tie: implementation. 77; 83
  focus on accident prevention. . . . 84; 85
interaction with quantitative risk
  analysis modelling. 75; 76
preparation. 66
  identification of barriers or
    control measures 67; 68
  identification of consequences. 68
  identification of escalation factor
    controls 68
  identification of recovery methods . . .68
  identification of threats or causes . . . 67
  identification of top event 66; 67
problems of limiting size 76
ranking of risks and controls. 73; 74

Bushfire inquiry 93; 213
coroner's findings of fault 213
counterfactual analysis, coroner's
  failure to apply 214; 215; 223
counterfactual analysis in disaster
  prevention. 222; 223
decisions perceived as contributing
  to disaster

Page

blameworthiness of decisions . . .221-222
failure to attack southern fire . . .215-219
failure to warn public 219-221

Challenger disaster 14; 167

Change management — see
  Management of change

Chemical and petrochemical industries
commercial pressure. 150
communication and employee
  involvement 144
good housekeeping. 146
judgment-based decision-making of
  experienced manager. . . . 155; 156; 157
levels of operational discipline . . .136; 147
maintenance of high standards in
  procedures 144; 145
management of change. 143; 144
organisational assistance to
  decision-makers 174-178
professional judgment of
  operational managers 168-172
roles of personnel 155
safety as sociopolitical requirement. . . 150
strong leadership promoting
  culture of safety and pride. . . . 139; 141
types of rules 165; 166; 167
up-to-date documentation 142; 143
well-defined and resourced
  procedures 142

Collection and analysis of information
accident analysis methods. 179-192
  AcciMap method 193-212
  counterfactual analysis 213-223
airline industry
  accident analysis 179-192
incident reporting and
  investigation systems 98; 99
participative network
  resolution 111-114
risk assessment as organisational
  risk resilience. 107-111
role of risk managers 100-108

Page

Airservices Australia
hazard registers 60-63; 76
incident reporting. 33-49
integrated risk management
bow tie 76-85
response to incident reporting. . . .50-55
capacity of organisations. 12
consultation and sharing of experience
of decision-makers 176; 177
nuclear power industry
follow up and action 127-129
learning from incident report
data. 131-133
reportable matters. 123

Columbia disaster 5; 15; 16

Commercial considerations
potential conflict in decision-
making 150; 177; 178
potential conflict of organisational
goals 21; 22

Communication
consultation and sharing of experience
of decision-makers 176; 177
incident reporting — see **Incident
reporting**
management and employees,
importance 144
operations experience feedback
meetings. 128

Confidential reporting. 34

Culture
normalisation of deviance. 167; 176
pride in one's work. 139; 141
recognition of areas of
organisational ignorance 105-107
reporting culture 38-40; 140
risk blindness theories 96; 97
safety awareness 20; 21; 34; 54; 55;
59; 77; 123; 150; 156; 157

Decision-making — see **Operational
decision-making**

Page

Diablo Canyon
electricity company/nuclear power
station operator as HRO. 6

DuPont chemical company
operational discipline . . .90; 135; 136; 147
characteristics 137; 138
communication and employee
involvement. 144
good housekeeping 146
maintenance of high standards
in procedures. 144; 145
management of change 143; 144
strong leadership promoting culture
of safety and pride. . . . 138; 139; 141
up-to-date documentation . . . 142; 143
well-defined and resourced
procedures. 142
process safety management wheel. . . . 137

Event reporting 37; 38

Frontline operations
communication and employee
involvement 144
decision-making by firefighting
supervisor 216
decision-making by shift
managers. 91; 92; 152-162
deference of HRO management
to expertise 13; 14
frontline operator sensitivity and
willingness to report 13
good housekeeping. 146
incident reporting — see **Incident
reporting**
learning from incident report
data. 131; 132
maintenance of high standards in
procedures 144; 145
organisational assistance to
decision-makers 174-178
strong leadership promoting culture
of safety and pride. 138; 139; 141
unwarranted blame for errors . . . 135; 213
vetting of reports by shift manager . . . 127

Page

up-to-date documentation 142; 143
well-defined and resourced
   procedures 142

Hazard management — see also **Risk
management**
adequacy of reporting systems 33
deference to expertise by mindful
   organisations. 13; 14
development of individualised
   reporting systems 33-58
development of safety management
   bow tie 77-85
hazard registers. 60-63; 76
reactions of mindful organisations 13

Hazard registers 61; 62
HAZLOG database system. 59; 84
disadvantages of hazard registers. . . 63; 76

Hierarchy of controls 70
escalation to higher level. 71

High reliability organisations (HROs)
characteristics. 3; 6; 9; 15
Columbia disaster evaluation . . . 5; 15; 16
commitment to resilience. 13
concept of "mindfulness" 9; 10
deference to expertise 13; 14
definitions 6; 15
origin of term. 5
preoccupation with analysing
   failures 10; 11
problems with definitions. 7; 8
reluctance to simplify interpretations . . . 12
sensitivity to operations 12; 13
United States examples. 6
willingness to learn. 14

Housekeeping
importance of tidiness in workplace. . . 146

Incident reporting
airline industry study 89; 95
   assessment of incident reports 99
   content of reports 98
   follow-up and response 99; 100

Page

incident reporting and
   investigation systems 98
role of risk managers 100-108
Airservices Australia 3; 33-58
   assessment of incident reports 42-49
   confidential reporting on safety
      concerns 34
   event reporting system 34; 37; 38
   immediately and routinely
      reportable matters 34; 35-37
   incident reporting as
      performance indicator 48-49
   monitoring effect of
      organisational change 55; 56
   monitoring safety performance. . .54; 55
   reporting culture. 38; 39; 40
   response to event report 54; 55
   response to incident reports 50-54
collection and analysis capacity of
   organisations. 12
DuPont chemical
   company. 91; 140; 141
frontline operator sensitivity and
   willingness to report 13
implications of Bird's safety triangle
   model 119; 123
implications of Reason's Swiss
   cheese model. 119; 120; 123
nuclear power industry. 90; 123
   coding and investigation by
      safety staff 127; 128
   immediate vetting by shift
      manager. 127
   learning from incident report
      data 131-133
   "near miss" situations 124; 125
   OHS and nuclear incidents,
      no differentiation. 125; 126
   operations experience feedback
      meetings 128
   overlap with operations support
      programs 130; 131
   prioritisation. 129
   reportable matters. 123
   willingness to report 134

Page

warning signal/noise
    differentiation 10; 11

Incident reporting and investigation
    systems (IRISs) 98
participative network resolution. . . 111-114
procedure 99; 100
risk assessment as organisational
    risk resilience 107-111
role of risk managers. 100-108

IRIS risk managers
analytical tactics 101
    drawing connections 103
    making patterns 101; 102
    recognising novelty 104
    sensing discrepancy 104; 105
assessment of incident reports 99
assumptions behind interpretive
    vigilance 100
detailed knowledge and intuitive
    approaches 106
limited authority 100; 111
participative network resolution. . . 111-114
recognition of areas of
    organisational ignorance 105-107
risk assessment as organisational
    risk resilience 107-111
safety briefings and reporting 99
study methodology 98

Injury reporting systems
inadequacy as hazard management
    indicator 33

Leadership
leadership by example. 139

Learning organisations
airline industry study
    approach to incident
        analysis 100-107
    approach to risk
        management 107-114
    learning from errors 114-115
Airservices Australia
    learning from incident reports. . . .50-55

Page

learning from incidents,
    examples 25; 26; 29
learning from survey results. 40
HROs' willingness to learn. . . 14; 114; 117
nuclear power industry
    learning from errors or
        organisational weaknesses . . . 140; 141
    organisational failure to improve
        practices 133; 134
    staff learning from incident
        report data. 131; 132
organisational assistance to
    decision-makers 174-178

Legislative requirements
airline industry 19
Airservices Australia 20; 150
nuclear power stations 132

Longford gas plant explosion
inadequate indications of hazard
    management 33

Maintenance and repair
reduction of safety barriers 154; 157
timing decisions 154; 159

Management of change
Airservices Australia 55; 56; 170
chemical and petrochemical
    industries 143
nuclear power industry. 143

March v E & MH Stramare case
coroner's reliance 215

Mindful organisations
characteristics. 10
commitment to resilience. 13
deference to expertise 13; 14
preoccupation with analysing
    failures 10; 11
reluctance to simplify interpretations . . . 12
sensitivity to operations 12; 13

Page

National Aeronautical and Space Administration (NASA)
Challenger decision-making
errors 14; 167
Columbia disaster evaluation . . . 5; 15; 16

Near misses
incident reporting 35; 124; 125

Normalisation of deviance 167; 176

Nuclear power industry
communication and employee
involvement 144
Diablo Canyon as HRO model 6
good housekeeping. 146
incident reporting 90; 118
coding and investigation by
safety staff 127; 128
immediate vetting by shift
manager. 127
learning from incident report
data .131-133
"near miss" situations 124; 125
OHS and nuclear incidents,
no differentiation. 125; 126
operations experience feedback
meetings 128
overlap with operations support
programs 130; 131
prioritisation. 129
reportable matters. 123; 124
willingness to report 134
levels of operational discipline . . . 136; 147
maintenance of high standards in
procedures 144; 145
management of change. 143; 144
operational decision-making
compliance with operating
rules 152; 153
"line in the sand" judgment
decisions 153; 154
organisational assistance to
decision-makers. 174-178
professional judgment of
operational managers. 168-172

Page

types of rules. 165; 166; 167
roles of personnel 151
strong focus on safety. 150
strong leadership promoting
culture of safety and pride. 139-141
up-to-date documentation 142; 143
well-defined and resourced
procedures 142

Operational decision-making 149
Airservices Australia
compliance with procedures . . . 158; 159
supervisor's judgment 159; 160
chemical manufacturing plant
judgment of experienced
manager. 155; 156; 157
decisions, risks and barriers. 173; 174
good and bad decisions. 172; 173
interplay of rules and professional
judgment 161; 162
nuclear power plant
compliance with operating
instructions 152; 153
"line in the sand" situation-
specific decisions 153; 154
organisational assistance to
decision-makers 174
clarification of boundaries. 175
clarification of safety/production
goals 177; 178
emphasis on barriers (controls)
rather than risk 178
formalising judgment-based
decision processes 175; 176
recognition of consultation 177
sharing professional
knowledge. 176; 177
organisational entity v professional
identity. 163; 164
professional judgment 168
experience and expertise 168; 169
importance 174
relationship with peers 171; 172
trust of senior management. 170
safety focus of chemical, nuclear
power and airline industries 150

Page

trade-offs between safety and
   production goals 150; 177; 178
types of rules 165
   goal-based (boundary). 165
   process-based (judgment) 166; 167

Operational discipline 90; 135; 136
characteristics. 137; 138
communication and employee
   involvement 144
good housekeeping. 146
integral part of process safety
   management wheel 137
levels observed in different
   industries 136; 147
maintenance of high standards in
   procedures 144; 145
management of change. 143; 144
strong leadership promoting
   culture of safety and pride. 139-141
up-to-date documentation 142; 143
well-defined and resourced
   procedures 142

Organisational entity of managers
clarification of goals 177; 178
role in decision-making 163; 164

Piper Alpha platform fire
decision-making errors 14; 164

Procedures
absence of shortcuts 146
adequate resourcing 142
clear definition of management
   processes. 142
decisions made in compliance 152;
                        153; 158; 159
guidance to decision-makers. . . . 175; 176
maintenance of high standards. . . 144; 145
up-to-date documentation 142; 143

**Process safety management (PSM)
wheel** 137

Professional judgment of managers
clarification of goals 177; 178
factors 168-170

Page

fostering by organisations 175-177
importance. 174
role in decision-making 163; 164

**Quantitative risk analysis (QRA)
modelling** 75
use of bow ties to display results 76

Risk management
airline industry approaches. 95
   analysis and learning from
     errors. 114-115
   assessment according to
     likelihood/severity matrix . . . 99; 109
   follow-up and response 99; 100
   incident reporting and
     investigation systems 98
   participative network
     resolution 111-114
   risk assessment as organisational
     risk resilience. 107-111
   role of risk managers 100-108
bow tie diagrams 60; 64
   advantages. 65; 68; 69
   analysing controls and possible
     failure .70-73
   interaction with quantitative
     risk analysis modelling. 75; 76
   preparation 66-68
   problems of limiting size. 76
   ranking of risks and controls 73; 74
development of Airservices
   Australia bow tie 77
   phase 1: data collection 77-83
   phase 2: implementation into
     safety management system. . . . 84; 85
hazard registers. 61; 62
   disadvantages 63; 76
   HAZLOG database system 59; 84
importance of interpreting and
   learning from errors 97; 114-115;
               117; 134; 140; 141
individualised incident reporting
   system. 47-49; 123; 124
   assessment according to
     likelihood/severity matrix . . . 42; 129

Page

prioritisation of incidents . . .43-46; 129
response to incident
   reports. 50-54; 127; 128
normalisation of deviance. 167; 176
operational discipline model. 135-147
organisational assistance to
   decision-makers 174-178
quantitative risk analysis modelling . . . 75
theories of risk blindness 96; 97
value of counterfactual
   analysis 222; 223

Risk resilience 89
approach to risk assessment 107-111
participative network resolution
   to risk management 111-114

Safety awareness
development of risk management
   bow tie 77
incident reporting 34; 123
industry record. 150
monitoring performance 54; 55
primary goal of air traffic control . . .20; 21
professional pride of shift
   managers. 156; 157
risk assessment systems. 59

Safety triangle accident causation
model. . . 118; 119; 121; 122; 125; 134
diagram. 118

Sensitivity to operations
antithesis of "silo" thinking. 13
communication and employee
   involvement 144
fostering of professional judgment
   in decision-makers 175-177
recognition of areas of
   organisational ignorance 105-107
strong leadership promoting
   culture of safety and
   pride. 138; 139; 141

Signal/noise differentiation. 10; 11
detailed knowledge and intuitive
   approaches to interpretation 106

Page

fostering of professional
   judgment 175-177
recognition of areas of
   organisational ignorance 105-107

Singapore Airlines crash
causes. 181-183
perceptions of apportionment
   of blame 186; 188; 189; 192
Singapore Ministry of Transport
   analysis 187; 188
systemic and non-systemic
   approaches 188; 189
Taiwanese Aviation Safety Council
   analysis 183-186

Space shuttle disasters
Challenger decision-making
   errors 14; 167
Columbia disaster evaluation . . . 5; 15; 16

Swiss cheese accident prevention
model. 43; 67; 89; 90; 118; 119;
               120; 123; 125; 134
diagram 120

Three Mile Island nuclear power station
effect of public outrage on
   HROs. 18; 19
warning signals. 10

United States Federal Aviation
   Administration
air traffic control system as HRO 6

United States Navy
nuclear aircraft carrier operations
   as HRO 6; 20

Warning signals
assessment of incident reports. 42-49
detailed knowledge and intuitive
   approaches to interpretation 106
development of individualised
   reporting system 33-58; 123
development of safety management
   bow tie 59-85

Page

professional judgment of decision-
    makers 164; 168; 175-177
recognition of areas of
    organisational ignorance 105-107
signal/noise differentiation 10; 11
response to incident reports 50-54

Watchdog bodies
effect on HROs 19

Page

Waterfall train accident
AcciMap representation 202
exposition of AcciMap
    representation 202-204
formulating safety
    recommendations 204
list of safety recommendations 205
synopsis 201